MW00483155

The Art
of
Sex Coaching

A NORTON PROFESSIONAL BOOK

The Art of Sex Coaching

EXPANDING YOUR PRACTICE

Patti Britton

W. W. NORTON & COMPANY

New York · London

The MEBES model is the exclusive intellectual property of the author. All references to MEBES should cite Dr. Patti Britton.

Copyright © 2005 by Patti Britton

All rights reserved
Printed in the United States of America
First Edition

For information about permission to reproduce selections from this book, write to Permissions, W. W. Norton & Company, Inc., 500 Fifth Avenue, New York, NY 10110

Production Manager: Leeann Graham
Manufacturing by Haddon Craftsmen

Library of Congress Cataloging-in-Publication Data

Britton, Patti O.
The art of sex coaching : expanding your practice / by Patti Britton.
    p.   cm.
    "A Norton professional book"—T.p. verso.
    Includes bibliographical references and index.
    ISBN 0-393-70451-3
    1. Sex counseling.   2. Sex instruction.   I. Title.

HQ60.5.B75 2005
613.9'6'071—dc22   2004057507

W. W. Norton & Company, Inc., 500 Fifth Avenue, New York, N.Y. 10110
www.wwnorton.com

W. W. Norton & Company Ltd., Castle House, 75/76 Wells St., London WIT 3QT

1 3 5 7 9 0 8 6 4 2

*This book is dedicated
to the loving memory of my daughter,
HOLLIDAY,*

*who, after a long struggle
with HIV/AIDS, died on
September 23rd, 2004.*

*May we each do whatever we can
to eradicate sexual ignorance
in our lifetime.*

*May we create, instead,
a world in which sexual responsibility,
wisdom, and celebration prevail.*

Contents

Appendices

Foreword

LIFE COACHING IMPLIES coaching the whole person. Well-trained coaches are capable of creating conversations about any and all areas of a client's life, and then creating multiple action plans (MAPS) to achieve the desired result or change. One of the joys of life coaching is addressing the client as a whole person, getting to know him or her in every facet of life, and turning all of him or her toward the desired goal.

Even as we aim to address the whole person, good life coaching often will address particular topics or specific aspects of a client's life. Sometimes the focus of coaching may be the client's spouse or intimate partner, and how the state of the relationship supports or does not support the client's life goals and intentions. But I suspect that when discussing relationships, more often than not, inquiries about the *sexual* relationship are avoided or not clearly discussed. Sex and sexual satisfaction is often the elephant in the room that people walk around, pretending it is not even there. Once sex and sexuality are removed from the conversation, we lose the *whole* person whose *whole* life we are working to support and enhance.

Sex coaching is a natural development in the growing field of life coaching. Sexual expression and sexual intimacy are crucial components of human life and certainly important aspects embodying the principles of living well and healthy living. Sex coaching is thus a unique but highly valuable niche within the life coaching profession.

In writing this foreword for Patti Brittons's book, I was tempted to call it *foreplay* instead of a *foreword*. Foreplay is the preparation, the welcoming, the invitation, and the beginning to a good sexual experience. I want to have you, the reader, get ready for the pages to come and your introduction to the field of sex coaching. It is my pleasure to introduce you to the wisdom of Dr. Britton and her informative guidance and coach approach to better sexual expression.

Sex. It is a word that is ubiquitous in our society. The word jumps out at people wherever they go and whenever they hear it or see it. Yet many people can't even say comfortably the word itself or, if they can, they can only do so in a whisper. We plaster our billboards with sexual images and fill our television hours with sexual innuendo. Yet in our personal lives there is likely no topic we discuss less. Sex, for all its ubiquity, remains the most misunderstood form of human expression.

The pervasive and enduring misunderstandings regarding sex are both paradoxical and impoverishing. Intercourse and other forms of sexual expression are brilliant symbolic representations of what most humans seek—connection, union, and integration (both within us and with others). (After all, where would we all be without sex? Our very creation came from such a moment.) Sex is also the human expression of the life force or *élan vital*. In Eastern traditions, this energy is called *chi* or *ki*. It is the core energy of our being and the unique expression of our humanness. Sex is thus not only the manifestation of our desire for connection and unity with another but is also be a source of transcendence in its most glorious experience. Yet, in societies worldwide, sex often continues to be the most misunderstood and dissatisfying form of human experience.

In *The Art of Sex Coaching*, Dr. Britton brings a new view to helping persons get more satisfaction out of their sexuality and their sexual experience. Be forewarned. This is a no-holds-barred approach to the topics of sex and sexuality. Dr. Britton believes that accurate information allows clients to make intelligent choices. This goes not only for clients but also for coaches. Dr. Britton is clear that in order to be a sex coach one requires specialized training, knowledge of ethical guidelines, and a developed professional network. All of these things are requisite if one is to be the best one can be at the art of sex coaching. Dr. Britton also emphasizes that sex coaching is not psychotherapy. Coaches are not therapists and not all issues which clients raise can be addressed in coaching. The first rule of coaching is to give clients proper referrals if they are not coachable or have therapeutic issues.

Some who read this book will be called to explore specialized training to become sex coaches and take their specialized training in sexuality and develop a sex coaching niche. Other readers will integrate techniques and insights from the book into their current coaching practice and help clients avail themselves of sex coaching resources when they would benefit from coaching that directly addresses sexuality. Therapists and counselors will also find *The Art of Sex Coaching* helpful as a source of information and guidance when working with clients whose therapeutic concerns involve sexual behavior and dysfunction.

Dr. Britton shows you how to discuss sex and sexuality with clients in a coachlike manner. My belief has always been that coaching is an ongoing series of conversations about any and all areas of my clients' lives, and this may include sex. Similarly Dr. Britton is clear to state that sex coaching is a process, not a single event—it is a conversational process taking place in the larger context of the client's life. When that coaching process requires addressing sex, *The Art of Sex Coaching* shows you how to expand the conversation in this direction in order to assist your client. The book is full of case examples and illustrative material that lets readers into coaching conversations and get a feeling for the frank and transformative conversations that occur in sex coaching.

This wonderful guide provides all that a reader needs—good, factual information as well as professional guidance in the techniques to use when you are actually coaching clients. There are many lessons the reader can take away from this book, even if the intent is not to become a sex coach; whether you are a coach, therapist, or counselor, this book should be on your library shelf. Together with further training, however, the lessons from *The Art of Sex Coaching* point the way toward becoming an informed, skilled, professionally-trained, and ethical sex coach.

Dr. Patrick Williams
Psychologist, Master Certified Coach
Founder, Institute for Life Coach Training

Acknowledgments

First and foremost I wish to thank my editor at Norton, Michael McGandy. Michael inspired the co-development of the concepts for this book; he contributed his intellectual acumen to the structure, content, and style, while lending a humanitarian and respectful approach to the creative process. Above all, I will never forget his patience and kindness during the first-pass editing of this book, which occurred while my daughter was dying. Amazingly, the editing of the manuscript was my anchor in that storm. I will always regard Michael with the utmost admiration, respect, and appreciation.

I wish to thank all of my clients, who showed up in my sex coaching practice with courage, trust, and dedication. Without them, this book would not exist. I honor each and every one of them for the gift of sharing their healing journey with me.

I also want to thank my literary agent, Jessica Faust, who is my warrior guardian in the book publishing business. I thank Casey Ruble for her talented and sensitive editing of a complex book. I also wish to thank my peers, who, at the very last moments while searching for research citations, rallied within the AASECT list serve, especially Kim Airs, Martha Cornog, Bill Kelly, Lou Paget, Jacob Pastoetter (from Germany); and kudos to my special friend/colleague Linda de Villers. I honor my pocket editor, Susan Crain Bakos, sex writer/editor supreme, for her assistance on this book. Finally, I so thank my partner, Robert Dunlap, who patiently listened while I read my *Inside Story* passages aloud, and who has undauntedly been there at my side as my best fan.

The Art
of
Sex Coaching

Introduction

TALK ABOUT SEX is as ubiquitous as cleavage on newsstands today; it is a constant focus of attention in American culture. The lead stories in women's magazines or teasers for television shows might lead you to assume that everyone is having great (and frequent) sex. Want the truth?

According to compelling recent statistics, sex is often problematical and certainly not satisfying for many, many men and women. Unlike previous generations, these sexually dissatisfied people are popping pills to get an erection, buying books to learn new bedroom tricks, and surfing channels and the Internet in search of a quick-fix solution. Eventually many of them turn to professionals trained to help them resolve their sexual concerns.

If you are a therapist, your practice may be suffering because the dollars allotted by consumers and insurers for talk therapy is steadily declining. As either a therapist or a life/personal coach, you are probably struggling to address the complexities of your clients' sexual issues. But you won't be able to help as much as you would like if you don't know how to function as a sex coach. Clients—men, women, or couples—can only overcome their sexual concerns when a sex-positive, client-centered, empowering approach is used.

Sex coaching—a field that grew, of course, directly out of coaching itself—is that type of approach. It is another route for overcoming sexual challenges, difficulties, and problems. Sometimes the sex coach simply gives permission, empowers, reframes negative messages, or disseminates accurate information. Coaching reinforces, guides, and directs the client to a result. Until now, no one has written a specific guidebook for sex coaching.

This book will take you on a journey of personal discovery as it teaches you how to become a sex coach. You will surely discover some aspects of human sexual expression that surprise you. And you may have to confront some personal biases about sexual behavior that you didn't know you had. You will find the book's vignettes, which are anonymous composites based on the true stories of clients who have overcome tremendous obstacles to attain sexual fulfillment, to be emotionally uplifting; and you'll find the sex coaching models, which include specific exercises, to be helpful for expanding your repertoire as a therapist or coach. Regardless of what led you to explore sex coaching, this book will give you more than you expected to find.

WHY A BOOK ON SEX COACHING NOW?

When I talk to clients, I emphasize that I am a sex *coach*—meaning I use a results-focused approach to help them reach their sexual potential. In the first session, I tell them that sex coaching is "outside the box," incorporating educational processes, home assignments, field trips, rituals, and many other resources. I'm amazed at the courage and sheer daring my clients show in plunging enthusiastically into this work. And I'm impressed with their hunger for more. When I describe coaching to them, I am careful to avoid the term *therapy*. If I do introduce that word, they shudder. *Therapy*, although an important part of the mental/emotional/physical/psychological healing professions, connotes pathology to many consumers.

When I interview a new client, I often discover that he has been or is currently in therapy. Many therapists and coaches are ambivalent about explicit discussion of sexual issues. They consistently avoid dealing with their clients' sexual concerns whenever they can. I can't tell you how many clients—even clients who've been with the same therapist for years—say, "Oh, yes, I'm in therapy, but we *never* talk about *sex.*" If you are a professional who winces at the thought of frank sexual discussion with a client, this guidebook may be the tool that finally helps you help them.

Why Should You Want to Add Sex Coaching to Your Practice?

Your clients need that help. The landmark 1999 *JAMA* study claimed that four out of every ten women and three out of ten men admit to a sexual dysfunction. Recent data from the Kinsey Institute data said that 26% of all women in their study had sexual problems, which are often a softer manifestation of emotional or psychological issues that typical medical models fail to address. That the vast majority of women never reach orgasm through intercourse alone is an accepted fact. And new statistics report that 40 million Americans are in sexless marriages. Even Viagra and its more potent cousins Levitra and Cialis haven't been the panacea they were expected to be. Instead, couples now realize that the relationship, not his flagging erection, may be the real problem. They need a sex coach, not a prescription.

If you want further proof that people are seeking sexual help in record numbers, look at the billion-dollar adult video/DVD industry. The average couple turns to videos and DVDs for help in adding variety to their sex lives or educating them on specifics, like how to be a better lover. The explosion of self-help materials (including books and websites) indicates that people's appetite for stimuli, information, and new tricks is enormous.

People want sexual fulfillment so much that they are willing to share painful truths with someone who can help them. That someone is a sex coach.

COOKBOOK LEARNING OR AN ART FORM?

This is not a paint-by-number approach to launching a sex coaching practice or integrating that skill into your current practice. More creative and flexible than traditional therapy models, sex coaching is an art. This book includes descriptions of my coaching method, as well as the methods of others, all of whom work in their own unique ways. Some rely solely on explicit bodywork and place their hands on (or inside) the bodies of their clients as part of the intensive coaching experience. Others elicit responses through massage or energetics. Most use talk-only methods in an interactive way.

Sex coaching is not sex therapy wrapped in a different ribbon. It is a solid, independent approach designed specifically to help clients resolve their particular sexual concerns at their particular stage of life. In Chapter 6, I describe MEBES, the coaching model I developed, which includes assessment and the creation of an action plan for each client. MEBES is founded on the idea that helping a client with a sexual concern usually involves their mind (M), emotions (E), body and body image (B), energy (E), and sometimes spirit (S). You will probably construct your own model, perhaps from pieces of this one and several others.

Think of sex coaching as a class on painting. You will learn how to prepare the canvas and decide which brushes and types of paint will best help you achieve the results you desire. As you learn various artistic techniques, you will become a master of composition. You'll be guided on how to access your palette, pulling inspiration from all the elements around you and gaining insight into the design of the techniques that best suit each client. Most importantly, you are the artist, creating a unique assessment and action plan for your client. Forget about strict rules. Absorb the information given in this book, and then just paint!

MY PERSONAL JOURNEY INTO SEX COACHING

I redefined my own knowledge, skills, and approach to clients in the early 1990s when I opened my first private practice in Manhattan. At that time I was fortunate enough to study under the pioneer sex educator and courageous, outspoken proponent of women's orgasmic potential, Betty Dodson. I was also a student of Thomas Leonard, founder and brilliant crafter of the emerging field of coaching at his original Coach University. Leonard crystallized coaching as its own profession, beyond sports. His thoughts, views, confrontational personal style, and radical approaches to self-help, personal growth, and entrepreneurial spirit were imprinted on the coaching model. Sex coaching takes all of that one step further. What I found troubling, however, was the fine line between coaching and therapy. Where did one begin and the other end? How did the coach know when to stop and send the client on to someone more qualified?

One of the great influences on my personal coaching style was my own personal coach, Cheryl Richardson, who was also Oprah's life coach and the author of numerous best-selling books on life coaching.

Empowering me with her methodologies and philosophical expectation of the highest personal good, Cheryl helped me discover my own potential. As part of her intake process she required clients to write their own autobiography—a daunting task! She also insisted that they list what she called (and is now widely used in coaching) *tolerations*, those energy-draining tasks or responsibilities one is required to do. Tolerations may be items consistently on the to-do list, like fixing the broken printer, making that mammography appointment, or writing a living will. But they also can be draining experiences, such as the lack of resolution to a relationship conflict or the absence of orgasm with your partner. Tolerations are often forever dangling as a want—like waiting and hoping for sex to happen in an overly scheduled life. Use the tolerations list as a regular self-exercise as well as an exercise for your clients. It's a powerful tool for recognizing what may be blocking you and then moving forward toward your goals.

I also was coached personally by Julian Cohen, an outstanding leader in the coaching field. He, along with Cheryl, influenced my thinking about myself, which has had a deeply positive impact on how I coach my clients. As my first coach, Julian showed me how to become the entrepreneurial thinker I am today. For example, he used printed intake forms to direct each coaching session. He insisted that I complete the form, even if only mentally, to arrive prepared. He went through each step of the form with me: What was accomplished, what wasn't, what was in my way, what opportunities were pending, a numbers report (such as cash flow or number of appointments set), goals for the current session, and commitments for the following session. Julian's system helped me organize my thinking as his client.

I don't use this particular technique of establishing accountability and preparedness for my own clients before each session. You may want to develop your own form as a tool for getting your client organized and prepared for a coaching session. I use a more intuitive approach than Julian's because it works for me. I verbally check in with the client early in the session before launching into the work of the day. I follow up most sessions with a handout, such as a personally written index card of their home assignments. It's also not unusual for me to send a client home with a small goodie bag filled with a book, a DVD, or even a sex toy that a company has asked me to test drive.

Julian was also a role model of wisdom and self-confidence. When his own client list was thin, for example, he increased his fees, saying, "My value has increased and I'm ready to attract richer clients." He coached me to shift from a *fear-based operating system*, common for most people, to a *faith-based operating system*, a positive pattern of thinking modeled on the operating system of a computer. He empowered me to overcome my fears and have faith that my visions could be manifested. And over time, they were. His coaching approach and its positive influences on my thought processes have helped me in ways that I will never be able to measure.

Julian also taught me that a coach is a resource and a guide, not an instant fix; that coaching requires personal responsibility on both the macro level (big picture issues) and the micro level (showing up for your session on time); and that a coach needs to have her own agenda, pursue her own goals, and stay attractive and diligent. In one of his creative twists on coaching, Julian taught his clients to "inspire the coach—in good times and in bad." I let my clients know that they can inspire or influence my coaching by telling me what they need, what has gone well, and where they feel stuck—and by sharing their successes.

I am grateful to each of these innovative, inspirational teachers; they each have had a profound effect on my own approach to sex coaching. The more we integrate the teachings of our own elders into our coaching approach, the more rich and authentic our work becomes.

MY SEX COACHING PHILOSOPHY

My work as a sex coach integrates the principles and practices of both coaching and sexology. My philosophy and style developed as I began working with clients. I was trained in sexology and studied the various techniques for sex therapy and counseling (see Chapter 2 for more about these treatment models), but I never felt that any one of these methods stood out as the best way to assist clients with sexual concerns. In my early years in private practice, I realized that the tenets of coaching fit with the ideas, methods, and approaches I had discovered in sex therapy, sex education, and sex counseling. I happily married the disciplines.

When I created my sex coaching philosophy, I defined it in my original brochure:

- We are all affected by the increasingly sex-negative cultural climate. Sex coaching is a way for you to share sex positivity, get the sexfacts, and celebrate your sexual power.
- Sexual fears, ignorance, confusion, and the many stressful pressures on our lives today are killing sexual pleasure. Sex coaching offers a safe space where you can heal your pain, reclaim your birthright to enjoy sex as pleasure, and regain sexual mastery for your own success.

In the next panel of the brochure I listed various sex therapy methods as well as some of my own methods, such as the use of the intuitive (discussed further in Chapters 6 as well as in Chapters 7–12). I would then go over these methods with the client. The brochure included the following information on style and methods:

- *Style.* Most therapy today is all talk. Sex coaching is designed to integrate the mind, heart, spirit, and body with specific experiential education.
- *Philosophy.* Sexual enhancement for maximum fulfillment; personal empowerment; sex positivity; experiential techniques; and a comfortable, healing, and safe environment.
- *Counseling approach.* Integrative; intuitive; based on proven techniques such as Masters & Johnson, Hartman & Fithian, and Jack Annon; holistic, whole-person centered.
- *Personalized sex education.* Specially designed for your needs; accurate, explicit, complete, up-to-date sexual health facts.
- *Bodywork options.* Breath training; self-examination; clinical sexological self-exam; pelvic posturing; PC muscles development; vibrator techniques; orgasm-directed coaching; ejaculation control.
- *Referral network.* Psychotherapy; extensive bodywork; MDs and healthcare centers; sexual enhancement products; co-practitioners such as licensed massage therapists, surrogates, physicians, and psychotherapists.

You must have a referral network, regardless of your professional training and skill base. Perhaps a client needs a chiropractor, an Ob-Gyn, a massage therapist, or a tantric teacher. Whatever happens in

MORE ABOUT THAT

As a sex coach you must have an extensive resource and referral base for your clients. The following list serves as a good starting point for such a resource and referral base which go well on a brochure or Web site.

Resources
• DVDs and videos
• Appropriate websites
• Selected books
• Sexual enhancers (e.g., clitoral gels, vibrators, and herbal supplements)

Referrals
• MDs
• Psychiatrists
• Psychologists
• Massage therapists
• Nutritionists
• Chiropractors
• Tantric workshop leaders
• Health clubs
• Health stores
• Gyms
• Yoga centers
• Adult entertainment venues
• Sex shops

Promote concrete results from the sex coaching process, such as joy, self-appreciation, personal empowerment, and, of course, better sex! Finally, you may choose to display client testimonials, using real quotes from real people. These are always a good means of validating your talents.

Initially I called my work *sexual health and fitness training* instead of sex coaching. Within a year I realized the influence that coaching had on my style of working with clients who came in with sexual issues or concerns and *sex coaching* became my shingle.

your assessment and actual sessions with the client, you, as a sex coach, must work holistically to offer a range of options both inside and outside of the sex coaching office.

THE FUTURE OF SEX COACHING

Although sex coaching may appear to be an old idea wrapped in new packaging, it *is* a new phenomenon to call oneself a sex coach. Thanks to the coaching principles and practices inspired by Thomas Leonard and his followers, coaching has become an institution in the American culture of business and personal development. It is not unwise to expect that sex coaching will become another avenue for men, women, and couples of any sexual orientation to find guidance and direction for resolving their sexual concerns and discover new ways to heighten their pleasure.

As you expand your coaching or therapy practice, you may decide to use sex coaching as an add-on or you may morph your current practice into that of a sex coach. If the trend toward seeking personal help with sexual issues continues, the profession of sex coaching is bound to grow.

PART ONE

The Broad Stroke of Sex Coaching

CHAPTER ONE

The Influences of Coaching on Sex Coaching

SEX COACHING DERIVES from the general coaching profession. The primary objective in coaching—and sex coaching—is empowering the client. Coaching does that in a different way and to a higher degree than most therapy does, making sex coaching quite different from most therapeutic approaches to treating clients' sexual concerns.

THE BASIC PRINCIPLES OF COACHING

The late Thomas Leonard, author of *The Portable Coach*, established Coach University and laid the foundation for the coaching profession. These principles can be followed by a life coach, a business coach, or a sex coach. CoachVille, one of several organizations dedicated to carrying on Leonard's vision, provides the following 15 "coaching proficiencies":*

1. Engages in provocative conversations
2. Reveals clients to themselves
3. Elicits greatness
4. Enjoys clients immensely
5. Expands the clients' best efforts
6. Navigates via curiosity
7. Recognizes perfection in every situation

* Excerpted by permission of CoachVille (http://www.coachville.com).

8. Hones in on what is most important
9. Communicates cleanly
10. Shares what is there
11. Champions clients
12. Enters new territories
13. Relishes truth
14. Designs supportive environments
15. Respects clients' humanity

Sex coaching embraces many of these themes from coaching:

The Client is the Focus of Attention

In coaching, the client, not the coach or the program, drives the process and determines the pace of progress. She may agree or disagree with your observations or coaching suggestions. You must meet the client on her terms and adjust assignments and expectations to suit her *willingness* and *ability* to do them. For example, you may think that Joan can recite personal affirmations (about improving her conflicted sexual relationship with Mark) every morning before work, but she may never be able to set aside the time or, more importantly, adopt your belief in the power of affirmations as a way to achieve her desires.

The Client is Encouraged to Build Attraction

"Be as attractive as you can be" is one of the mantras of coaching. One path to empowerment is moving the client away from goal seeking and toward becoming attractive. That may sound like cognitive dissonance, but it's a brilliant life philosophy. What does it mean? The gist of coaching is this belief: If you become the most attractive *you* you can be (physically, mentally, emotionally, in your attitude, communication style, ability to negotiate), you will ultimately get what you want for yourself. Setting goals and striving to meet them is a process of pushing against resistance. Being attractive, on the other hand, is all about developing yourself as a magnetic force field. You aren't pushing—you're pulling. Remember the catch phrase from the movie *Field of Dream*: "Build it and they will come."

Empowerment is Central

It's worth repeating: Empowering the client is the hallmark of all coaching, including sex coaching.

• *Teach clients the art of saying "no."* Help them set healthy boundaries. Coach them to ask for what they want, and distinguish *want* from need, prefer, or desire.

• *Use empowering words.* Say: "I know you can do it" or "keep going." Suggest: "Here's how you can improve. . . ." Give "I'm here for you" messages.

• *Keep the process short.* Unless they have a complex concern, get clients *out* of your calendar as quickly as possible. Plan for the end of sex coaching in the beginning.

• *Encourage acceptance of personal responsibility.* Help clients realize that freedom comes through choice/responsibility. Teach: "You are responsible for your own erection/orgasm/pleasure." Act like their sidelines coach, speaking to them as they progress.

THE BASIC PRINCIPLES OF SEX COACHING

As I have said, although sex coaching may be inspired by certain therapeutic approaches, it is a different animal from therapy or education. Rather, it is a unique approach to helping people experience more (and better quality) sexual fulfillment, pleasure, and joy. Following are what I like to call the *ten principles of sex coaching.*

1. Sex coaching moves the client *toward future outcomes and results.* It is based on looking at what is and deciding what the client wants to be, do, or have. The client, not the sex coach, is the one who determines the outcome.

2. Sex coaching relies on *positive reinforcement* of the client's dreams, wishes, goals, and desired outcomes. Whether it's a more intense orgasm, any orgasm at all, sustaining arousal, or experimenting with a threesome, what a client wants is up to him.

3. The sex coach is the *guide.* She helps the client overcome sexual blocks in thinking, feeling, and behavior and opens up the possibility for free flow of sexual energy in whatever form of expression the client desires.

4. The client is *not a patient.* This is not a pathologizing model. The sex coach is a collaborator on the journey toward a client's goals. Sex coaching models cooperation with the client, even participation, not a top-down hierarchical style of relating.

5. The *client will always set you straight.* The arrow of attention is always focused on the needs for the client, not the sex coach. Any

personal disclosure by the sex coach is appropriate only when it facilitates healing for the good of the client.

6. Sex coaching works in a *short span of time*. No long-term therapy here! In some cases, a client's concerns are resolved in one or two brief sessions. For other clients, sessions may last several weeks, either once a week or every two weeks, giving the client enough time to do the necessary home assignments. When sex coaching involves bodywork, such as orgasm-directed coaching with women, the process can take weeks or sometimes months if the client is resistant to doing the home play.

INSIDE STORY: THE TWO-SESSION MAN

Pete came to me because he couldn't have sex with women. "I have a fetish," he said, "and I can't tolerate the thought of a woman being revolted by my terrible secret." Pete was aroused by wearing women's clothing. I was trained in transgender issues, so this was no big deal.

"Would it be helpful if I let you come dressed in your outfit to the next session?" I asked. He said that it would. "Then we can talk about how you feel dressed in women's clothing. And I may be able to help you with your fetish."

Pete arrived with a small tote bag. He went into the bathroom—the client changing room—to put on his woman's outfit. He then marched out: a six-foot-tall white man, stark naked except for a pair of size-thirteen black patent-leather pumps. Rather high ones, in fact.

I smiled, invited him to sit down on the couch (where all clients sit), and continued our session without skipping a beat. We talked as though nothing were amiss. He shared how he felt in the outfit. He moved his leg up and down repeatedly, the motion distinctly changing his demeanor. He seemed quite feminine and smiled often. He spoke at length about his shame, discomfort, and fear that he'd never be accepted by a woman. Aside from the fact that he was naked and in heels, the coaching session seemed quite normal. Afterward, Pete changed out of the heels and into his clothes. He stood at the door for quite a while before saying, "This was what I came here for. You are amazing. I feel like if I could do this with you, I can now face doing it with any other woman. You never winced, you made it okay, and I can now go on with my life."

I never saw Pete again. When we spoke next on the phone, I asked if he wanted to book a session. He replied, "I got what I needed. How can I ever thank you? I feel like I'm going to be okay. Bless you, Dr. Patti." That was that.

Of course, I'm not suggesting that it's okay for the Petes of the world to break into female shoes on the first date, clothed or unclothed. However, the permission to be and the acceptance of the "miss" in Mister Pete was all he needed at that time for his personal transformation.

7. The word *homework* is always changed to *home assignments*, to avoid any negative emphasis on sex as work. The idea is that sex is play.

8. Sex coaching is *highly experimental* and *highly experiential*. The client will be asked to try new things as the sex coach takes him to the desired outcomes. Usually information/education is not enough. A rehearsal or redirecting of certain behaviors (their home play) is a necessary component in successful sex coaching.

9. The sex coach is a *participant in the healing process*. It's a 50/50 role. Interactive sessions occur with a sex coach as facilitator, not in a passive role. It's okay to give advice, to give an opinion, to disagree with your client for her own good.

10. Sex coaching is often a *vehicle for containing the client's emotionality*. Deep past emotional issues are not its focus. The focus is on the present and where the client wants to be sexually. Clients with deep emotional issues or childhood concerns often require referral to a therapist. If you are trained as a therapist, these aspects can be handled as part of the overall care. One female client came to me because she couldn't achieve orgasm: Emotional blocks in her body were obstructing her orgasm.

INSIDE STORY: THE WOMAN WITH A GLACIER FOR A CHEST

Sarah, a woman in her late sixties, came to me after years of no sexual pleasure. She had no recollection of ever having a real orgasm. But she'd just met a new man who brought out the romantic in her, and she was determined to open up sexually. Minimally employed, Sarah had lots of free time alone and was eager to push through her barriers to orgasm.

In her sex history, she'd reported being raped at age 16. I knew that was part of her problem. In our brief review of her past, she recalled some of the positive erotic sensations she'd experienced before that traumatizing incident. Having her breasts stimulated was part of her sexual arousal, but since the rape she felt as if her breasts were in solid ice, with no feeling. No wonder she didn't have orgasms.

During a guided imagery journey that I use to promote relaxation and self-awareness (Appendix A) in our third session, Sarah went inside her body and bravely melted those glacial walls of her chest. That day she went home with a daily masturbation assignment due before her next session. Three days later she called, with a new elation in her voice.

"Dr. Patti," she blurted out, half laughing, half in tears, "I did it! I had my first orgasm. I kept going and I had three! I'm so excited, I had to call you." Through sex coaching Sarah discovered the key to her liberation and ultimately her sexual pleasure.

In short, the sex coach pushes/guides/directs the client toward his or her results. Like all coaches, the sex coach holds a positive vision for the client. She can act as mirror for that client's desire to reach exquisite goals for sexual pleasure.

SEX COACHING GUIDELINES

A sex coach plays an active role with clients, engaging them in role playing, taking a stand for their highest good, and holding the progress bar high. This is not a passive profession! There are seven key sex coaching guidelines.

Careful Boundary Setting

Keep clean, clear boundaries between you and your clients. You need to walk your talk by looking fit and sexy yourself, but your appearance and behavior can't be provocative. Don't blur the roles by, for example, going bowling with your client or hiring her as your accountant. However, taking coaching outside the office or studio (for example, escorting a client to a sex toy shop) is not only acceptable, it's also often a good idea, as long as your role as coach remains distinct.

Personal Disclosure

A traditional therapist does not disclose anything of a personal nature to a client, but as a sex coach, you may do that if you choose. The art and timing of self-disclosure is everything. If you do share personal information, only do so for the good of the client, never for your own benefit. This may be the most powerful information you ever transmit to a client—as long as you follow that golden rule of disclosure.

Instruction in Selfishness

When a person takes charge of his life, he has to become self-centered. That's not bad behavior or a weakness. The self-centered person can take responsibility and behave in empowering ways. Teach clients: By paying attention to yourself first, you will be able to give to others.

Assessment, Not Diagnosis

Coaches assess concerns; therapists diagnose dysfunction and problems. Be familiar with mental health issues and disorders; for example, know the symptoms of chronic depression, borderline personality disorder, and psychotic behavior. Pay attention to your own comfort level with a client, and trust your observations (seen/heard/felt.). If you suspect a client has a mental disorder, you may have to terminate coaching. Your work as a coach is not providing therapy or medical advice.

Evaluation, Not Analysis

During the intake process and regular ongoing assessment of the client's progress you are evaluating the situation, not analyzing the client. The evaluation process is a more neutral way of looking at the client. Analysis can be judgmental and lead you to play a therapist's role. If you are trained as a therapist, you may want to use those skills with coaching clients. But move out of one mode before moving into another.

Positive Encouragement and Feedback

Complimenting clients is acceptable, as long as your compliments are sincere. For example: "You're looking relaxed today, Susie"; "You look really handsome today, Marco"; or "Have you lost weight,

Fran?" As their sex coach, you may be the sole source of positive feedback in a person's life, especially about appearance.

MORE ABOUT THAT

In the late 1980s I served as the national director of the HIV/AIDS teacher-training model program for ETR Associates, a health education and training firm. My mentor there repeatedly told trainers: *You must be able to create an elegant design for each training program.* He meant that programs must have tightly woven agendas with depth and meaning, flow in a certain direction, incorporate many different activities, emphasize personal growth, include humanity and the element of fun—and be personally transformational for all participants. Whew!

When I realized that I could create those elegant designs, I saw how they could apply to my work as a sex coach. Whether I am constructing a weekly home assignment or planning a multi-month program for a client, I try to make it elegant. Personalized sex coaching is unique and alive because it begins with an elegant design.

Assignment-Driven Sessions

Give home assignments at the end of each session. Ask for feedback on home assignments at the beginning of the next session, unless there appears to be a crisis. Home assignments sustain the momentum of the coaching process and provide accountability for the client and you. Use your time with clients to review the progress they've made on their own, rather than doing most of the work together in session as therapists do.

HOW SEX COACHING DIFFERS FROM SEX THERAPY

Sometimes the philosophical differences between sex coaching and other forms of therapy seem clear-cut; other times they are barely discernable. The differences, even when slight, are critical in defining your work as a sex coach. The following list of sex coaching characteristics illustrates how it differs from most sex therapies and standard therapies.

- Unlike many traditional forms of therapy, sex coaching is *present-centered*. Coaching work begins in the present and works toward the future. Therapy involves the past. A traditional sex therapist will start in the past to find out *why* a client has a sexual concern, whereas a sex coach will focus on what's wrong now and how the client can make it work better tomorrow.
- Sex coaching is *client-centered*. As in Rogerian therapy and other models discussed in Chapter 2, the client drives the process and determines the steps and the pace.
- Sex coaching is *dynamic, with the sex coach playing an interactive role*. Most therapists do not make active suggestions, give advice, or, for example, accompany a client on a sexual field trip outside the office.

- Sex coaching is *a fluid process*. A sex coaching action plan is a creative work in progress.
- Sex coaching is *collaborative rather than hierarchical*. The sex coach and the client (individual or couple) are equal parts of the team.
- Sex coaching is *independence-oriented* and *empowerment-focused*. The client is not dependent on the sex coach. In the first session the coach begins fostering the attitude: "I can do this alone."
- Sex coaching is *healing, not pathologizing*. Sometimes sex coaching is fully directed at promoting healing from an emotional or spiritual wound, without labeling it as wrong, bad, or shameful.
- Sex coaching is mostly a *cognitive-behavioral approach* and can involve esoteric practices. It's more like baking a souffle or casserole and adding certain spices or special ingredients to basic dishes than it is like grilling a steak or roasting a chicken.
- Sex coaching is about *personalized education*. Rather than fitting the client into the therapeutic program or theory, the coach designs the program specifically for the client.
- Sex coaching is *psychoeducational*. It includes the psyche or personality in the action plan.
- Sex coaching is *creative behavioral therapy*. Home assignments drive the process. In-studio sessions focus on skill development. Music may be used in session with some clients for its relaxing value. Free 10-minute check-ins are provided as needed.
- Sex coaching allows for *flexibility in the length and periodicity of sessions*.

INSIDE STORY: BE MY HEALER

A highly motivated man, Dave devoted himself to healing from a failing, sexless marriage. He was looking to me for redemption from his past failures. Because I knew Dave had been in treatment with a psychiatrist before coming to me, I asked him during one of our earlier sessions why he wasn't talking to his psychiatrist.

I thought he might need a clarification on the difference between sex coaching and therapy, so I said, "Dave, I want to be sure you understand that I'm not a psychotherapist. I don't do textbook therapy."

He sat up straight in the chair, looked as if he were collecting his thoughts as he put his hand to his chin, then looked straight into my eyes and said: "That's why I'm here. I've had other therapists, and they used the textbook approach. You are a healer. That's why I'm here. I want to be whole. I know you can help me get whole."

Humbled by his faith and trust, I said quietly, "Thank you, Dave. You are in the right place." And we moved on.

SEX COACHING METHODS

You have a wide range of coaching options regarding where, how, and when you work with clients. Unlike a traditional therapist, you are not tied to the basic office visit with the client sitting opposite you or lying on a couch facing the wall.

In Person

The obvious model: You and the client sit face-to-face. This is perhaps the most powerful mode, as you are wholly involved with the client and engaging all five senses. However, if geographic proximity is a problem, in-person coaching is not ideal.

Telephone

Thanks to the variety of modern phone options, some coaches may never meet a client in person! I find that the telephone sometimes promotes the deepest work: The client can spill his guts because you literally will never see him. That aspect of anonymity provides a cushion of comfort that some clients prefer. The telephone method also cuts down on time commitments and travel constraints for clients. Do not use the telephone for highly emotionally dependent clients, for clients prone to lying (such as someone who hides an obesity problem that is contributing to sexual problems), or, obviously, for clients who dislike telephones in general.

Group Sessions

Usually conducted in a workshop setting, group sessions can be held everywhere from a coffee shop to a cruise ship, where I often do them. I like groups. The dynamics of a group can shove a quiet person into the limelight, offering support and sometimes the courage for breakthrough. Of course, with most groups, especially public classes or workshops, opportunities to provide clients with individual attention are limited.

Online

Email, instant messaging, interactive video conferencing, and new technology to cyberlink from anywhere with anyone are making online coaching a highly viable option. Online sex coaching has just begun. In the early days of my Web site, I offered online appointments for a fee. I was way before my time! Email and online signups can help you develop your practice and build a client base faster than traditional print media or personal networking can. However, just as with the telephone, if you decide to do online sex coaching (such as instant messaging), host a live chatroom or posting forum, or even write back-and-forth emails as your process, you may never know the truth about your client's real identity. That's a hazard of cyberspace.

Advice Columns and Television or Radio Spots

Writing sex columns for newspapers, magazines, Web sites, or other forums, or hosting or appearing as a regular guest on television and radio programs, is a wonderful method for building your brand as a sex coach. It also enables you to serve a broad audience with one action. You have to be on your toes with the latest news and also be able to field questions on the spot to do this work. That can be stressful, which is a drawback.

Body Sessions

Body sessions are always conducted in person. As the coach, you are an observer and often must comment on or document the client's sexual technique. You will learn more about bodywork in the chapters that follow. For some clients, this is the most intense and powerful gift you can give. However, it can be scary for you and even pollute your other career paths.

Seminars

Seminars are typically conducted in person in a group format. But you can also offer seminars online or through teleconferencing. The dynamics of seminars are different than those of one-on-one work. If you love speaking in front of groups, this may be a good option for you. If not, stay away from this venue. A benefit of seminars is that they build your name value, especially if they are publicly announced.

Teleclasses

Teleclasses, a new format for reaching thousands of clients at once using long-distance telephone as the connecting link, usually are live, hour-long sessions that allow interactive dialogue among many listeners. They often result in the production of a CD or live Internet link for archiving. Teleclasses can boost your book sales or sale of other products you develop considerably. The downside is that they take some work to plan and advertise (usually on your Web site) and the outcome can be limited. Obviously, you must be able to talk on the telephone with ease if you are to conduct teleclasses.

HOW A SEX COACH CAN BE A POSITIVE ROLE MODEL

Perhaps one of the most significant distinctions between a sex coach and a therapist is your level of participation. A therapist isn't expected to be a positive role model; a sex coach is. Some of the clients you will encounter as a sex coach may shock you, even when you think you've seen it all. You will often find that what happens during the sex coaching session (and may never occur in traditional therapy) places you in the unique role of the positive role model. For example, sharing one of your client's experiences (anonymously, of course!) can encourage personal risk taking for another client or provide that magical permission to go further. As mentioned earlier, your personal disclosure may be the single most powerful ingredient in a coaching session. Revealing to clients that you are a breast cancer survivor, or have had abortions, or have suffered from vaginal dryness, can lend authority, authenticity, and compassion to your work, as you are speaking from the *I* voice. A caveat: Remind your client that confidentiality applies to your personal disclosures as well as theirs. Stress the rule of safe disclosure for everyone at the start of the coaching process.

Though not for the faint of heart, sharing your own body through body coaching is often the ultimate way of being a role model. This may or may not show up on your list of client services, and don't feel guilty if it doesn't. Be very selective in your choice of clients for this type of work. As you read the vignettes in later chapters about how I've served my clients, with and without personal body revelation, you will develop a clearer idea of what you can do in your work.

WHEN SEX COACHING BECOMES LIFE COACHING

Occasionally a client will come to you for sex coaching and stay after the sexual concern has been resolved. Sometimes the focus shifts away from sex in such a subtle way that you don't see it happening at the time. Before you realize it, you are no longer sex coaching the client—you're life coaching.

Before that happens, decide if you want to be a life coach. Many books and good training programs (see Appendix E) can help prepare you for the job. Read *Therapist as Life Coach*, one of the very best books on this helping profession. I offer life coaching to long-term clients who use me for intermittent (sexual and general) tune-ups, but I do not currently offer those services to new clients.

> **MORE ABOUT THAT**
>
> This is a fun way to remember what your role as a SEX COACH is all about:
>
> S is for smart, sex-positive, informed, and a quick study
>
> E is for experienced in sexuality and trained to address sexual concerns
>
> X is for expert in identifying and treating a range of sexual concerns and being open to all forms of sexual expression
>
> C is for compassion toward your client
>
> O is for open to whatever the client wants within reasonable boundaries or expectations
>
> A is for actively participating in the process with the client
>
> C is for committed to the client's highest good
>
> H is for holding the bar high for the success for the client

Get It!

1. What are three elements found in coaching that integrate well into sex coaching?
2. Discuss what you think empowerment really means for your clients' greatest good.
3. What have you learned from this chapter that informs your approach in working with clients?

CHAPTER TWO

Sex Therapy Models
That Inform Sex Coaching

I HAVE TAKEN a variety of models and approaches from several disciplines and adapted them both theoretically and practically to create my own methodology for sex coaching. My techniques for assisting clients in resolving their sexual concerns and reaching their ultimate sex goals have been informed and influenced by the different schools of sex therapy, education, and counseling. The schools include cognitive behavioral, rational emotive, behavioral, psychoanalytic, voice dialogue, Gestalt, intuitive, and ego states therapies—and some nontraditional approaches, too.

This chapter outlines the various methodologies I have incorporated into my approach to sex coaching; they are taken from the fields of clinical sexology, traditional therapy, New Age philosophies, and self-help therapies. My hope is that this basic structure will help you create your own personal style.

CLINICAL SEXOLOGY

According to Ted McIlvenna, founder and president of the Institute for the Advanced Study of Human Sexuality (IASHS) in San Francisco, sexology is the study of what people do sexually and how they think and feel about it. Trained clinical sexologists do not pathologize sexuality. The discipline not only tolerates but also embraces the full range of consensual adult sexual behavior. In fact, sexology promotes sex, as long as it is not coercive, violent, or abusive.

Very few trained clinical sexologists are at work in the world. Many who call themselves sexologists come from other disciplines, such as social work, massage therapy, psychology, sociology, and medicine. Often their only education or training in sexology consists of a few college courses or a weekend workshop. My coaching philosophy is based in the pure clinical sexology perspective.

The SAR Process

Developed in the late 1960s for training professionals at IASHS, the Sexual Attitudes Reassessment/Readjustment/Restructuring (SAR) process is an experiential model for self-awareness, learning, and growth. SAR was designed to help people working in the field of sexology change their attitudes so they could become tolerant and accepting of diverse kinds of sexual behavior. That can be, and has been, a life-altering process for many participants.

> **MORE ABOUT THAT**
>
> Membership in and certification by sexological organizations will add to your credibility as a sex coach. Following is a shortlist of organizations devoted to assuring quality control in the field of sexology:
> - American Board of Sexology (ABS): known as the Diplomate status, this certification is well regarded in the field of sexology.
> - American Association of Clinical Sexologists (AACS): the sister organization to ABS.
> - American Association of Sexuality Educators, Counselors and Therapists (AASECT): has strict guidelines for becoming certified as a sexuality educator, counselor, or therapist.
> - American College of Sexologists (ACS): the least well known of the certifying bodies. Most of its members are graduates of the Institute for the Advanced Study of Human Sexuality.
>
> All certification requirements are posted on the organizations' websites (see Appendix E).

The multidimensional, multimedia, and multifaceted SAR process usually takes place over at least a weekend, with two day-long sessions. At IASHS the process is taught in 60 hours (six 10-hour days) and includes personal sharing by people living the lifestyle, films, videos, and DVDs about all aspects of sexual behavior, as well as intense small-group activities. Elements of the SAR process are taught in short workshops at the AASECT annual conference and intermittently during the year by those few qualified SAR leaders in their private workshops.

The elements of the SAR process include the following:

PROCESSING YOUR STUFF

Experientially based exercises help you get out of your head and into your guts (i.e., feelings). You also need to develop an authentic self, getting past the denial that keeps you from seeing who you really are.

HEARING REAL STORIES

Listening to real people tell their own sex stories helps expand your thinking and help you embrace other sexual behavior, overcoming the pain, discomfort, ambivalence, or disgust you may feel about that behavior. In the late 1980s at one SAR event I heard a man who was a female-to-male (FTM) transsexual speak about living as a new man with a small penis-like clitoris, watched a demonstration by an S&M (sadomasochistic) rope master, and heard many gut-wrenching talks by persons living with AIDS, (PWAs). The more you hear other perspectives, the more open you become in your views, feelings, and values.

TRYING IT OUT

Experimenting with different aspects of your sexuality moves you beyond your own personal comfort zone and helps you break free of your personal boundaries. Through experimentation, you will have discoveries and revelations. In SAR trainings at IASHS, participants may be nude and may touch or be touched (with permission).

MIXING WITH PEOPLE

Mix with positive role models for sexual tolerance and diversity— the kinds of people you are likely to meet at AASECT and IASHS. Seek opportunities for socializing with people whose sexual lifestyles are different from your own. Attend lectures and workshops conducted by sexual liberators and change agents; engage them in conversation when you can.

WATCHING IT

Sexual image saturation is part of a SAR process weekend. Fuck-O-Rama, a total-immersion experience, shows over 24 sexually explicit films simultaneously. That kind of experience forces you to confront your biases, alters perception, and takes you out of the judgmental state by moving you to the site of emotions in your brain. You can break down your own prejudices, assumptions, and barriers to understanding other forms of sexual expression by exposing yourself to available material on cable television, DVD, and video.

The SAR process helps you understand and accept the wide range of human sexuality. "The only unnatural act is one which cannot be performed" was the signature email sign-off from Xaviera Hollander, the former Happy Hooker, sexuality educator, *Penthouse* columnist, and advocate for sexual rights.

The PLISSIT Model

Jack Annon's PLISSIT model is the sex therapy modality that has contributed most to my sex coaching approach. I've adapted it to the PLISSIC model, outlined here:

P: FOR PERMISSION

The greatest gift you can offer clients (or anyone else) is the permission to be who they are, to do what they desire, and to express the fullness of their human sexual potential. Some clients may only need a single session to gain the permission they never had. Permission is also the first step for all other work with clients.

LI: FOR LIMITED INFORMATION

Some clients want clarification on a confusing issue, specific information about a sexual concern, or even a reframing/affirming of what they already know. You may stop at LI, if this is why the client came and she has received what she came to see you for in the first place.

SS: FOR SPECIFIC SUGGESTIONS

If information or clarification isn't enough, the sex coaching really begins at SS. Give the client directed processes, exercises, and activities that he can do as a home assignment or in your coaching sessions. These exercises may be the pivotal force for healing or personal change.

IT: FOR INTENSIVE THERAPY

In Annon's model this level is called IT, for intensive therapy. I like to call it IC, for intensive coaching. I can't overstate the importance of a vast referral network in meeting each client's unique requirements. If you are a trained therapist, move into that role for the client's therapeutic needs. If you're not, refer out.

Intensive coaching often takes longer than a few sessions. As you develop your own skills, you will learn how to determine when or if your client is open to receiving IC by the first or second session.

Masters and Johnson

Sex researchers William Masters and Virginia Johnson are often credited with pioneering sex therapy in the 1960s at their clinic in St. Louis, Missouri. They developed sensate focus, the backbone of therapeutic techniques aimed at improving couples' sex. Employing physical and mechanical means for measuring, recording, and reporting human sexual response in the laboratory, they defined the four-part sexual response cycle and described orgasm by counting the contractions and measuring the intervals between them.

They prohibited clients from engaging in sexual intercourse at the start of therapy, teaching them instead to use sensate focus, in which they focused solely on the pleasure of being touched. Delaying intercourse is often the key component in restoring sexual functioning and resolving couple's sex concerns.

Later, Helen Singer Kaplan, trained by Masters and Johnson, added the desire phase onto the beginning of the sexual response cycle. As discussed in Chapters 7 and 8, low or inhibited sexual desire is the most prevalent sexual concern for women and is increasing for men.

Hartman and Fithian

Marilyn Fithian and Bill Hartman spoke at IASHS when I was attending classes in the late 1980s. They described how they had augmented the Masters and Johnson sex therapy model, integrating more sensual touch and lengthening the residence program. I was riveted by the stories of personal transformation experienced by participants at their clinic in Long Beach, California. In their 2-week intensive residential program, they performed extensive testing and assessment of couples and helped them change their sex lives through drawing activities, body image processing, educational films, body touch exercises (escalating from light caresses to full sexual exchanges), and sexual function training, especially for erectile/ejaculatory control.

Much of my sex coaching work is inspired by the Hartman and Fithian model. In Chapter 9, on couples' sexual concerns, you'll read more about how some of these techniques—such as the hand caress and the personal erotic drawings of both self and partner—work with real couples in sex coaching.

TRADITIONAL THERAPY

Following is a potpourri of traditional therapy models that particularly influenced me. I have tried to capture the essence and nuances of each model to illustrate how they differ and have contributed to my sex coaching approach.

The Schnarch Model

David Schnarch, author of *Passionate Marriage,* is a leader in psychoanalytic tradition and a popular sex therapist/author. His approach to sex therapy is to treat everything as an intimacy issue. If something is wrong with sex, the problem is one (or both) partner's inability to tolerate intimacy. According to Schnarch, real intimacy requires emotional bravery to sustain heightened states of emotional closeness that engender what he terms *wall-socket sex.* (But, he says, few people get to enjoy that kind of sex.) I attended a workshop conducted by Schnarch and his wife, Ruth, who is also a therapist. What I recall most vividly is their insistence that couples learn to have sex with the lights on. Not for the faint of heart, their method of lights-on sex uses a directive therapeutic model, taking the clients through many intensive steps to confront their intimacy capacity. Although I don't agree that every sex problem is an intimacy problem, I have taken something from the Schnarch model. I am perhaps more directly confrontational with some clients than I would have been had I not learned about this method.

Rational Emotive Behavioral Therapy

Albert Ellis, author of numerous books and a great-granddaddy of sexual education and treatment, developed one of the most widely used and reliable methods of the cognitive behavioral technique. I attended some of his lectures and demonstrations in New York City, and had two personal sessions with a partner, learning firsthand from a pro how to sort through the cognitive garbage we carry in our minds and then master the confrontation of self-deprecating judgments. The theory put forth by Ellis and other pioneers—that thinking leads to feelings, which lead to behaviors—informs much of sex coaching. The work of both Betty Dodson and Joe Kramer (discussed later in this book) also owes a debt to Ellis, though their emphasis is on bodywork.

I use rational emotive behavioral therapy (REBT) in coaching clients. By helping clients sort out what they are thinking—and what they are *shoulding* on themselves and their partner—you can help them redirect their thinking. That leads to a change in feelings, and in behavior. REBT employs both writing and self-talk. Through writing, clients see how their internal dialogue creates feelings about a

MORE ABOUT THAT

When someone tells Ellis that his partner should respond in a certain way, he asks, "Why should she?" The following story illustrates the power of this question.

John wished his wife, Amanda, would initiate sex more often. Instead of telling her that he wanted her to initiate sex and felt rejected when she didn't, he retreated into silence, watching television and ignoring her. She consequently became withdrawn.

Using REBT, the coach helped John realize that he was thinking: "She *should* want to have sex with me." The coach had him ask himself, "Why *should* she?"

That led John to let go of his expectations about what Amanda should think/feel/do. He then changed his behaviors, conversing with her during dinner and lingering over their coffee. He showed her more affection, including erotic touch. This created in her the desire for him that he craved.

person, incident, or situation. They can then change the dialogue, taking the first step toward freeing themselves from those limited views.

Gestalt Therapy

Founded by Fritz Perls, Gestalt therapy is one of the most popular psychodynamic methods for personal growth. Gestalt focuses on the present, on the whole person—and, like the therapy approach developed by Carl Rogers (Rogerian), on allowing the client to direct the therapy. A Gestalt therapist asks, "What's going on now?" rather than "What did you mother do when you were 5?"

In treatment, the coach or therapist helps the client read the clues expressed by the body. For example, a woman wringing her hands as she talks about how anxious her mother makes her feel may really be wanting to wring her mother's neck. A woman kicking up her leg as she outlines her conflicts with her husband might love to give him the boot. Breathing techniques also help clients access those emotions and deal with them. *Gestalting it out* is a two-chair exercise that frees and expresses emotions. The client imagines her parent, for example, sitting in the vacant chair and talks to him; then she shifts chairs to complete a dialogue long overdue. Gestalt therapists are body readers. I read my clients' body language in my coaching, too. Telling them what I see often opens emotional doors faster than asking questions would do.

Ego States Therapy or Transactional Analysis

Developed in the 1950s by Eric Berne, transactional analysis (TA)—the analysis of the dynamics of relationships—was popularized by his best-selling book of the 1970s, *Games People Play: The Psychology of Human Relationships*, and by Thomas Harris's *I'm OK, You're OK: A*

Practical Guide To Transactional Analysis. According to TA, we are always in one of three ego states when relating to others:
- Parent Ego State (P). Variations are: the critical parent (criticizing the other or self through negative self-talk; the critical parent says "I/you can't") and the nurturing parent (helpful, loving, offering guidance and supportive self-talk; the nurturing parent says "I/you can").
- Adult Ego State (A). The adult offers information and is neutral in matters of can/can't.
- Child Ego State (C). The child can be adaptive, codependent, and have no boundaries, no self-identity, or needs, like good girls. The child can be angry and prone to acting out, like bad boys. Or the child can be free. Your free child is the part of you who plays during sex.

In the early stages of romantic love, we tend to be child meeting child, or C-C. In time couples often slide into P-C relationships, filled with resentment rather than sex play. But A-A relating also kills desire. This couple shares the news reports of their day and reviews their laundry list of chores. Passion, emotion, and intimacy are lacking. Clients stuck in poor relationship dynamics can benefit greatly from learning to recognize and acknowledge the ego state patterns of their primary (and other) relationships.

Active Dialogue Techniques

This technique is taken from Gestalt therapy's "Gestalting it out" approach. The client enacts a dialogue with another person (or persons) who has caused him emotional or psychological pain. The client may also work out a dialogue with parts of himself, for example, his inner critic and his nurturing parent. Classically, he envisions the other, then acts as if that person were in the room by moving from one chair to the other and using different voices. Dialogue is a useful technique

MORE ABOUT THAT
Most therapists base their treatment approaches on their own experiences in therapy. In the late 1970s, when being in therapy was not something you discussed, you were lucky to find a competent therapist with more than one trick in his bag. That's when I had my early encounters with therapy—and I was lucky. After my husband left me for his secretary (cliche!), I sought help. That divorce was the greatest gift. In therapy, I worked through my feelings about losing him, addressed my family of origin issues, identified my destructive behavior patterns, and tore into my belief system (B.S.)

My first therapy session was with two open-minded, delightfully humorous nuns. Their program combined Gestalt and TA. I continued working with their best protegee, who introduced me to neurolinguistic programming. All three modalities influenced my own style of sex coaching.

for sorting out the various voices inside that give negative or conflicting messages. The speaking roles help clients learn how to balance positive and negative messages, enabling them to realize how influential past messages are in their life today.

I sometimes briefly use this method when counseling clients who are blocked by internal negative messages.

Neurolinguistic Programming

Widely used in sales and marketing departments as a tool for decoding communication styles, neurolinguistic programming (NLP) is also a popular methodology for understanding personal communication styles and changing behavior based upon that understanding. In coaching, I use this model with clients who argue with their partners about who said/meant what. NLP helps create new responses to the same old questions and remarks. Special NLP techniques also encourage painful past events to recede in their importance in memory, as well as change thought-and-feeling patterns in the present.

I often use the Primary Mode Test with clients to help them learn if their style is primarily visual (V), auditory (A), or kinesthetic (K). When they understand how they primarily speak and listen (or otherwise communicate), they gain insight into how they can adapt their speaking and listening styles to be better understood by—and more understanding of—their partner. Changing communication styles often changes partner dynamics. I integrate some NLP techniques into sex coaching when it fits the needs of the client.

In the early 1980s I was privileged to be in the very first Fire-walk: Turn Your Fear Into

MORE ABOUT THAT

Each of us has one primary modality which predominates—visual, auditory or kinesthetic. When someone is primarily visual, he sees and speaks from a vernacular based on sight, such as "I see what you mean." If his partner is primarily auditory, they may face communication conflicts when he says "You look hot in that teddy" and she is longing to hear, "I love how you talk to me!" Primarily kinesthetic people have to feel everything first, whether it's touch or emotions. To test your clients (or have someone test you). Here is how it works: Watch the movement of the eyes in one of three directions (in accessing a memory) to assess the correct primary modality. Ask your client to recall an incident, such as asking, "So, Fred, when did you and Ralph first meet? What happened that day?" His eyes will shift in one of three ways: up, indicating visual; to the side, indicating auditory; or down, indicating kinesthetic. Though not foolproof, this test usually is accurate in pinpointing the primary mode of any individual. Once you clarify their primary mode, share it with them, and begin to concentrate of allowing the client to address how this can help achieve the goals ahead. You as their sex coach will also have the advantage of being able to align your own speech to include their primary mode, by reflecting back in ways such as "I notice that . . .", "I hear you when you say . . ." or "I feel how difficult that must be for you."

Power all-day workshop, facilitated by famed motivational leader and NLP master trainer Anthony Robbins. That experience inspired me to solidify my approach with clients who rely on their "I can't" excuse to avoid change. Telling them about walking barefoot the 10-foot-long fire bed (hot enough to melt steel into a liquid) generally gets their attention. "When I got to the other side," I say, "I felt an overpowering sadness about how much I had missed in life by making excuses. Walking on fire showed me that I could never go back to my old way of living. I was freed from the tyranny of excuses for the remainder of my life. If I could walk on fire, I could do anything." When I finish this story, clients usually smile, wince a bit, and then breathe. That breathing is the cue that they understand. They don't have to walk across hot coals themselves. My fire walking helps them let go of their excuses and decide to walk on their own personal fire.

HOLISTIC/NEW AGE

The influx of New Age philosophies through books, videotapes, and television have greatly enhanced what we know today about the healing arts. Following is a brief look at aspects of New Age technologies, such as bodywork practices, and a discussion of some of the writers who have influenced my thinking.

Esoteric Models

Esoteric therapies often are rooted in energy flow and healing, like the ancient art of acupuncture. Carolyn Myss, whose work on modern energy healing mirrors my understanding of how the concepts work, teaches healing the past through using energy medicine. I took part in the workshops that preceded the publication of her recent book, *Sexual Contracts: Awakening Your Divine Potential*, which is a profound text on understanding the power of archetypes in our lives. Myss's books and tapes are part of my lending library for clients.

Eckhart Tolle presents a similar healing method in the popular book *The Power of Now*. The central idea—becoming now-focused rather than past-or-future-focused—is an essential teaching of sex coaching. One of the biggest names in esoteric healing therapeutic models is Wayne Dyer. His books, tapes, and audio programs [see Appendix E] teach human personal growth dynamics and the elements of healing on a high level. I use his CD programs as an active part of my teaching with clients.

Bodywork

Bodywork methods known to release emotional blocks include Rolfing, Feldenkreis, Alexander technique, Trager, and more. Unless you are trained in this kind of bodywork, refer clients to licensed practitioners. Many forms of professional therapeutic touch can be helpful for sex coaching clients who experience a lot of tension surrounding their sexual concern. The range of options includes spas, alternative healing centers, licensed independent practitioners of massage, and, of course, bodywork therapists. The history and scope of massage are discussed in my book *The Complete Idiot's Guide to Sensual Massage*.

The most controversial and misunderstood aspect of bodywork in healing sexual concerns is the use of sexual surrogates. The International Professional Surrogates Association (IPSA), founded by Vena Blanchard in Los Angeles, has been teaching qualified surrogates in body-on-body skills that they provide clients, hopefully under the care of a trained clinical sexologist. Surrogacy is not prostitution. The use of a surrogate can be the most powerful component in a sex coaching program if the client is unskilled and single, is in a sexless relationship, or has poor sexual performance skills. Typically clients are male and surrogates female, but there are a few male surrogates who work with women.

Healing Arts

The healing arts are growing in popularity. You need to be familiar with what's available in your community and recommend only those that feel right to you. Your clients will always tell you what they will and will not accept when you make suggestions and referrals.

I often refer certain clients for outside work in the healing arts, including Reiki energy work, in absentia pain management treatment, emotional/spiritual cleansing, colonics, nutritional counseling, body alignment, shamanic readings, Native American sources for animal medicine, astrology, numerology, prayer circles, Goddess worship, flower power (Bach flower remedies or other live essences), chanting, yoga, meditation, and others. In addition, I may recommend healing products such as stones, crystals, essentials oils, ritual objects, toning forks, Tibetan bells or bowls, Fengshui, herbal sexual enhancers, and homeopathic remedies. Study these products—and use them if you can—before you recommend them to someone else.

SELF-HELP THERAPY

With the explosion of self-help materials and resources, there are many to choose from. I have homed in on those self-help trends and on one particular phenomenon, John Gray's model, to illustrate other important influences on sex coaching today.

Gray's Model for Male/Female Communication

John Gray's Mars/Venus books have sold worldwide in the millions. He is a paradigm-shifter for the modern age. Beginning with the groundbreaking *Men Are From Mars, Women Are From Venus*, his books have altered our understanding of the gender gap and are helping heal the pain that gap has caused both men and women.

Gray has greatly influenced the way I coach individuals or couples who have relationship dynamics issues. I was fortunate to train under him in two programs following his intensive seminars. As I explain to clients, men go into their cave when they get upset and try to slay their dragons without talking through the pain, whereas women, as Gray says, just pick up the phone and talk about their upset until the cows come home. Of course, this is a generalization that doesn't apply to everyone, but there is significant truth in the assertion that in conflicts men avoid and women pursue.

One element of Gray's teaching that I often use with clients is his masterful Love Letter technique. I first learned of it during Gray's *Heart Seminar* in 1983. It broke through a family relationship block, changing for the better the pattern of relating between my father and me for the remainder of his life. What a blessing! I also benefited from learning about the anger process, and I often coach couples to try it. Discharging their pent-up angers and resentments safely through this process is cleansing and healing.

Self-Help Books, Videos, and DVDs

America has always been a self-help culture, and the Internet has made it even easier for people to buy sexually explicit educational material. This is a burgeoning market; you need to review or at least browse the products before you recommend them. (Not all sex advice is created equal.) Review Appendix E for a comprehensive list of books, videos, DVDs, websites, and other sources for self-help.

If there is a cornucopia of advice available today, there is also a culture of confusion surrounding that advice. The media distorts sexual reality—from porn videos (and mainstream films) featuring women who orgasm instantly to overly optimistic articles in women's magazines about reviving the passion in seven easy steps. You may notice the continual trend toward sexual braggadocio prevalent in men's magazines and the surely false stories of celebrity sex in other media outlets from *Us* and *People* to *Entertainment Tonight*. No wonder many people need to find a real person they can trust to advise them face-to-face on their sexual concerns. Most of your clients will have some sex information, but they may need your help in sorting myth from reality. And some may be suffering from information overload. How do they mine the gold from that trash heap of sexual information? They come to you because they need a sex coach to help them do it.

12-Step Models and Programs

One of the most successful therapeutic—but not therapy— programs is the 12-step model. Twelve-step programs are free of charge and ubiquitous. You can even find 12-step meetings for various addictions aboard cruise ships! The movement began with the *Big Book* written for alcoholics in the 1950s. Now millions of people use the steps to help them heal the damage from a multitude of problems from drug abuse to gambling.

I have found that some of these programs, such as the ones for eating disorders, drinking, and drugs, can be a healthy adjunct to the sex coaching process. I particularly believe that CODA (Codependents Anonymous) and ACA (Adult Children of Alcoholics) help people set healthy boundaries in intimate relationships.

Why do you need to know about 12-step programs as a sex coach? You will find it nearly impossible to continue to coach an alcoholic/addict or a partner of an alcoholic/addict. They need outside help. Insist that your client get that help—in a 12-step program if that seems to fit the need.

What about Sex and Love Addicts Anonymous? Chapter 11 discusses the highly controversial concept of sexual addiction. As a sexologist, I do not believe addiction is an accurate definition of the condition of compulsive sexual behavior.

To summarize, you are free to pick and choose the philosophies and schools of practice that resonate with your own training, belief system, and comfort zone. You may want to integrate many therapeutic models as you develop your sex coaching style, or simply tweak your already fully developed approach in order to become skilled at sex coaching. It is a process of dabbling into the paints on your palette, adding some new colors, and then using different brushes to get the desired effects from different strokes. Remember, sex coaching as an art is a matter of expressing your unique style.

Get It!

List three therapy approaches that may inform sex coaching and one main point about each.

1.

2.

3.

Now, in one sentence, write about what most influenced your thinking as you read about other therapy models and discuss how it could influence your own unique style of sex coaching.

PART TWO

Becoming
a
Sex Coach

CHAPTER THREE

Preparing Yourself
on a Personal Level

ARE YOU READY to make some personal discoveries as you prepare to become a sex coach? I hope so, because what you learn about yourself will inspire you and illuminate your path. Who you are determines how you will coach.

A client once told me: "Who I am with one person is who I am with every person." I thought that was an interesting adaptation of the old musical refrain: "I gotta be me!" As I have said, my coaching style is a very personal amalgam of other coaching models and therapy approaches. Yours will be too. And that's why you need to hone your attitudes, freshen your thinking, and make the necessary distinctions between what feels right for you and how other people work.

These distinctions are one of the hallmarks of coaching. As you read, imagine how you might approach each of the topics we cover. How would you infuse each coaching situation with your own sensibilities? Taking on the most intimate concerns of another human being calls for a special person. If sex coaching really is your calling, I hope this chapter gives you the information, inspiration, and courage to become a sex coach extraordinaire!

Personal preparation for coaching includes these big steps: (1) learning the three levels of language usage and the terms appropriate to coaching; (2) developing your own personal comfort with all aspects of sexuality; and (3) understanding the full range of human sexual behaviors and sexual expression.

SEXUAL LANGUAGE

The three levels of sexual language are:

1. *Medical/clinical* [often in Latin], such as *clitoris, vagina, penis, cunnilingus, fellatio.*
2. *Neutral,* such as *love button, canal, member, oral sex on her, oral sex on him.*
3. *Slang,* such as *clit, hole, cock, eating out, going down on.*

MORE ABOUT THAT

In the 1970s when I was training in a family planning clinic, I discovered a group desensitization activity that neutralizes sexual slang. First you list five to ten medical/clinical terms (single words or phrases) on sheets of newsprint, one term or phrase on each page. Divide the group of people into smaller groups of no more than five. Ask each group to write down all the slang terms, *dirty words,* they can for the clinical terms you've given them. Then ask each small group to rise in turn, stand in front of the whole group, and, in unison like a chant, yell out the slang terms from their sheets. This activity is an excellent and meaningful way to neutralize the negative charge that certain words hold. The word *pussy,* for example, is an oppressive word for some women but an empowering and erotic word for others. As Ibsen wrote, "There's no accounting for tastes!" You can modify this activity for use with clients, especially in situations where the couple disagrees about use of sexual slang.

A sex coach must accept a wide selection of sexual language to do his job effectively. Some clients use one or two levels of language; others use all three. You must be a safe container for all of their expression, verbal and nonverbal. How you respond to Jack's telling you about his *soft cock* will facilitate his healing. If you respond to some words with disgust or shame, you won't be able to hide it from a client. I often repeat the words my clients use, starting with the neutral words, and echo their linguistics. That method can help you meet clients where they are and keep the focus on their needs, not yours.

Acquiring a Comprehensive Sexual Vocabulary

Learning the language of sexuality may seem like a serious challenge. I am a firm believer in the power of laughter. Not only does it let you experience the feel-good chemicals in your body, but it also promotes learning—the student enjoys what he learns. That's what inspired me to include in my original sexual help Web site a multiple-choice test called the *sex quiz.* The reader was asked to choose the correct definition of a sexual term from a list that included riduculous answers that would make them laugh. For example:

1. A gonad is:
   A. The first line of a bebop tune sung by the Cadillacs ("Gotta gonad . . .")
   B. A rare species of leaping tree frogs from the Andes
   C. A reproductive organ, such as the testes or ovary
   D. The chant used at the 30-yard dash line in a home game
   Answer: C

2. The foreskin is:
   A. The covering over the handle of a golf club
   B. The movable skin surrounding the penile shaft that protects the glans (head) of the penis and is cut back during circumcision
   C. Furrows on the brow of the human forehead
   D. A home remedy used to shrink warts that appear on the foot
   Answer: B

These questions help readers learn learn the correct definitions while enjoying the humor of it all. You may not want to do a sex quiz, but you will need to familiarize yourself with a wide range of sexual terms, because your clients will use them.

Making Language Distinctions

Sex coaching, unlike other approaches to treating sexual concerns, does not pathologize behaviors. I have reworded many terms that have a judgmental tone to be more neutral. For me, changing negative language is an element in sex coaching. How can you become a supportive container and advocate for your clients if your language pathologizes them?

The following list (though not exhaustive) is a sampling of problematic terms and their more empowering, nonpejorative counterparts.

PATIENT VERSUS CLIENT

Your client does not have an illness or disease. (If she does, you should refer out and coach her to handle it.) You are not a medical doctor. *Client* is a neutral word that is more centered on growth than *patient* and is reflective of the less hierarchical client/coach relationship.

LOVEMAKING/MAKING LOVE VERSUS HAVING SEX/BEING SEXUAL

I avoid the term *lovemaking*. Not all clients are in love or feel love. *Having sex* focuses on pleasure—and on sex for its own sake. If the client says *lovemaking* or "I'm in love," that's fine.

PROMISCUOUS VERSUS SEXUALLY EXPERIENCED

Promiscuous is a damaging and judgmental term. A *sexually experienced* person has had more than a few sexual partners. The word *experience* gives a positive spin.

SEXUALLY ACTIVE VERSUS PASSIVE

This can be confusing. A *sexually active* person is more physically engaged in the sex act than a *passive* person. But *sexually active* also describes someone who is having or has had sexual activity (usually with a partner, not just solo sex). Finally, a *sexually active* person is not a virgin (someone who has not had sexual intercourse).

NORMAL VERSUS NATURAL

Use *natural* instead of *normal*, a word derived from research in which a *norm* or *normative* behavior is defined by statistics. *Natural* is a softer term that doesn't compare one person's sexual behavior to that of another.

WIFE/GIRLFRIEND AND HUSBAND/BOYFRIEND VERSUS PARTNER

We lack good words to name a sexual *partner* (my favorite term) when he or she is not married. In a heterosexist society like ours, *husband* and *wife* are the sacred names. Nonmarital relationships are denigrated as *boyfriend* or *girlfriend* regardless of age—or sometimes as *lover*. In gay culture, defined by sex, *lover* means partner.

SAFE SEX VERSUS SAFER SEX

In the HIV-prevention movement the phrase has been: "The only safe sex is no sex." Perhaps there's some truth in this. The preferred term now is *safer*, indicating levels of personal risk in being sexual with another person and risking contracting an STI, especially HIV/AIDS.

NEED VERSUS WANT/PREFER/DESIRE

Clients often use language that pushes their partner away from providing what they are seeking. For example, a partner's saying he *needs* something can make him seem need*y* to his partner. Coach your clients to speak from the *I* voice, empowering them to request what they want. If they ask that their *wants* or *desires* (requests) be met, they will not seem needy or too demanding—and they will be more likely to fulfill their sexual dreams.

SELF-CENTERED VERSUS SELFISH

Coaching emphasizes the self. Being self-centered implies egotistical, self-promoting behavior. Taking care of yourself is a critical part of being ready to share your life (or pleasure, or flesh) with another. Being extremely selfish is a good trait, placing the responsibility for your life and its results on you, not letting you wallow in the blame or complain game.

PREFERENCES VERSUS SEXUAL ORIENTATION

When working with lesbian/gay/bi/trans clients, help them and those around them make the critical distinction between *orientation* and *preference.* Our sexual orientation is *not* a choice or a preference. We can choose the sexual activities we prefer, but we can't choose our sexual orientation. Sexual attraction is inherent, not an option. Whether or not we act on our erotic attractions is always a choice. Part of your job as a sex coach is dispelling the myth that people choose sexual orientation. Above all, respect the language your client is using about herself; if she believes *sexual preference* best reflects her sexual orientation, honor that.

STD VERSUS STI

In the language of epidemiology, we have moved beyond VD (venereal disease), and STD (sexually transmitted diseases). Now it's STI, for sexually transmitted infections. Some of the conditions that your clients face are not diseases but rather infections or imbalances, many of which can be transmitted back and forth between partners. The new terminology is meant to help deflect social stigma.

Think about what other terms you may want to help your clients reframe, such as HIV versus AIDS, impotence versus erectile dysfunction, or premature ejaculation versus early ejaculation.

DEVELOPING A SEXUAL REPERTOIRE AS YOUR BASE

This may sound like preaching, but as a sex coach, you should you have a sexual repertoire of your own as a base of experience. You don't have to disclose anything about yourself that you don't wish to share. However, personal disclosure about your own sex life can sometimes provide the pivotal moment in coaching or provoke a breakthrough in healing for your client. If you haven't experienced much more than tepid vanilla sex (see Chapter 12 to learn more about *non-vanilla sex*) it's time for you to *sexplore* and *sexperiment*!

You owe it to yourself and your clients to break free of your own body image issues, sexual inhibitions, or concerns from a sexually charged past. Moving forward on your own personal growth trajectory as a sexual being is a necessary prerequisite for coaching. Be the ultimate role model for sexuality; you will serve your clients better. Of course, you don't need a penis to coach men on erectile dysfunction issues or to have given birth to coach a woman with pregnancy-related sexual concerns. A male sex coach doesn't have to be a master of multiple orgasms to guide clients on that path. And a woman can serve clients who play with S&M without having *professional dominatrix* on her resume. But the more you practice what you preach, the more authentic you are. Your coaching will have greater impact and reach. Expand your own sexual horizons before hanging your shingle. Your clients can only grow as much as you have grown.

Get Your Feet Wet

One of the caveats for training in clinical sexology is this: Never ask a client to do what you haven't done. Familiarity breeds better skills! To broaden yourself as a wide container for what the client asks of you, here is a checklist of suggestions for you to explore in your own personal journey of sexual development. What can you do to add to your palette of colors?

EXTRACURRICULARS

You certainly will never be expected to sign up for nude tennis or become a porn star. Let yourself explore realms that are unfamiliar to you, the knowledge and experience of which will enrich your ability to serve your clients' needs for your embracing their fullest sexual expression.

Naked resorts. They call themselves *naturists.* Go to a nudist resort, try being in a group of people without clothing, and check out how this makes you feel. You may be surprised to feel nothing. Or embarrassment. Or even a little erotic tinge. Don't, however, be shocked to find that there is *no* erotic tension flowing at all—just a bunch of bags of skin on bones, romping and sunning and doing all the natural things that people (even families) do when they want to relax and play.

Gentlemen's clubs. Visit a gentlemen's club. These may show women half-clad in costumes while pole dancing, or you may find women who prance on the stage in a strip show, leaving you panting at their bodies in mere thongs or nothing at all! I assure you that you need to experience being in the presence of open erotic enticement, in the flesh. Going to a strip club, an exotic dance salon, a burlesque ballroom, or an intimate playroom—wherever dancers are taking off their clothing and probing the audience erotically for cash—is something that will tell you a lot about your own erotic zone. And be assured that you are going to meet clients who spend many hours and dollars in this type of venue. So know about it.

Swinging. Lifestyles.org is the ultimate Web site for swinging. They offer a huge number of outlets where the full range of swinging attitudes and behaviors take place. It may be a swingers-only cruise, a play party, a special secret party at a person's home, or a resort hotel where the conventions are held. Know how it feels for you to be in the openness of a whole community of people who like to share their intimacy openly with others. Remember that if you go, you will never be touched against your will or be expected to do anything other than gawk. If you ever decide to be touched by someone other than your own partner, if you have one, this is a good venue to explore that option.

S&M venues. Even if you only walk into a store with S&M gear on the shelves or watch a video that teaches about dominance and submissive practices, you need to *feel* the erotic tension field that S&M is all about. In most major cities S&M groups hold monthly meetings or classes, such as the JANUS or Eulenspiegel societies. You may want to take an educational seminar or sign up for a special track at one of the AASECT annual conferences. You could find a local dungeon (the term for a play space where S&M activities occur in private) and witness the action. Or you can read the works of the Marquis de Sade or rent *The Story of O*, if that is closer to your learning style.

Spiritual-sexual workshops. At the other end of the sexuality spectrum from S&M is sexuality and spirituality. This feels softer, is anchored in accessing the inner self, and promotes a sense of spiritual union with your partner. You can find tantric (or other spiritually based teachers of sexuality) near you (see Appendix E), or read your local New Age magazines for listings. You may want to travel to Hawaii, where several spiritual teachers reside and offer in-residence workshops in the beauty of paradise. Whatever it is that you do, do something that takes you into this form of personal sexuality/spirituality connection. Even a simple tape of sitar music or reading the sacred literature of the East (think *Kama Sutra!*) will help set you into that realm.

Online porn. You may shudder to think that you have to cruise the Internet and then, as a lasting reward, get spam for months once you click onto the triple-X Web sites. Do it anyway. If you don't know what your clients are watching, how can you best serve their needs? Internet porn ranges from explicit photos to live sex acts and everything imaginable in between. The more raunchy and explicit, the more likely you have to pay a price—actual cash. You may want to browse a selection of adult sites online to give yourself a quick schooling in what's out there. Be sure to clear the cache on your computer after your home triple-X schooling to avoid any future trouble with your children or your work agency!

Triple-X movies. This may sound like a shocker, but I am a proponent of porn for couples and individuals who are either lacking in their own sexual repertoires or who may be unable to make up great fantasies during masturbation. Triple-X movies come in all different types: amateur style, high-quality Hollywood-style films, for women only, for gay men only, fetish, and so on. In the doctoral program at IASHS, students are required to view 100 hours of porn and code what they see. That process teaches a tolerance and understanding of the almost limitless range of human sexual expression. Even if you don't attend the classes at IASHS, you owe it to yourself to do some home sex schooling and watch as many kinds of porn as you can.

Believe it or not, these are just a few suggestions. The world of sex is enormous. I hope that your appetite for self-expansion and personal growth in the realm of sexual expression takes you to places I haven't mentioned. Online dating, strip poker games, board games for romance, books on tape, sensual massage, cross-dressing—the possibilities are like a storm of dandelion fur.

ADOPTING SEX COACHING ATTITUDES

Adopting the attitudes for being a sex coach may at first require a personal cleansing. After you review the following information and encouragement, you should be ready to move up to the actual steps necessary to apply sex coaching knowledge and practical skills.

Right-Brain Thinking

Sex coaching is a balanced set of right-brain and left-brain tasks. The left brain hemisphere controls our linear side—the part that counts numerically, uses logic, and gathers information. Our right brain is the part that we rely on for intuition and nonlinear thought, feeling, and sensing—in a word, art. Sex coaches, not unlike life coaches or therapists, get to use their right brain a lot!

Art is a right-brain process. I first studied Betty Edward's, *The New Drawing on the Right Side of the Brain*, during a drawing class I was taking. I was shocked at one of the initial exercises in the class: Our teacher told us to take a specific drawing from the book, turn it upside down, and draw it. It worked like magic—we were all able to replicate the image. Imagine being able to draw a Michelangelo pen-and-ink in fine detail on the first three tries! As she explained, it was because we could see shapes and the bigger picture when we got out of our left-brain thinking patterns. We learned to draw what we saw, not what we thought we saw. Just the simple act of turning the image upside down and studying it freed our perceptions on the right side of our brains. That's what a great sex coach can do as well.

It is inevitable that you will want to experiment as you develop your sex coaching practice. By shifting your focus and thinking to the right side of your brain, you will be better able to create your own design.

Unpack Your Baggage

You may be coming from a business or personal coaching background, seeking to expand the range of your coaching services. If you've been coaching organizations, businesses, persons, or groups, you know that your own *stuff* is going to show up along with your greatest skills. If you are working as a therapist, you're quite familiar with the personal growth necessary to become a helping professional.

Years ago therapist and author Barbara deAngelis hauled a baggage cart full of labeled luggage onto the set of her television show. The luggage bore large labels, including *guilt, fear, hatred, self-loathing, unrequited love, lost hope,* and *failures.* She used that luggage to make her point that we all bring a load of baggage into our relationships. You, too, will be hauling your past issues about sex and sexuality into your professional relationships with clients. And you must find a way to get rid of the baggage and heal your own concerns before you begin practicing.

Don't think that working as a sex coach will be your path to healing. Much of my work elevates me to a higher level and makes me feel so good that I sense I am being healed too. But I would never go *into* a sex coaching session or relationship expecting that for myself. Neither should you. As the sex coach, you must clean up your baggage cart before you enter the train station.

Start with your attitudes about yourself. This will make it easier for you to stop judging others, especially about something as complex, vast, and deep as sexuality. How do you define yourself sexually? You need a positive self-definition before you can begin helping others express their sexuality. This is perhaps the most amorphous part of the task of preparing yourself to coach.

Embrace the following qualities to develop the healthy attitudes that are a prerequisite for being a sex coach:

Tolerance	Intensity
Patience	Laserlike thinking
Acceptance	Articulateness/good communication
Unconditional love	Sensitivity
Liking people	High hopes
Compassion	Taking a stand for the clients' great-
Passion	est good
Honoring humanity	Taking a stand for your greatest good
Believing in magic/knowing	Keeping tight and clean boundaries
that miracles can happen	Showing up (on time) and being
Forgiveness	fully present
Understanding	Keeping a "no matter what" affect
Playfulness	Upholding "act as if" as an art form
Lightness of being	Adopting an "up until now"
Quick wit	approach

Get It!

What are three basic personal characteristics that could make you a better sex coach?

1.

2.

3.

CHAPTER FOUR

Preparing Yourself on a Professional Level

PREPARING TO BE a sex coach on a personal level is perhaps more daunting than on the professional level; both are critical to your success. Now that you're more comfortable with the personal issues, you're ready to learn everything necessary to start a sex coaching practice or integrate sex coaching into your existing coaching or therapy practice. The guidelines in this chapter will help you address the professional basics, including:

- Guidelines for sex coaching, including resources for updating your knowledge on sexual function and dysfunction, sexual anatomy, and physiology
- Understanding the diversity of sexual orientation and sexual expression
- Thinking outside the box
- Starting your own sex coaching practice

In addition, you'll learn why some coaching experiences are regarded as failures and how you can cope with them.

This chapter is not a panacea for your training. The appendices of this book supplement the material presented here by providing resources and tools for both personal and professional development. Someday you may even want to share your training and expertise as a sex coach with other professionals. You'll have everything you need here for designing a sex coaching training template, including the training and certification tools listed in Appendix E.

When you enter the practice of sex coaching, you enter the field of sexology. The client work demands mastery of a complex knowledge and skill base. And (I can't emphasize this enough!) you are shifting your perspective from other forms of coaching or therapy to join a community of professionals from many disciplines in a field with its own unique perspective.

GUIDELINES FOR SEX COACHING

As a sex coach, you are going to confront a vast array of attitudes, values, beliefs, and facts about human sexuality. Once you soothe yourself of your own misgivings or limitations about doing this work, the rest of your preparation follows. Several key organizations have developed helpful guidelines to set you on course for being ready to handle the challenges ahead as a sex coach.

Beyond the Personal

In sex coaching, perhaps more than in any other occupation, you not only have to know your stuff but also know how to let go of your stuff. As mentioned in the previous chapter, you have to get your baggage off the cart before you can serve the special needs of each client. In the increasingly competitive marketplace of professionals treating sexual concerns, clients make their choices based on a sex coach's personality, life experience, coaching skills, knowledge of sexual concerns, and contacts and connections.

Before you can take clients, you have to know who you are as a sexual person and what you can offer as a sex coach. Explore all the educational options available to you, including a SAR course (at IASHS or AASECT), explicit teaching videos, recommended books, and many conversations and interviews with people who have different sexual lifestyles. Those are the minimal steps for career preparation.

The Bricks and Mortar of Sex Facts

Although I'm tempted to offer a mini-course in facts about sexuality, I prefer to teach you how to integrate them into a dynamic sex coaching practice. This book isn't a textbook on the bricks and mortar of sexuality. It is a map for where to locate what you need to know. There are many excellent books, DVDs, videos, websites, and courses online or in person that will teach you about sexuality topics. Many of these resources are cited in the Appendix E. They will inform, educate, and prepare you for the ABCs of S-E-X.

What follows are several sets of standards and guidelines for becoming a well-trained sex coach, as well as some principles to augment your professionalism for this complex work.

Sexual Attitude Reassessment Standards

The AASECT guidelines for a sexual attitude reassessment (SAR) offer an overview of the range of topics in human sexuality that you should know to some extent. Review Chapter 2 for a description of the essence of the SAR process, which was created to help sexology professionals process themselves as individuals before helping others. How far you go in acquiring information on sex-related topics will be driven in part by your personal interest in addressing or targeting niche populations. If, for example, you decide to serve pregnant/post-partum women, or the transgender community, you'll want to learn more about relevant topics through varied resources.

THE PC EXERCISE MODEL

A sexologist should know about topics such as pregnancy prevention, STI protection, and sexual techniques, among others. You need to master any topics that seem relevant, from A for abortion to Z for zoophilia and everything in between, including the PC Exercise model found in Appendix D. AASECT has prepared standards for a SAR for certification that include suggested topics. Review the lists that follow and choose the topics that you think meet your needs. If you decide to become certified by the AASECT as a sexuality educator, counselor, or therapist, you will be required to attend a SAR and show mastery in all of the mandatory topic areas, along with five elective subjects in the broad field of human sexuality. Make mental notes as you read the AASECT guidelines that follow.*

* Reprinted by permission of the American Association of Sex Educators, Counselors and Therapists (AASECT); as approved by Board of Directors, 1999. SAR standards are currently under revision.

PURPOSE

AASECT requires the completion of an Attitude/Values Training Experience as a portion of the requirements for certification. Certification candidates most often satisfy this requirement by participation in a SAR seminar.

DESCRIPTION

The SAR is a process-oriented, structured group experience that promotes participants' awareness of their attitudes and values related to sexuality and assists them in understanding how these attitudes and values affect them professionally and personally. Because the primary purpose of SAR is the examination of attitudes and values, it is not a traditional academic experience designed to disseminate cognitive information, nor is it psychotherapy directed toward the resolution of personal problems.

PROGRAM OBJECTIVES

The primary objectives for participants in SAR seminars include:
• Exposure to a wide spectrum of human sexual arousal and behavior, followed by the opportunity to express their feelings regarding the range of human sexuality, including the identification of areas of comfort & discomfort
• Exploration of participants' attitudes and biases related to various sexual expressions and how these attitudes and biases may affect personal expression and professional interventions
• Increasing participants' comfort in discussing sexual matters
• Providing a nonjudgmental and respectful forum for the exploration of others' sexual values and differences
• The opportunity to better understand the sexual attitudes and values of persons whose sexual interests or physical or cognitive abilities are different from those of the participant

TOPIC AREAS

The basic SAR includes required topic areas, as well as elective subjects determined by the SAR presenter. Mandatory topics, presented in a topical, timely, relevant, and unbiased manner are:
• Masturbation
• Sexual orientation
• Sexuality across the lifespan

- Sexual variations
- Sexual ethics and morals
- Sexuality and physical and developmental disability
- Negative sexual experiences

Elective topics can include at least five of the following:

- Sex roles
- Sexual language
- Gender roles
- Pornography
- Sexually transmitted diseases
- Paraphilias
- HIV
- Touch
- Sexual dysfunction
- Intimacy
- Body image
- Jealousy
- Fantasy
- Religion
- Gender dysphoria
- Spirituality
- Sexual development
- Sexual potential
- Sexual assault
- Coupling
- Monogamy and multiple partners
- Cultural influences on sexuality
- Pregnancy
- Childbirth
- Abortion

The Institute for the Advanced Study of Sexuality

This second set of guidelines is extracted from graduate student competencies from the Institute for the Advanced Study of Sexuality (IASHS) programs.* It can be used as a guide for self-study and a means of self-assessment.

Clinical skills and competencies:

- To be able to choose a method of clinical intervention that is most appropriate for dealing with and presenting clinical problems.
- To have the skills to use any of the contemporary therapeutic techniques in their newest form based on the differential diagnostic methods used by such people as Bill Masters, Albert Ellis, and Marilyn Fithian
- To have the competency to be able to choose between clinical sexological interventions and more traditional therapy and to be able to refer when necessary
- To have the competency not to be noticeably judgmental when facing a client's unusual sex orientation or practices

* Guidelines excerpted with permission of the Institute for the Advanced Study of Human Sexuality (IASHS; www.iashs.edu).

- To have the competency to take a complete sex history using sexological coding systems that protect the privacy of the client
- To have the competency to be able to use the knowledge of developmental sexology for people in different parts of their life cycle
- To have the competency to deal with the situational factors that affect sexual values, sexual situations, and sexual functioning

Anatomy and physiology skills and competencies:
- To have the competency to deal with gender (identity and gender role) differentiation
- To have the competency to be able to interpret both the uniqueness and the similarities of male and female sexual anatomy
- To have the competency to explain the sexual response cycle
- To have the competency to understand the danger of vested interests of the other helping professions in dealing with presenting sexual issues

Legal issues:
- To have the competency to be able to sort out and interpret the various legal responsibilities of a sexologist

Sexuality Information and Education Council of the United States

The Sexuality Information and Education Council of the United States (SIECUS) lists the characteristics that define healthy adult sexual behavior. Like Planned Parenthood Federation of America (PPFA) and AASECT, SIECUS often leads the pack as a national organization establishing sexual health policy, pragmatic criteria for educational and clinical work, program development, professional training, and advocacy. I highly recommend visiting their Web site and becoming a member, which enables you to receive the *SIECUS Report*, a periodic journal that is one of the finest in the field. Other recommended journals are listed in Appendix E.

As you review the SIECUS *Life Behaviors of a Sexually Healthy Adult*, let yourself reflect on your own attitudes and responses to each statement. These are attitudinal statements, created in part to drive the content and spin on sexuality education and training programs. For your unique sex coaching practice you may want to promote these behaviors.

SIECUS LIST OF LIFE BEHAVIORS OF A SEXUALLY HEALTHY ADULT

A sexually healthy adult would:*

• Appreciate one's own body
• Seek information about reproduction as needed
• Affirm that human development includes sexual development that may or may not include reproduction or genital sexual experience
• Interact with both genders in respectful and appropriate ways
• Affirm one's own sexual orientation and respect the sexual orientation of others
• Express love and intimacy in appropriate ways
• Develop and maintain meaningful relationships
• Avoid exploitative or manipulative relationships
• Make informed choices about family options and lifestyles
• Exhibit skills that enhance personal relationships
• Identify and live according to one's values
• Take responsibility for one's own behavior
• Practice effective decision making
• Communicate effectively with family, peers, and partners
• Enjoy and express one's sexuality throughout life
• Express one's sexuality in ways congruent with one's values
• Discriminate between life-enhancing sexual behaviors and those that are harmful to self or others
• Express one's sexuality while respecting the rights of others
• Seek new information to enhance one's sexuality
• Use contraception effectively to avoid unintended pregnancy
• Prevent sexual abuse
• Seek early prenatal care
• Avoid contracting or transmitting a sexually transmitted disease, including HIV
• Practice health-promoting behaviors, such as regular checkups, breast and testicular self-exams, and early identification of potential problems
• Demonstrate tolerance for people with different sexual values and lifestyles

* Life Behaviors of a Sexually Healthy Adult is reprinted by permission of the Sexuality Information and Education Council of the United States, 130 West 42nd Street, Suite 330, New York, NY 10036, 212-819-9770, http://www.siecus.org.

- Exercise democratic responsibility to influence legislation dealing with sexual issues
- Assess the impact of family, cultural, religious, media, and societal messages on one's thoughts, feelings, values, and behaviors related to sexuality
- Promote the rights of all people to access accurate sexuality information
- Avoid behaviors that exhibit prejudice and bigotry.
- Reject stereotypes about the sexuality of diverse populations

Think through each of the behaviors and determine for yourself the answer to these self-assessment questions:

- What does this statement mean to me?
- What are the implications from this statement?
- How can I use this statement to better my sex coaching practice?
- What can I learn from this statement?
- What more do I need to study?
- How can this statement help me with my clients?
- How can this statement help my clients directly?

Let's look at one example: "Affirm one's own sexual orientation and respect the sexual orientation of others." You will have clients whose sexual pleasure is impeded by homophobia or sexual orientation confusion. By acknowledging this behavior of a healthy adult, your care for this client will become influenced by the move toward self-affirming beliefs and attitudes about his or her sexual orientation. You may realize that pushing this client toward affirming his sexual orientation will help him overcome shame, guilt, or his inability to perform sexually, alone or with a partner. Having this list of behaviors as part of your preparation for sex coaching expands your base of awareness, gives you materials for client handouts, and may lead you to training others in sex coaching methods.

World Association of Sexology

The World Association of Sexology (WAS) provides a more global perspective on sexuality. I attended the 2001 World Congress of Sexology conference in Paris, France—one of the biannual WAS meetings. At these international gatherings you will meet a smorgasbord of humanity—the world's best in sexology! The sheer volume of people, along with the massive amount of information shared and the glorious diversity, make it worthwhile to invest the time and money for attending a world meeting.

The meetings include a seemingly endless array of presentations on all aspects of human sexuality—including medicine, the law, cultural values, sociology, anthropology, politics, psychological models, clinical treatments, new drugs, ethics, feminism, and sexuality education. It's a dazzling cross-cultural variety of topics. I find that attending a meeting outside of the United States sheds new light on old subjects, from women's rights to the effects of clinical trials on new pharmaceutical drugs, to burgeoning trends in sexuality education programs to condom distribution programs to the erotic uses of poetry or the romantic cuisines of Europe! It's all there to titillate your thinking and shift your stodgy attitudes. Be sure that you go to a World Congress meeting at least once. See Appendix E to locate the next one.

You will derive great benefit from reading and absorbing the WAS guidelines that follow. They have been carefully distilled through a lengthy process and represent the amalgamation of disparate views of many people into one harmonious doctrine.

DEFINITION OF SEXUAL HEALTH

These set the guiding standards of practice in sexology worldwide. Use them to guide your own thinking and direct your one-on-one work. As a sex coach, part of your role is to advocate for sexual health and sexual rights. WAS uses the World Health Organization definition: Sexual health is the experience of the ongoing process of physical, psychological, and sociocultural well-being related to sexuality. Sexual health is evidenced in the free and responsible expressions of sexual capabilities that foster harmonious personal and social wellness, enriching individual and social life. It is not merely the absence of dysfunction, disease, or infirmity. For sexual health to be attained and maintained, it is necessary that the sexual rights of all people be recognized and upheld.

The definition of *sexual well-being* differs from client to client. As a sex coach, it's your job to promote the client's well-being, even if his or her definition is not your own. That is what I mean when I say you must coach for the highest values and wellness possible for your clients.

THE DECLARATION OF SEXUAL RIGHTS ACCORDING TO WAS

Sexuality is an integral part of the personality of every human being. Its full development depends upon the satisfaction of basic human needs, such as the desire for contact, intimacy, emotional expression, pleasure, tenderness, and love.

Sexuality is constructed through the interaction between the individual and social structures. Full development of sexuality is essential for individual, interpersonal, and societal well-being.

Sexual rights are universal human rights based on the inherent freedom, dignity, and equality of all human beings. Because health is a fundamental human right, so must sexual health be a basic human right. In order to assure that human beings and societies develop healthy sexuality, the following (abbreviated) sexual rights must be recognized, promoted, respected, and defended by all societies through all means. WAS states that sexual health is the result of an environment that recognizes, respects, and exercises these rights.*

1. The right to sexual freedom
2. The right to sexual autonomy, sexual integrity, and safety of the sexual body
3. The right to sexual privacy
4. The right to sexual equity
5. The right to sexual pleasure
6. The right to emotional sexual expression
7. The right to sexually associate freely
8. The right to make free and responsible reproductive choices
9. The right to sexual information based upon scientific inquiry
10. The right to comprehensive sexuality education
11. The right to sexual healthcare

UNDERSTANDING SEXUAL DIVERSITY

As you read Chapter 10, you will gain more understanding of sexual diversity than you perhaps had before. Let's review the message in Chapter 3: To be a great sex coach, you must expose yourself (not that way!) to an array of sexual behaviors and a wide range of human sexual expression, along with differing viewpoints, attitudes, and

* Reprinted by permission of the World Association of Sexology (http://www.worldsexology.org).

ideas, before you can adequately respond to the variety of demands that clients will ask of you. Beyond reading, go to places and events where you can meet people who are different from you in sexual orientation and proclivity. Sexuality evolves from a context. It does not exist in a vacuum. By talking to people, you will begin to see how and why their sexuality evolved. The powerful WAS sexual rights statement manifests a basic belief you must have as a sex coach: Everyone deserves the right to express their unique sexuality in whatever way they can, safely and appropriately. Your job is to help them make good choices for themselves and others.

You may have to attend conferences on transgender, for example, to serve those clients. Or you may wish to take classes in S&M or tantric sexual practices to become more savvy about those environments and the special behaviors of practitioners. The choices for broadening your knowledge and skills base are yours, but you must make some of those choices to stretch and grow.

That growth is an ongoing journey, not a destination. Be open to other cultures and diverse communities as you explore them. This fieldwork will help you develop your ability to become a safe haven for authentic sexual empowerment and acceptance. As you grow personally and professionally, you become that container for handling the concerns of your clients—and the range you can handle will expand, too.

THINKING OUTSIDE THE BOX

This section is designed to kick-start your thinking as an artist. Use your right-brain and let go of your linear ways!

The Artist's Way

Back to our art theme. As an artist, you might try different mediums—whether oils, acrylics, or watercolors—on the surface you choose for your expression. You could opt out of painting and use another medium altogether—pastels, charcoal, clay, mosaic tiles, wood, or even video. You get the point, don't you? Art is a creation made out of something. You are never going to paint like Picasso, Lichtenstein, Vermeer, or O'Keefe. Like any other artist, you are going to test drive different methods, styles, and nuances that come from both your personhood and your professional preparation for sex coaching. At the end of the day, though, you will do it *your* way. Your painting or other art form will reflect the flair that's one-of-a-kind yours.

I have shown you my own personal evolution; yours will happen in a different way. Whatever path you walk, you have to invent yourself in your own style. That uniqueness is what will set you apart in the marketplace from others who purport to offer similar services.

Sometimes that means going outside the box. Taking chances or risks to do it your way may be just the ingredient you need to freshen a stagnant therapy or coaching practice. Being highly creative can mean that there is no net under your trapeze act at times. That's fine. It's when we trust ourselves to fly that the outcome is usually the best. I encourage you to give yourself permission not to do it the way others have done it before. And dare to use techniques, approaches, exercises, recommended resources, and even your own personality that is not the standard fare. Being a sex coach is absolutely an open road.

STARTING YOUR OWN SEX COACHING PRACTICE

Once you have prepared yourself personally for sex coaching (through a SAR and other means) and have expanded your knowledge, attitudes, awareness, and skills as a sex coach, you have the opportunity to frame how you will actually conduct your practice.

Think about what you have learned so far. Let yourself integrate the personal and professional aspects of your coaching preparation into your own portfolio of methods. Make a checklist of questions that might include:
• What is my vision for my practice?
• Do I want to serve everyone or find a niche market, for example serving only singles, or couples, or restricting it to heterosexuals?
• Will I serve fetish or S&M clients or those who are involved in esoteric sexual-spiritual practices?
• Do I want to be telephone-only? Or will I have a private studio in which I see all clients?

• Do I want to be open on a 24/7 basis with ongoing email and phone contact, or set aside specific hours for communication with clients?
• Will I offer body coaching or stick to talking as my sole modality?
• Who will act as my client referral network, sending me new clients?
• When will I make referrals to offer as comprehensive a service as possible?

Further Training

Ask yourself what further training is needed for you to open your doors to sex coaching clients. You may want to take classes in, for example, NLP or active-dialogue technique, which you may find in local training programs or by attending IASHS or an AASECT meeting. Maybe you want more training in the clinical or pharmacological aspects of medical treatment for sexual problems. Perhaps you are seeking intensification of your therapeutic skills base by learning EMDR or hypnotherapy or becoming licensed in therapeutic massage. But to be ready to become a sex coach you will have to *feel* ready to address any sexual concern. Whether you seek better coaching training in a teleclass through CoachVille, more training in the therapy domain, or just want to add another medium to your artistic wares, you are in charge to self-determine which add-ons you want for being magnificent at what you do.

WHEN SEX COACHING FAILS

As you prepare yourself for this career path, expect some bumps along the journey. As with all professions, you may learn all you really do need to do a superb job at it. And, as with life itself, sometimes things just don't happen the way you wish. What exactly constitutes a failure? Sometimes it is a client with whom you don't click, or a client who simply cannot seem to budge from along his own continuum. Other times it's more subtle—a feeling you get or a pattern of missed appointments that gives you the sense, usually accurately, that this isn't working for you or the client. In those special cases where you have given your best and progress is not being made, it may be that the terror of facing the truth, and the compelling need to make a significant change, is the point of no return for a client. Sal was one such client.

INSIDE STORY: SAL'S PAIN

Sal suffered from psychologically triggered erectile dysfunction (see Chapter 7). His abusive, alcoholic girlfriend belittled his manhood, stopping sex when he went soft. His drug addicted brother was draining resources from the family business and crashing at Sal's house. His life, not his erection, was his problem.

When he asked for coaching on his erectile problem (this was before the days of Viagra) after being referred by a competent urologist, I said (with compassion) in our third session: "You have to face your life crisis. Until you are willing to let go of your damaging relationships, I cannot really help you." We argued for half an hour.

Then, abruptly, he said, "Dr. Patti, you're right. But I can't let them go. I guess I'll just go on like this."

Sal walked out of the studio that day, despondent. He knew that his inability to face the truth and make a huge life change was costing him his sexual identity and his life's pleasure. I never heard from him again.

Sometimes change is too hard. As a sex coach, hold up the truth for your clients, even if it costs you that client. Did sex coaching fail? I think so, but I'll really never know.

No matter how skilled you are, your sex coaching will sometimes fail. Sex coaching is intense, direct, and often confronts the client at the core of their resistance. Some clients will not be able to push through that resistance, no matter how many good suggestions you offer or techniques you apply. Unless you are doing a poor job at sex coaching, know that the difficulty isn't within you. Forgive yourself.

In some of my early trainings as a student of Anthony Robbins, I learned about the pain–pleasure continuum. People move toward pleasure and away from pain, especially emotional or psychological pain. Your clients are pain avoiders as much as they are pleasure seekers. I've discovered that a client quits when he can't face the pain of real change. The pain of change exceeds the reward (pleasure) that a new way of behaving would give him. Sometimes the clients who quit—our failures—leave the sex coaching process early on but return again later.

Get It!

Name three areas for your professional training that you are ready to explore now.
1.
2.
3.
What do you need to add to your tapestry of knowledge and skills to be available to work as a qualified sex coach?

CHAPTER FIVE

Toward A Successful
Sex Coaching Practice

BEFORE YOU ACTUALLY conduct sex coaching, you need to set up your practice. This chapter provides helpful guidelines for establishing a new practice or integrating sex coaching into an existing practice, including tips on building your client list. It also gives suggestions on marketing and publicity, especially on effectively promoting yourself in the media to attract clients and gain credibility as an expert in the field. The appendices supplement this chapter with handy reference guides, giving you useful tools for sustaining a sex coaching practice and implementing the information in this book.

PUTTING YOUR SEX COACHING PRACTICE TOGETHER

The first issue you will confront as a new businessperson (if you are just starting a practice) and as a new sex coach is the question of fees.

Setting Fees

The fees you can charge depend on several factors, primarily your range of professional experience and the going rate for commensurate professionals in your marketplace. The following principles have served me well, both in earning a decent living and letting me live according to my own principles of fairness to myself and my clients—one of the important coaching principles discussed earlier in the book.

MAKE YOUR FEES AFFORDABLE

As an entrepreneur, you must set reasonable fees so that you have clients! Don't under- or overcharge. I charge $120/session, which runs for about an hour. For double sessions, the fee is doubled, and so forth. I have conducted (though rarely) 7-hour sessions, at seven times the hourly rate, plus travel.

SLIDING SCALE

Especially if you are a coach and not a licensed therapist, psychologist, or social worker with the capacity to accept third-party payment (insurance)—you need to have a sliding fee scale, with fee based on ability to pay. That is fair and reasonable for both you and the client. Give your client a range and ask what he can afford. If you are out of the client's range, you may want to engage in barter.

BARTER

I've had many clients with cash flow deficits, particularly early in my practice. Instead of paying cash, they paid in kind. Before sex coaching began, I discussed fees and modes of payment. I suggest that you never agree to a barter of a client's services. That can lead to a tricky dual relationship. Approach barter as a primitive means of payment, predating actual coins and dollars, and go for goods. I've been paid in hats, wearable garments, jewelry, and art—all negotiated ahead of the first session. (One colleague in Hawaii is often paid in the currency of fresh mangos!)

PAYMENT PLANS

If you have a website and/or credit card fulfillment options, make that option available to your clients. Having them pay for the session with a credit card in advance is a common practice. You may also want to do a three-quarter payment plan. I let clients whom I will see more than a few times pay for four sessions in a 4-week period for the cost of three. That 25% reduction is often the dealmaker for financially constrained clients. Devise your own payment plan based on your client's ability to pay and your flexibility. My motto with clients is: "Money is never a reason for you not to work with me."

VALUE VERSUS COST

In coaching the question of cost versus value often arises. You have paid X dollars for an item, or an experience, such as trip to Paris or an educational seminar of great value to you or your career. Wouldn't you value that experience as being worth more than the actual cost? Years ago, as a working single mother with almost no expendable income, I enrolled in Transcendental Meditation. When I begged for a waiver of the $35 initiation fee, the teacher told me, as he'd been taught by Maharishi Mahesh Yogi: "In America, people don't value things they get for free. You have to pay something to make it have value to you." You will meet sophisticated clients who will avoid payment or genuinely not be able to pay full fare; ask them to pay something anyway or they may not value the service. The few times I gave away my sex coaching services to clients, I regretted the outcome. Don't get caught in that web.

CASH VERSUS CHECK IN SESSION ONE

I usually insist on cash payment rather than a check for the initial visit. This helps sort out clients who aren't that interested in coaching and will be wasting your time.

COUPLES VERSUS INDIVIDUALS

You may—as I do normally—charge more for a couple than an individual. Why? If you do spot coaching and check-ins, including frequent emails between sessions with each person, you may feel like you're being paid far too little for your double time. Consider setting your couples' fee at 25% higher than an individual's fee; then reduce it for any individual sessions you conduct with the couple.

SPOT COACHING THE FORMER CLIENT

What if you have raised your rates and a former clients contacts you for spot coaching? Raising fees for former clients can be difficult. They know the cost of everything else has gone up in two, five, ten years—but they think your fees should remain frozen in time. I suggest using the same guidelines you apply to other coaching or therapy clients. I often charge the old rate, or a rate somewhere between the old and the new, partly because I benefit from tracking their progress.

Recording Your Sessions

Whatever you do, keep records. I suggest that you keep a record, in some format, of each session. First, this is good business practice. It may serve you later if there is a dispute about what you provided. Second, it helps keep you focused on what the client is saying to you or what is taking place. Third, good note-taking or recording with technology will aid you in tracking your client's progress. It may also help you spot trends in your client's evolution and may inform you about your own sex coaching skills as they develop or change.

CLIENT RECORDS/INITIAL AND FOLLOW-UP

With each new client, I indicate their MEBES concern and some options for resolving the concern on the initial intake form (I color code them to distinguish the first from follow-up visits). I usually get the client's email address in the first session so I can send the male or female intake form immediately. On all follow-up forms I track the client's concerns, progress, and home assignments. Sometimes I also modify the action plan.

CLIPBOARD FOR NOTE-TAKING

I attach the forms to a clipboard that I have with me at each session. The name at the top is a code and never a full name (to protect my clients in case my files are requested for legal purposes). The clipboard suits my personal style. I say, "I will be taking notes on today's session, so I can review what's going on later. That allows me to focus more fully on your concern. I hope you are comfortable with that." No one has refused to let me take notes on their behalf. I think they are relieved to know that I'm paying full attention to what they say. I do, of course, set aside the clipboard and note-taking if clients are in emotional crisis (crying) or when I sense that I need to look into their eyes, listen intently, and be with them for that moment of disclosure. You will develop your own method of recording and listening. Preserving your observations about clients as you track their progress, however, is key to being a successful sex coach.

INDEX CARDS

I often use index cards to jot down a home assignment or clarify a recommendation for a book, DVD, or activity. You may choose printed handouts of your home assignments. I also refer clients to suggested activities on my website or print sections out for them.

> **MORE ABOUT THAT**
>
> You will develop working techniques that have your unique personal mark. When I worked with Albert Ellis, he used an ancient Rolodex card holder. He spun the holder on his lap while he lay back in his lounger. As he talked to me, he'd intermittently scribble notes on the little white cards. I'll never know if he was tracking my session—or if, for example, he was making notes to himself to buy more peanut butter for his frequent snacks or scribbling suggestions for his own writing. A giant like Ellis can get away with eccentricity, but a new sex coach probably can't. Be creative in your own approach to recording the sessions—but do record them.

TAPE RECORDING

An audio tape recorder may be required in sessions if you are under supervision by another professional or when you are working toward a degree, certification, or licensure. In my personal journey in therapy, I always audio-recorded every session with my therapists. Sometimes I did replay them, especially the very emotionally charged sessions when I feared that I wasn't taking in all the great information. But stick to a pen and paper unless your client requests that you tape him, you want proof of what was said (for a difficult case, for example), are under supervision, or prefer this method as a way to capture the content and nuance of each session.

VIDEO RECORDING

You may want to have a video recorder in the room. In my past family therapy, sessions were both videotaped and observed through a one-way mirror by a team of therapists-in-training. If you work in those circumstances, you may need videotaping. Or, as an entrepreneurial sex coach, you may videotape clients to show them exactly what they are saying, showing, and exhibiting. (Make copies of the tapes available to them at cost.) I've taped private sessions in my weeklong seminars aboard cruise ships. Sometimes these tapes are a documentation of the client's most important sex coaching encounters.

TELEPHONE SESSIONS

You may want to offer telephone sessions. They can be recorded into a sound file on a computer (for later download access) or even a URL designated for this. You may want to establish your own URL for such recordings, a private Web site where clients can access their live phone sessions with you. These files also can be transferred to CDs for your clients. Technology can be your best friend as a sex coach!

Other Considerations

Beyond how you keep track of the content and flow of your time spent with clients, there are other things to consider. Your role in relationship to your clients (and how to communicate your role and expectations to clients) will govern your success. Providing printed guidelines, taking care of your own safety, and assessing if you wish to expose your current lifestyle to a line-up of strangers marching through your private residence are some of the factors to evaluate before you start.

CONFIDENTIALITY

The greatest gift you can offer another person is to *be there* or *be present* for them, unconditionally. You become the safe container of what they express. Your role as a sex coach is to sustain and contain anything the client gives you. But when your client is suffering deep psychological pain or confusion, you may—as I've said many times in this book—want to refer out to a therapist. By setting good boundaries, defining your role, respecting confidentiality on both sides, and clarifying expectations from the beginning, you can be there for your clients. This is a step beyond offering your opinion. Treasure that responsibility and empower the client to uphold his end of this trust balance. Of course, in your initial handout or opening remarks, stress mutual confidentiality.

GUIDELINES FOR CLIENTS

Show your clients in writing what you expect from them and what they can expect from you. In the first session, give them a handout of your guidelines (See Appendix B). You may include your guidelines about on-time payment, sliding fee scales, keeping appointments with cancellation/rescheduling clauses for missed appointments, and mutual confidentiality requirements. List your credentials and contact information, such as your telephone numbers or specific hours of availability for full sessions and spot coaching. Sometimes I give handouts covering specific needs (for example, sexual rights information) or terms for loaning or selling my own books when appropriate. I write down their next appointment on my business card—giving them a handy contact reference.

MAIL-ONLY ADDRESS

If possible, have a neutral mailing address (such as a mailbox service) printed on your business cards. I *never* give out my actual home or office/studio address online or on my business cards. Be savvy about protecting yourself. Some people think that sex coaching is a cover for prostitution. Keep your public persona protected and your personal life safe.

HOME-BASED OFFICE OR STUDIO VERSUS AN OUTSIDE OFFICE

As telecommuting has become commonplace, many professionals, including coaches, work from their own homes or apartments. Working from home rather than an office building won't damage your status. I have never rented office space because I find sex coaching to be such intimate and delicate work that I can't imagine doing it outside a safe and warm environment. (I use a wicker screen to separate my desk from the session area in my home office.) However, there are some issues to consider, including privacy (you may not want to reveal where you live), housekeeping (having a home-based office or studio requires that you maintain a very neat, clean home), space (in a metropolitan area, space is limited), safety (you may feel safer working in a public space), support services (sharing office space with other professionals can give you access to a reception area and staff). Decide what is best for you given your personal living circumstances. I would never, for example, rent a sterile office and see clients dressed in a white lab coat, but you may need to be in a clinical setting as part of a comprehensive medical or coaching team. Or you may need to rent separate space if you have pets and children at home. Another option is to offer sex coaching house calls, which I do occasionally, especially for body coaching. These eliminate the need for an office at all. If you primarily rely on telephone sex coaching, you can even work from your cell phone in the car or at the beach as long as you provide your full attention and a clear line of communication for your clients. That is the joy of sex coaching in a virtual world!

GROWING A SEX COACHING PRACTICE

Sometimes a sex coaching (or any other coaching) practice fails for one simple reason: No one knows it exists! No advertising or networking results in no clients. I do a lot of national media, am listed on many search engines on the Internet, and have a listing in the website for AASECT. I get most of my clients through the Internet. They say, "I saw you on television [or quoted in a magazine article] and did a Google search." Or they went to the Internet in search of a local sexologist.

Some places where you can advertise or network:
• Holistic magazines
• Conferences with other professionals

MORE ABOUT THAT

I once did a workshop on female masturbation in New York City for a large adult learning group. Although nine registered in advance, only two women showed up. I was disappointed. However, one woman became a long-term client. Don't become discouraged when you don't make your bottom line amount on a workshop. Adopt a positive attitude. You are marketing yourself and someone—even if only one person— is listening. If you're good at what you do and have a passion for your work, you will succeed. Passion and good skills are client magnets.

- Weekly papers
- Organizational directories
- Websites
- Professional networking groups
- Paid workshops (such as *Learning Annex*)
- Free talks on sexuality in the community

The teamwork approach can help you build a practice too. Cultivate a referral base, including chiropractors, nutritionists, body workers, gyms, health clubs, MDs (OB/GYN, urologists), tantra practitioners, S&M societies, Crossdresser (CD) groups, swinging groups, Chinese doctors, herbalists—other professionals who will send sex coaching clients your way. Consider integrating your coaching services into a group clinic or sexual health center. After you've built a client base this way, you'll be able to go out on your own if that's what you really want to do.

EXPANDING YOUR PRACTICE

Although you may think that a sex coaching practice consists of one-on-one client sessions in your office or studio, it can be much bigger than that. Broaden your thinking about what you do and where you do it.

Add Services

If you don't have a ready-made audience or client base, you can expand your range of influence as a sex coach by learning more skills and adding to your range of services. For example, you may specialize in a combined practice, such as hypnotherapy and sex coaching, life or personal coaching and sex coaching, licensed massage therapy and sex coaching, esoteric forms of healing (Reiki, hands-on treatments) and sex coaching, reflexology and sex coaching. You will need additional training and probably advanced schooling, but that added education can pay big career dividends.

Certificates

You can increase your knowledge and prestige by earning certificates, for example from the Institute for Advanced Study of Human Sexuality, where you can be certified as a sexologist. AASECT awards certifications as sex educator, counselor, or therapist, one of my credentials. In the future you'll be able to earn sex coaching certificates at the website for Sex Coach University. You can always go to sexology conferences and earn continuing education credits (CEs) or even sponsor your own events for CEs. Consider obtaining a certificate in companion practices, such as Feng Shui or personal trainer, if you have added those services to your practice. The more richness you can bring to your sex coaching practice, the better.

Marketing, Spin, and PR

You can't be a real success in America without the media. I use the media on a global scale, but you can build up your practice by getting coverage in the local media. Not all sex coaches will be quoted in *Cosmopolitan* magazine or appear on national TV talk shows. You may cringe at the thought of speaking on camera. Sell yourself in a media outlet that matches your particular strengths. Just do something—anything, really—that showcases your talents and your business.

Markets and Venues

Following is a sampling of media markets and venues to explore:

LIVE RADIO SHOWS

Terrestrial (land-based) shows. Accept every opportunity to be a guest. Establish an ongoing relationship with local talk show hosts who know they can always count on you to talk about sex (coaching). If you're a good guest, you might be able to work into your own show or regular segment of a show.

SATELLITE RADIO

This new medium is very popular and growing. The shows are similar to their terrestrial counterparts, with commuter-hour shows that tend to be less family-oriented and more likely to air a sexuality-based show.

INTERNET RADIO

A growing trend, Internet radio has a worldwide reach and benefits from both advances in and consumer comfort with the concept of media in cyberspace. Visit www.surfnetmedia.com for options in being a guest and hosting your own show. Internet radio shows are archived, meaning they can be downloaded anytime. They last forever.

LIVE TELEVISION SHOWS

From local cable access to the networks, television uses many experts. And sex experts are particularly popular guests during rating sweep periods. Experts are frequent guests on talk shows, but even news stories and documentaries (on CBS News, the History Channel, by independent producers, and so on) weave commentary from experts into their programs. Hosting your own TV show is possible, especially if you are willing to start in local cable or university stations.

MAGAZINES

National magazines, especially women's magazines, run stories that quote experts on sex topics. If you have authored a book and can come up with fresh quotes, you will get your name in print, maybe frequently.

JOURNALISTS

Be courteous and accommodating to journalists asking for your help on articles! The more generous you are with your time, the greater rewards you reap in print. I always make time for a writer for a national magazine and sometimes for local news. And I truly enjoy talking to writers or journalists. Even if you are wary of the press, you can't afford to alienate them. A caveat: Beware of journalists looking for that one sensational quote they can take out of context—to your disadvantage. Speak carefully. You can ask to see final copy before print, but very rarely will a journalist agree to that. Don't make judgmental comments or accusations like: "I know the medical center director is lying about the number of patients who . . ." or "Our mayor is a jerk for letting kids. . . ." Be the consummate professional; speak honestly, with style and authority. When you want to share something spicy or personal, say: "Off the record, and I mean that. . . ." *Never* say anything about *your* sexual experience in print.

BOOKS

Write your own book, even if you self-publish. You must get your name out there for media coverage. One warning: Publishing is a tough business. Submit a solid, professionally written, unique book proposal to a literary agent. And keep trying until you get an agent. The competition for agents and publishers is stiff. Advances are notoriously low if you don't have what they call a *platform* or wide reach/name value. But you need a book. Consider it an investment in your future, like an advanced degree.

LOCAL NEWSPAPERS, ESPECIALLY WEEKLIES

Being quoted in local papers gives your practice visibility in the community. Keep up local ads/listings. Even consider pitching the editor a proposal for your own column. It won't pay much, but it will give you a high profile and name recognition that attracts clients.

WEB SITE

Above all else, have your own Web site. It acts like an online Yellow Pages ad for your services. Your website is also a great calling card for media looking for good quotes or spokespersons. You can make it simple or interactive; you can put it together yourself or hire talented (and fairly expensive) website development professionals.

The success of your sex coaching practice depends on how energetically you pursue expansion and on what some people call "shameless self-promotion." Remember the coaching guideline to become attractive. Be as magnetic as you can be and clients will find you. Think creatively about how to augment your range of sex coaching services. Get into the stream of public promotion and develop awareness about your practice. There are unlimited ways to make your practice grow and thrive. Just keep at it.

MORE ABOUT THAT

Once you develop a media presence, you will receive this request: "Can we use your clients for interviews?" Some reporters insist that you give them clients' names and contact information in exchange for featuring you in a story. Learn the art of saying "no"—without losing your opportunity to participate.

A national television news magazine wanted to use me for a story with one of my more extraverted clients. She agreed to discuss her sexual problems if I would appear on camera with her. After the show's producer quit, the new producer was preparing to air the story without me on it. I knew the segment would ultimately exploit my client. I threatened to sue. They threatened never to contact me again. I held my ground; protecting my client was my ethical duty. The segment didn't air. I will never again involve clients in situations where exploitation is even a remote possibility.

Get It!

Name three elements you can identify in setting up the structure of your practice:
1.
2.
3.

What are two ways in which you can expand or promote your practice using media?
1.
2.

PART THREE

Delivery
of
the
Service

CHAPTER SIX

Assessment Criteria for Clients and Sex Coaching Methods

THUS FAR THIS BOOK has provided you with an overview of the sex coaching profession and a discussion of the qualifications you must bring to it. Now you will see how the principles of sex coaching are applied to resolve specific sexual issues and concerns.

The sex coaching models covered in this chapter include:
• My own MEBES model, both a philosophy and method for assessment and for providing options for the resolution of sexual concerns
• The Dodson orgasm-directed coaching method
• Joe Kramer's self-pleasuring paradigm for men
• Energy-alignment techniques, including Reiki

What you learn here will prepare you for the detailed work in Chapters 7–12, which address the most common sexual concerns among men, women, and couples. Studying these coaching models will also help you construct a working template to use in your practice.

THE SEX COACHING PROCESS

There are many imaginative approaches to sex coaching. This chapter discusses those of Betty Dodson, Joseph Kramer, and my MEBES method, outlines specific steps to take, and provides information on sexual surrogates. But first, let's take a look at the actual sex coaching process.

What Is Sex Coaching?

I have talked about my philosophy and approach as a sex coach, especially using the MEBES model. Here is another way to look at what a sex coaching practice may offer clients:

1. Personalized information and education on sexuality
2. Redirective cognitive processes and mental reframing
3. Emotional balancing
4. Intuitive guidance
5. Behavioral training
6. Resource and referral management

Driven by clients' desire to set and reach goals for sexual fulfillment, sex coaching is not talk therapy. A sex coach doesn't look back at the stumbles and falls in a client's life. Instead, she takes the client's hand, guides and empowers him, and points him toward his expressed dreams. With a focus on future outcomes, sex coaching is a process, not an event. It involves not only talking but also accessing emotions, practicing a variety of specific exercises, conducting home assignments to do alone or with a partner, reading, watching videos, writing, and, most of all, daring to change.

How Does Sex Coaching Work?

In treating sexual concerns, five basic areas must be discovered, addressed, unblocked, and then aligned. For most people, all five elements must be in alignment for sex to be fulfilling. The areas are:

MIND

Information. Self-talk, thoughts about sexual performance, capacity for fantasy, and troubling thought patterns, such as compulsivity.

EMOTIONS

Feelings. Feelings that a person carries from the past about body and body image, what to suppress and express, how to express emotions, and capacity for intimacy.

BODY AND BODY IMAGE ISSUES

Physical. A person's knowledge of how her own sexual pattern works, understanding of her own body's sexual architecture and function, acknowledgment of her own sexual (dys)functions, and learning skills for how to be a successful lover alone or with a partner.

ENERGY

Sex is all about energy! The buildup, the containment, and the expression of energy. In my one-on-one work I observe energy patterns with the individual and with a partner (nonphysical relationship dynamics are energy exchanges too) and I give coaching feedback for handling this often overlooked part of sexuality.

SPIRIT

The essence of self. Esoteric moments or practices that transcend the moment (such as peak orgasm experiences), sacred sexuality, the more subtle and delicate manner in which people deny or reflect their inner self through sexuality, and the path of sex to experience the divine or God.

Who Can Use Sex Coaching?

Any adult could probably benefit from sex coaching. I work with men, women, and couples. Even teens are welcome to access the wide range of information available at my website for their protection and wellness. My work is gay/lesbian/bi/trans-friendly, although my website and my individual sessions are primarily heterosexually oriented.

HOW CAN SEX COACHING HELP SOME COMMON SEXUAL CONCERNS?

The nine most common sexual concerns for men are covered in detail in Chapter 7. They are:
• Low or no sexual desire (LD)
• Early ejaculation (EE)
• Erectile dysfunction (ED)
• Delayed ejaculation (DE)
• Sexual inhibition (SI)
• Body dysphoria issues (BD)
• Social/dating skills deficit (SDSD)
• Desire for enhanced pleasure (EP)
• Sexual trauma (ST)

Men often present with more than one of these concerns because the problems are intertwined. For example, men with EE often suffer from ED because they lose an erection with too-rapid release.

The ten most common sexual concerns for women are covered in Chapter 8. They are:
• Low or no sexual desire (LD)
• Preorgasmic primary (unable to reach orgasm, either alone or with a partner)
• Preorgasmic secondary (unable to reach orgasm with a partner)
• Dyspareunia (painful sex)
• Vaginismus
• Sexual inhibition (SI)
• Body dysphoria issues (BD)
• Social/dating skills deficit (SDSD)
• Desire for enhanced pleasure (EP)
• Sexual trauma (ST)

The eight most common sexual concerns for couples are covered in detail in Chapter 9. They are:
• The sexless relationship: little or no sex in the relationship
• Aversion to touch or misplaced touch communication
• Conflicts about desire/uneven desire (UD)
• Conflicting values about monogamy/affairs
• Performance skills deficit (PSD)
• Body image issues (BI)
• Communication style conflicts (CS)
• Negotiation skills deficit (NSD)

SEX COACHING WITH THE MEBES MODEL

I use the MEBES model as my assessment and action plan design tool. In the initial assessment the model works as a template for determining the issues, problems, or concerns the client brings to the sex coaching process. In other words, why is the client here? Again, MEBES is not a medical model or psychotherapy evaluation tool for diagnosing disorders. Medical and psychotherapy models often pathologize behavior that a sex coach views as natural within the broad spectrum of human sexual expression. I often code the intake notes with an M, E, B, E, or S to indicate the realm of each client's concerns. Once the assessment is made, I use the MEBES model to address the identified concern.

Reading the descriptions below should help you interpret situations and conditions that are blocking sexual fulfillment for your clients. You will also quickly become more savvy about developing action plans that utilize their unique skills and abilities for overcoming their obstacles.

How an Action Plan Evolves From the MEBES Model

Once you have identified which element(s) from within the MEBES model is affecting your clients, you can then construct an action plan. That is your guiding force for preparing steps to address the originating concern(s).

M (MIND OR MENTAL)

What a person thinks or thinks he knows, self-talk (what he tells himself), information, past held beliefs, current belief system (BS) that may impede satisfying sex.

Many clients in this category need a big coaching push. They are blocked by negative, self-deprecating talk, lack of sex information or misinformation, a sex-negative value system or set of personal beliefs (from family, church, or peers), or simply a lack of ability to fantasize better sex. I tell them that sex begins in the brain: Your mental realm can be your best ally or your worst enemy for sex. Through coaching they learn how to shut down the *bad sex* part of the brain by quelling the negative thoughts—about losing an erection, about looking fat naked—and correcting misinformation.

You will be a teacher with this client group, often devoting sessions to instructing, re-educating, and helping convert the negative mental chatter to positive internal messages. For example, you may change a client's "stinking thinking" (12-step lingo) into positive self-regard. Teach him to stop the "monkey mind" that tells him he isn't good enough in bed. Tell her that her clitoris is her primary site of pleasure and help her move from a vaginal-centric sex style.

INSIDE STORY: AN UNFORGETTABLY SAD WOMAN

In my early days in the 1970s as a rural outreach worker for a statewide Planned Parenthood affiliate, I counseled an unforgettable client. She was the classic case of sexual ignorance and confusion: When told to use jelly in her diaphragm, she obediently slathered it with grape jelly. She consequently became pregnant and subsequently had an illegal abortion, which left her scarred for life. A simple piece of factual information could have saved her from years of regret and sorrow.

E (EMOTIONS)

What a person feels, sexual history/emotional baggage and jubilant moments, past emotional disturbances revealed in the sex history forms, past incidents or patterns of abuse, the terrible three (fear, guilt, and shame), stuck feelings (which may come out in anger release).

Several coaching techniques can evoke feelings and clear them. For example, John Gray's Love Letters (from *Men Are From Mars, Women Are From Venus*) help clear and redirect blocked emotions. You may coach an angry woman to vent her rage by beating a pillow or screaming at the top of her lungs while alone in the car. I coach some clients to push through negative emotions by singing in the shower or boxing in the gym. Use your own imagination in constructing an option for your clients that addresses their E blocks.

In my own personal growth training I attended *Insight Transformational Seminars*, founded by John Roger. We learned to think about emotion as *energy in motion*, dispelling its negative charge. Emotions are neutral, not good or bad. The inside story of the woman whose emotions turned her chest to ice illustrates how emotions can be powerful friends or foes.

B (BEHAVIORS/BODY)

What a person does, how he feels about his physical self, body language, signs of affection, sexual performance and techniques.

Some clients don't know how to be a lover, good or bad. You will have clients who don't know the difference between a G-spot and the tip of their nose. Others will seek help for specific skills, like touching or kissing or oral sex. You will certainly have couple clients who want to put the passion back into their relationship. What their bodies do—and don't do—says as much as their words about their sex knowledge, skill, desire, and level of functioning.

You will also have clients with body image issues (discussed in depth in Chapters 7, and 8). A number of sexual concerns fall under the heading of B for "body"—but they are not always expressed verbally. Always pay as much attention to what clients do as to what they say!

INSIDE STORY: THE GIRL WITH THE HIDEOUS THIGHS

Celine could have stepped off the cover of Vogue—*lithe silhouette, luxurious hair, perfect face. I was stunned when she walked into my studio. This was the woman with the so-called hideous thighs and ugly body?*

When Celine called to make her appointment, she said, almost sobbing in a hushed voice, "Dr. Patti, I can't get past my ugly body. I can't have sex with the lights on and my boyfriend's bugging me to do something about it!"

As she sat down in the chair across from me, I tried not to focus on her extreme beauty. "Celine, can you tell me more?" I asked. After some discussion about her concerns, I attempted to soothe her discomfort by telling her how beautiful she was.

Suddenly Celine stood up, pulled down her slacks, pointed to her upper right thigh, where the panty line touched, and said, "It's this hideous thing. I can't let a man see me like this. I hate this piece of cellulite! What can I do about it, Dr. Patti?" she screamed.

Sometimes the life of a sex coach is heavy; sometimes it's hard not to laugh! There on this gorgeous woman's thigh was a whitish puffy spot no bigger than a dime. This so-called hideous body part had shut her down sexually for years.

We spent half the session discussing options. Would she be able to slide into self-acceptance, knowing that a seasoned sexpert was telling her this bit of imperfection was really no big deal? Would she insist on seeking out liposuction or cosmetic surgery? Would she confess that there was more to her concern than this tiny bump? She finally admitted that she'd feared being seen in the bedroom for as long as she could recall.

Over the next few sessions I coached her for self-acceptance and overcoming body shame and gave her a reliable dose of reality check. And, of course, I gave her permission to express herself as a sexual woman. That was one of her unspoken needs. And she blossomed!

On our last visit she beamed with pride as she told me about her lights-on escapade the night before. How a client feels about his or her body can determine whether sex is pleasure or disaster. A tiny thing—like a spot of cellulite—can change a life.

E (ENERGY)

What makes a person feel alive, chi or the universal life force energy that runs through every living thing, energetics/flow.

Everything is energy. That is the bottom-line message of noted author and speaker Wayne Dyer in his CDs on the energetics of emotions. He describes the vibrational scale of emotions, ranging from the low vibrations of guilt or shame to the highest vibrations of love. Energetics affect everyone, whether they know it or not.

As a sex coach, you may have to access your more subtle skills in noticing and observing—or sensing—your clients' energy flow.

S (SPIRIT/SPIRITUALITY)

A person's essence, spiritual belief system (not always the same as his religion), inner self.

Spirituality is everywhere. Not unlike chi (universal life force energy), our spirit runs through us. I often relate in a special way to clients open to overt discussions about the spiritual dimensions of both sex and their overall lives. They seem to understand the self that was always present, from birth to death, regardless of outside appearances. "It's the inner you," I say.

If you are comfortable in esoteric territory, sex coaching with these clients is definitely outside the box. Coaching a client to use I-statements with a partner, to access her intuitive side, or to sense more than intellectual knowing all are components of working in the spiritual realm. If you can give your client a glimpse of that aspect of life defined as *something greater than yourself*, you give her a key to the larger future, perhaps helping her form her search for the "sacred beloved" mate or simply turning her on to tantric sexuality.

Sometimes clients take slight turns down the ethereal road, for example, by feeling a connection with a past life or talking to their "spirit guide" for direction. Those twists and turns into the unseen realms can change some lives for the better. Clients who are stuck may respond to touching the depths of their being with you. Show them the way out and go crazy in your daring to be experimental.

You may meet clients who demand that you be their guide in the blending of sexuality and spirituality. As their sex coach it's partly your job to know local resources, sorting the real from the fake. Spiritual sexuality teachers abound, as do programs about this aspect of sexual expression, but many are not authentic. Review the Appendix E about qualified resources for spiritual sex, such as authors like Mantak Chia, Margo Anand, and Deepok Chopra.

INSIDE STORY: THE MAN WHO DANCED IN THE WOODS

I sensed that Gerval was an unusual client the minute he walked in the door. He was suffering greatly from what he perceived as the loss of his his manhood following recent prostate surgery. But the real issue was not erectile quality. It was his loss of ejaculate. Ejaculating made him feel like "a real man"—and no amount of coaching would restore that function for him.

"I'll do anything," he said. "I'm a spiritual man and I feel close enough to you to say this. I'm a wild man, even though I'm pushing 68! I'll do anything to feel like a whole man again."

I understood he was in a soul crisis. He could produce erections, but the missing fluids plagued him daily. His self-image had sunk to a profoundly sad level. I had to think in radical terms to design an action plan for such an open and radiant being who was in extreme pain but ready to take any suggestions to heart. We spoke about what he might do. He lived in a rural area and loved nature and hunting with his pals in the woods, which made him feel strong and masculine.

"Gerval," I asked, "do you ever hunt alone?" He smiled. "How'd you know what I have planned for Saturday?" He chuckled quietly. "Are you a psychic, Doc?" Laughing, I assured him that my instincts were not worthy of a psychic 1-900 line. "This is far out, but would you be will-ing to devise a special ritual to say good-bye to your ejaculate. . . . You know, come to completion with it and maybe, well, bury it? Like a cer-emony?"

"Sure, I'm game," he said, smiling more broadly than he had to date. "Let me think of what I'll do," he said, before leaving for the week.

Two weeks later, Gerval returned with a skip in his step and a broad grin. "Well, I did it! Wanna hear about it?"

"Of course . . . I can't wait! You look 20 years younger. What hap-pened?" I was so excited that I skipped around the room with him before he spoke.

"Well, I created a ritual. I constructed four wooden boxes and painted ritualistic figures—you know, like animals and trees and flow-ers and faces—all over the outside. I wrote down how I felt, putting my

words on small pieces of white paper, and set them inside each box. Then I did a long prayer, got naked, went to the woods near my house in the moonlight, and danced three times around the biggest tree I could find."

He stopped for a deep breath. I was spellbound. "Go on, please."

"Then, after about 10 minutes of singing, chanting, and dancing naked around this magnificent elm, I took out my shovel, made two great holes, and with ceremonial honoring, I did it . . . I (he started to choke up a little) . . . I buried my ejaculate. I said good-bye, and—here's the best part—I claimed my maleness back. I feel like I've been reborn. I love you!"

This was a heroic invention by a very spiritual being. He had created a way to say farewell to an essential part of himself and then found a new way to express the essence of his manhood. A simple act of closure in the woods that night restored this man's wholeness. I often think of the creativity and courage it took for him not only to think about but also act on his intuitive nature. This was a rare experience. I will always be grateful I risked going beyond the tried and true when I suggested a wild card to him—and grateful I had the privilege of working with a man of such inner beauty and strength.

In the following weeks Gerval's erections (with the help of his pump) grew strong. He even ventured into new relationships until he met the woman of his dreams. I hope they lived happily ever after. Jumping into that unknown realm of the spiritual was the risk we both took for his healing.

THE SEX COACHING FORMULA

I use a basic coaching formula for nearly every client. You will find this set of steps a helpful guideline for your work with clients—and you can alter the formula to create steps in closer harmony with your own training and, of course, to fit the unique needs of your own clients. I usually follow the steps in order:

Step 1. Define the Breakdown

For individual or couples coaching, define the sexual concern or, as I prefer to say, the breakdown. Where is the breakdown occurring? What is breaking down in the couple's sexual relationship?

This step takes place during intake (often done briefly over the telephone) and the first in-person session. If you are conducting sessions with a couple by telephone, rather than in person, make sure each partner has his or her own phone in a separate room.

Step 2. Conduct a Comprehensive Intake and Assessment

Use the intake forms (male/female) in Appendix C or amend them to conform with your own background and professional emphasis. You may also want to look at the sexual history forms in many of the books on the recommended reading list, such as Hartman and Fithian's *Treatment of Sexual Dysfunction: A Bio-Psycho-Social Approach.* The intake/assessment is an early investment of time that will pay off later in the sex coaching process.

I usually email intake and assessment forms to clients and ask them to complete the forms online and return them via email before the next session. I evaluate the intakes with the individuals in a private (not couples) session.

As you read the intakes, check or highlight any flashing yellow lights or red flags that catch your attention, such as early potentially traumatic incidents, persistent negative body image issues, failed attempts at pregnancy, a history of abortions, or sexual performance failures. Pay particular attention to first sexual experiences. Study the narrative essay (or notes they jotted down) of their relationship history. How little or how much the client writes in a relationship history may tell a revealing story about intimacy capabilities, number of partners, successful management of relationships, and aspects of sexual experience that might not otherwise be described in session. Some clients will find it a challenge, or even become averse to writing at all. Use an in-person (or telephone) session to gather this critical information, if so. Be a good detective and uncover clues.

Step 3. Create an Action Plan

What are the possible options for repairing the breakdown for the person or couple? Create an action plan before you begin. You can expect some clients to push for a fast fix, demanding an immediate estimate on the (lowest possible) number of coaching sessions involved. Say "I don't know," with both compassion and personal conviction. Involve them in identifying the causes of their concerns and addressing ways to overcome those causal factors—it will help them understand that they won't achieve their goals overnight.

A few clients may say they've comparison-shopped and discovered that some sexual help centers do promise results in a set number of sessions. That only means the counseling stops at a certain point— not that the breakdown is repaired. Many couples come to a sex coach after failing to get what they need in traditional therapy. They may be weary of therapeutic processes in general and eager for instant gratification after what they perceive to be a long time waiting for results. No matter what their reasons, you can't make the promise.

Setting a number of sessions with a promised outcome is a disservice to the client and the sex coach. The same formula will work in a different way and at a different pace for each client or couple. Coax all your clients into trusting your process.

Step 4. Construct, Review, and Revisit the Plan

Measure progress toward goals and make adjustments as you go along. Every session should give the client at least one concrete "takeaway": a specific observation, recommendation, or assignment. That gives clients a sense of moving forward—a sense of accomplishment. In talk therapy, a client may feel shortchanged without a take-away.

Step 5. Establish Some Optional Components for Each Session

Clients should focus on some of these components whether they are in coaching for days, weeks, or years:
• Education on accurate sexual information and realistic expectations about sex
• Development of communication and negotiation skills
• Sexual self-help options
• Sexual self-exploration and masturbation
• Specific, targeted cognitive and affective options for client (reframing for accurate information, relationship repair, belief systems, emotional blocks, healing the past, forgiveness, anger processing)
• Sexual behavior changes, including new activities with skills rehearsal and behavioral shifts for enhanced sexual pleasure; training for overcoming sexual problems and concerns
• Exploration beyond the comfort zone and experimentation with non-vanilla sex (see Chapter 12.)

• Self-help books, videos, and DVDs
• Consideration of bringing some aspect of spirituality into sexuality

Step 6. Go for Closure

If possible, complete your work with clients in a closure session that empowers both them and you. They will give you feedback about your sex coaching, letting you know where you were successful and perhaps where you need improvement. A closure session also gives the client a sense of completing the process with you. A good closure session seems to cut down on those post-coaching crisis calls.

Closure helps elevate the coaching process to an art form. It is like framing your painting or hanging it on the wall. Even if the session discloses shortcomings or apparent failings in the process, it still provides a feel-good moment. If you cannot do a closure in person, invite it by telephone, letters, or emails. Your clients will have the opportunity to thank you and you them.

OTHER MODELS FOR SEX COACHING

Unless you resonate exactly with the MEBES model, or are trained in other methodologies that will drive your sex coaching style, you will need to adapt others' work into your own.

Body Coaching

This is a form of sex coaching that usually involves explicit demonstrations, nudity, or touch of the client by the sex coach. Perhaps the two most widely known practitioners of body coaching are Betty Dodson, in New York City, who works with women, and her West Coast male counterpart, Joseph Kramer, in Oakland, California, who works predominantly with men. Dodson and Kramer both began their careers as sex educators with an emphasis on masturbation and then expanded into body coaching over the years.

You may or may not want to include body coaching in your practice. When you review the later chapters on treating the sexual concerns, you will see many instances where body-based sex coaching is both useful and appropriate for certain clients. You may decide to maintain a talk-only practice and refer out for body coaching. It is my hope that more sex coaches will find the courage to relate to clients in this difficult but rewarding way.

Seeing your client's nude body can be a daunting experience. I rarely offer viewing sessions as an option, but some men find this type of bodywork fundamentally life-altering. Shy single men who are isolated socially and sexually may be consumed by their body image concern. For these few special men, I offer a viewing session. I ask them to come prepared to show me their penis. I do not touch my clients; I only observe them. They may produce an erection, in carefully arranged conditions, including a special couch for sitting or lying down, towels, tissues, personal lubricant, and more often than not a porn movie to play for their arousal.

You may wonder whether the client directs his erotic energy toward the coach under these circumstances. That has never happened to me. I prepare them carefully for this special session so their attention will remain on their own erection throughout. I help them develop a mental fantasy or encourage their focus on the adult movie playing in the room. For men with penis size concerns, once they produce the erection, I comment positively on their penis. Usually I offer positive commentary on their overall physical self, including facial features, physique, fitness and masculine qualities.

Body coaching requires personal comfort and self-confidence in your sex coaching ability, training, and perhaps months or years of exposure to a wide range of sexual expression in clients and on screen. Most importantly, you must be able to distance yourself from all that erotic energy in the room and not be uncomfortable if some of it is directed at you. Transference and countertransference can crop up in sex coaching just as they do in more traditional forms of therapy, but they may be harder to tolerate here. You may never want to be involved in body coaching, and that's okay.

BETTY DODSON

A sexual education pioneer and explicit sex teacher, Betty led all-women workshops from the 1970s into the 1990s. The main characteristics of her coaching method are: masturbation techniques for sexual discovery and enrichment, orgasm-directed coaching practices, female genital awareness/acceptance, and encouraging sex for the sake of pleasure. Dodson's landmark book, *Liberating Masturbation*, established her as the authority in the field and led her to write the book that I send all female clients with orgasm concerns out to buy: *Sex For One*. Her sequel, *Orgasms For Two*, shares her radical views on sex for couples.

In her private sessions Dodson touches clients, often probing or tweaking them as an explicit sex teacher, with literal body coaching for arousal to orgasm. Her body-directed coaching is the subject of her videos—used widely by open-minded sexuality educators and highly recommended by me for my own clients. Videos include *Self-Loving*, *Celebrating Orgasm* (my favorite step-by-step female orgasms guide) and *Viva La Vulva!* These explicit videos feature groups of women with exposed genitals and beautifully showcase the Dodson style: upfront, personal, direct, and assertive.

JOE KRAMER

In a way, Joseph Kramer is the Dodson for men. He focus on male genital self-massage and anal pleasure. Kramer also offers an erotic bodywork training program at the Institute for the Advanced Study of Human Sexuality. According to the cover copy on his DVD *Fire On the Mountain: Male Genital Massage*, characteristics of his coaching include: Self-erotic massage demonstrations, including anal eroticism; practical sex wisdom on healing the heart-genital connection; transforming sexual shame; and enhancing and prolonging orgasm.

His spiritualized approach to male sexual body coaching is in a class all by itself. In 2003 Kramer began teaching the first California state-certified course in erotic bodywork (see www.eroticmassage.com/gradschool for a course description).

In his *Introduction to Masturbation Coaching* (an online course) he writes, "Betty Dodson wrote me recently that, 'It is my belief that hands-on sex coaching during masturbation is how we will be teaching sex in the future. I've been doing this with groups since 1973 and with individual clients since the mid-eighties.'"

If Kramer and Dodson had their way, sex coaching would all be done hands-on.

Surrogate Partners

Sexual surrogates (or surrogate partners, as some practitioners prefer to call themselves) have been in business for years. In ancient times, the sacred temple prostitutes, revered and worshipped for their gifts, often served as sex surrogates for entire populations of men. Today's sacred prostitutes are professional women trained to use their bodies (along with their minds and hearts) to serve the sexual development needs of their clients, under the guidance and referral system of a well qualified sexologist. *Women of the Light*, by author and groundbreaking teacher Ray Stubbs, is the best resource on the subject. Ray was my personal trainer on sexual bodywork at the Institute for the Advanced Study of Human Sexuality in my doctoral program. Linda Savage's *Reclaiming Goddess Sexuality*, a one-of-a-kind resource, is another important study of the marriage of sexuality and spirituality within the female sacred sexual context.

There are, of course, some caveats regarding the use of surrogates in your own coaching practice. Before you arrange a surrogate for one of your clients, learn the laws governing the use of paid sex partners in your state, and access the national website for surrogacy hosted by the International Professional Surrogates Association (IPSA).

Be wary about going online for more than information. Many women who advertise themselves as sexual surrogates or body coaching professionals are prostitutes in disguise. Referring to their services may land you in jail! Remember, a sexual surrogate should be working *with* you as a sex coach; you *both* direct the process. Only a few women are qualified as both surrogate and sexologist. It isn't difficult to check the credentials of anyone claiming she is.

Negotiate fees and terms with the surrogate before she meets the client. Following your action plan, she will work alone with him (or her), using shared guidelines jointly developed for each client. She (or he in rare cases) may teach sexual skills or social/dating skills. Often a surrogate helps a sexually inexperienced man gain sexual confidence. She may even be the first woman he's seen naked or touched intimately.

The range of care surrogates provide can be extensive. Whatever services you contract from her, expect her to debrief you after each client session and follow your suggestions for continued care based on that conversation. If you don't keep tight control of the situation, you are in for trouble. Use weekly (or periodic) client check-ins to determine whether or not the surrogate involvement is effective. Handled properly, the use of a surrogate can alter your client's sex life, especially if he is an inexperienced, sexually shy, or poorly performing male.

Nonsexological Approaches To Body Coaching

You may supplement your menu of services with nonsexual bodywork, reflexology, Feng Shui, or any number of holistic approaches to improving life. I refer out for nonsexual bodywork such as Reiki and Feng Shui. Some clients will find, for example, that the use of Reiki (energy balancing) improves their sense of physical or emotional well-being, making them more receptive to sex coaching and home assignments. You can find reliable Reiki practitioners in holistic directories. A knowledge of Feng Shui, as funny as it may seem, may help you coach clients about clutter or misplacement of objects in their living space, which may be negatively affecting their sex life.

Whether you offer these services or refer out is your call. I do not offer nonsexological services, but some coaches do. You may, for example, acquire training in techniques that are performed clothed, such as reflexology (which puts physical pressure on certain points on the foot or hand, some of which can activate sexual energy or quell too much) or acupuncture/acupressure (using the pathways of energy in the body, some of which are specific to sexual function, such as the kidney system). Acupuncture in traditional Chinese medicine is often accompanied by herbs, which can be formulated for positive sexual effects. For postmenopausal women, for example, you could recommend dong quai, black cohash, or wild yam derivatives to address sexual concerns.

Talk-Only Sex Coaching

With talk-only clients, you can use body-based self-help ideas, including home-based mirror work, self-recording in audio or video, and explicit teaching through videos or DVDs. Though you won't be body coaching, you can still get client feedback during coaching sessions from intensive bodywork at home. Some clients will be working with other helping professionals, including psychologists, psychiatrists, social workers, and marriage and family counselors—people with whom they have not shared their sexual concerns, at least not in specific detail. These types of talk-only professionals are rarely as well trained as you are in coping with clients' sexual concerns, and they certainly aren't as comfortable doing it. Your version of talk-only sessions is quite different from theirs.

Sex Coaching as Life Coaching

You will have some clients, like Doug in the following inside story, who morph from a sex coaching client into a generic client for life or personal coaching. If you are currently a therapist or counselor, you may find this difficult. If you are already a coach, you probably won't. When the sex coaching client has completed that part of her work with you, continue as you normally would as a life or personal coach.

INSIDE STORY: THE SHY GUY

Doug had just ended a bad relationship and sought coaching to help him overcome his sexual shyness before he started dating again. After developing his self-confidence over a few months, dating other women, and exploring sexual options, he initiated the shift to life coaching by asking different kinds of questions.

Instead of talking about sex, we often discussed his various romantic relationships and a few sexual interludes. At first I used my sex coaching skills to refocus our work on sex, but I soon realized that he wanted to skip what he termed "the sex stuff" and focus on getting both his career and living situation on track. We are still working together 3 years later on an occasional basis, using spot coaching.

Spot Coaching

I also call spot coaching sessions *tune-ups*. The sessions occur sporadically and infrequently. Spot coaching typically takes place over the telephone, with perhaps an occasional in-person session. I offer this option to all clients on a lifelong basis.

An out-of-the-blue phone call from a former client is not an uncommon event for me. The conversation typically begins with: "Hi, Dr. Patti, Phil Smith here. Remember me?" I often, for example, hear from transgendered clients who have hit a rough spot, found the love of their life, or done the "downstairs" surgery. Disheartened husbands whose wives did not sustain the changes they made in sex coaching sometimes call. Single guys who've finally found the guts to move into a certain social situation may phone in the good news. Clients may call after a hiatus of several weeks, months, or, like Justin, after 4 years to say, "Hi, just checking in with you. Saw you on TV the other day and started wondering what you were up to. . . . Oh, and by the way, that issue we worked on? Well, it's gone, but now I've got this other thing that is bothering me and I was wondering if you could . . ." And so it goes. Just like sexual development itself, a client's relationship with a sex coach can be a lifelong journey together.

Get It!

1. Describe the MEBES model and how you think it would apply to your work as a sex coach:
2. Name two people known for their work in body coaching and explain their focus:
3. Discuss the use of surrogates and how they can be used in sex coaching:

CHAPTER SEVEN

Men

Common Sexual Concerns and Resolutions

YOU CAN TREAT *all* male sexual problems, concerns, or dysfunctions with the sex coaching process taught in this chapter. Whether the male client suffers from serious ED or is merely seeking information and guidance for enhancing his own and his partner's pleasure, he is treated with the same approach. It begins with the intake process, supplemented by the forms in Appendix C. As you gather pertinent information in the sex history, you'll determine the client's outcome goals. An action plan based on that information will direct sex coaching throughout the client's participation in your program. In every session you will chart his progress toward achieving the goals established in the plan.

Many men who seek sex coaching have already seen a urologist. If your client hasn't, refer him to one. Before you get started, you must rule out any possible physical or physiological causes of his sexual concerns. Of course, coaching and medical care can be effectively combined to treat a problem.

There are nine areas of sexual concern most common to male clients. You will be given sample options for resolving concerns in each area. The chapter also provides information and resources for further study.

As noted in Chapter 6, the nine concerns are:

• Low or no sexual desire (LD)
• Early ejaculation (EE)

- Erectile dysfunction (ED)
- Delayed ejaculation (DE)
- Sexual inhibition (SI)
- Body dysphoria issues (BD)
- Social/dating skills deficit (SDSD)
- Desire for enhanced pleasure (EP)
- Sexual trauma (ST)

Men often present with more than one of these concerns because the problems are intertwined.

Before you read further in this chapter, review the material in Chapter 2 on sex therapies that inform the sex coaching process, specifically PLISSIT/PLISSIC, Jack Annon's model (P for permission, LI for limited information, SS for specific suggestions, and IT/IC for intensive therapy/intensive coaching).

HOW DO YOU SEX COACH A MAN?

Sex coaching for men is similar to women. We are all sexual creatures, with more similarities than differences. Men do suffer from unique concerns, given their anatomy and physiology, along with cultural and social upbringing. Your coaching of male clients will focus on what specific concerns they bring to your practice and how you—based on your gender, training and life experience—best relate to helping your male clients to thrive.

Focus on Results

Most men don't like to dwell on the past. They *do* want to achieve fast results once they have identified a problem and committed themselves to resolving it. Men respond well to sex coaching because it meets their need for taking action.

The sex coaching philosophy and action plan model is based on the present and the future, not the past. As already mentioned, sex coaching places minimal emphasis on the past aside from the brief assessment in the sex history part of the intake process (covered in Chapter 6). Coaching emphasizes the current status of a man's sex life and his desired outcome in working with you.

As a coach, you must find out: What is working? What is not working? What does he want to happen? Focus on determining what actions will help the client achieve his desired outcome, not on therapy issues. The sex coaching process is personally empowering and sex-positive. You are like an athletic coach, helping the client become the best lover he can be. And that's a concept every man can understand and embrace.

Watch Your Language

Language is particularly important when the client is a man. Words like *problem, dysfunction, breakdown,* and *failure* are typically perceived as threatening words, especially by men. Some men respond to those heavily negative words by becoming defensive or retreating into wounded silence.

I use the most nonjudgmental terms possible to describe a client's situation. The last thing I want to do is imply that the man I am coaching is a failure as a person. I usually say *sexual concerns.*

The medicalization of sexuality is a discomforting new trend in the field of sex therapy. Concerns become conditions, and goals are translated into diagnoses, with treatments relying on prescription pills and devices. The emphasis in sex coaching is on empowering the man, not the problem. A good sex coach emphasizes the positive in the areas for improvement.

No More Easy

Remember that today you won't see easy cases in sex coaching any more than you will see them in traditional forms of sex and marital therapy. Ten years ago, before the arrival of Viagra, clients often presented with basic sexual problems. Now with the advent of the little blue pill and the sex information explosion, men who need basic help can find it in drugstores, bookstores, magazines, via the Internet, and through educational sex videos. Sex problems are discussed in many venues. The average man with the average sexual problem knows he has a variety of options for resolving the concern, medically and otherwise.

The problems of men seeking sex coaching are typically more complex. These men may have been in traditional therapy, tried products available online, employed self-help strategies, and been in sexuality workshops—all in an effort to help themselves. By the time they show up on your doorstep, they are savvy, demanding consumers who won't be impressed with basic information and a few simple how-to steps.

Male sexual concerns can be as simple as a single body dysphoria issue—for example, a negative sexual image fueled by anxiety about a small penis—requiring one coaching session as the entire action plan. At the other end of the spectrum, the presenting concern may be just one factor in a complex amalgam of erectile and ejaculatory difficulties exacerbated by a lack of dating or relationship skills. That client will need a multisession action plan. The range of male sexual concerns and options for resolution is obviously quite wide; again, they can all be treated by the same coaching model.

You have to know your stuff. And you need a variety of tools in your kit to pull out for your clients' care. As mentioned earlier, you are also going to need to assemble an extensive resource database. A sex coach has to be the most sophisticated purveyor of the best information in the helping professions.

How Does Sex Coaching With Males Work?

I tell my clients that coaching is like drivers' ed. "I am in the car with you, sitting in the other front seat, guiding you, and keeping you safe, but you are driving the car," I say. The message is: We are equals, client and coach, but I am helping you become the best driver you can be. As a sex coach I hold my client to his highest expectations and help him overcome the obstacles in his way as he moves toward his goals. I offer specific suggestions on what he should think, feel, say, and do to get where he wants to go.

Some of the basic elements in coaching men include:
- Reviewing or teaching new information on the facts of life, such as safer sex, birth control, female sexual anatomy, male sexual anatomy, male orgasm, and ejaculation.
- Updating sex techniques on how to arouse and satisfy a female partner or another male. Many men achieve their own arousal and satisfaction primarily or at least initially from seeing and experiencing their partner's being aroused and satisfied. That's the *catch-22* for most males.
- Promoting self-acceptance, self-awareness, and self-love. Men, as well as women, often have body image issues and other anxieties about not being good enough.

• Teaching that masturbation is the foundation for all partner sex as well as its own sexual outlet.

THE NINE CONCERNS

The rest of this chapter is an in-depth look at the nine most common sexual concerns for men. Each section will:
• Define the concern
• Outline the most common causes of the concern
• Present options for resolution
• Provide inside story case examples
• List other useful information in sidebars

Concern 1. Low or No Sexual Desire

I call this concern *low desire* (LD). According to reports published in the *Journal of the American Medical Association* and the *Journal of Sex Research*, approximately 15% of men ages 18 to 59 suffer from low desire. Your client will probably say that he doesn't desire or think about sex as often as he (or his partner) wishes he did. He may be in a relationship with a woman or man who has a stronger sex drive than he does. His desire level is low in comparison, though not necessarily low as measured against statistics on sexual desire for his age group. Other clients may rarely think about sex, feel desire, or have the energy for expressing sexual drive when the opportunity does occur. Most men are somewhere in the middle of these two extremes, reporting infrequent sexual urges, a situation that frustrates them and their partners.

CAUSES

Following are some common causes of LD, many of which can lead to a shutdown of sexual desire if the concern is left unresolved.

Physical/physiological issues. Two of the biggest culprits are—low range of total testosterone (total T); low concentration of *bioavailable* or *free testosterone* in a clients blood testing sample. Certain drugs and physical exhaustion can also dampen libido.

Psychological issues. Poor self-esteem; low sexual self-esteem; low feelings of sexual self-worth and feelings of not being adequate for themselves or as a lover to their partner.

Mental issues. Misconception about what is a normal frequency of sexual desire; conflicts with partner in a relationship with mismatched sexual desire levels.

Emotional issues. Internal conflict about masculinity or self-image issues; external conflict in the primary sexual relationship, such as unresolved anger/resentments; physically/emotionally abusive relationship history or current relationship dynamics; conflicts in the relationship unrelated to sex, such as issues concerning money, family, childrearing, or general power struggles, that are leaking into the bedroom.

Poor sexual performance problems. History of erectile failure; poor ejaculatory control; inability to please partner; inherent emotional suffering from failing to perform adequately.

Body image issues. Such as: fear of revealing vulnerabilities, often caused by ridicule, humiliation, or past negative judgments about his body.

Intimacy issues. Poor intimacy management skills or an ingrained tendency to avoid intimacy.

Exhaustion or stress, and anxiety. Feeling so worn-out or distracted, there is no energy for sex.

Sexual ignorance. Lacking information or awareness about sexual realities—clueless!

OPTIONS FOR RESOLUTION

As with all of the nine sexual concerns for males, there are a variety of options for resolution at your disposal. Choose what you think and feel the client will best respond to and then combine options as you determine which best fits each client's needs. My first step with LD clients is to make sure that there is no medical condition present.

Use prescription drugs or natural herbs to stimulate the libido. Some men do well on a testosterone supplementation plan. To make appropriate medical referrals for that treatment, you need to have good contacts in the medical community. As noted earlier, all your male clients should have seen (or be seeing) a competent urologist, hopefully one who will share information about the client with you (with the client's permission, of course). Learn all you can about the different modalities of testosterone treatment, including topical creams, injections in low and high dosages, pills, lozenges, and other forms. You should be familiar with the side effects of testosterone replacement therapy.

There is also a huge and growing marketplace in natural male sexual enhancement products. Many of the products available are good, but the manufacturers of others make false claims. Some may even be harmful. It's your responsibility to know this marketplace so you can discern the helpful products from the ineffective or dangerous ones.

The products that are effective *and* safe usually are made of homeopathic compounds or of natural herbs used for centuries to enhance sexual performance or stimulate desire. There is, for example, a rich history of using Chinese medicinal herbs for treating sexually related ailments. Be sure that any product you recommend has been tested (preferably endorsed by a competent, credentialed clinical professional) and that you are familiar with its properties and claims. Otherwise you put your client at risk and leave yourself open to a lawsuit.

Remove the relationship blocks to desire. Help him identify the desire blocks in his relationship. Maybe he needs to acknowledge the connection between his past sexual failures and his current avoidance technique. As you work with the client in identifying the places where (and the reasons why) he puts up the libido roadblocks, also help him separate desire from the emotions stifling it. He needs to release the pent-up anger and hurt that is damaging his sexuality.

Build his confidence in himself as a lover. Focus on his erotic technique. Teach him to become a more skilled lover. Being a better and more confidant sexual performer may motivate him to be sexual more often.

Encourage the use of arousal devices. Erotica, porn, and sex toys can liberate stifled male sexuality. If he can reach orgasm easily through using these devices, he is likely to have more frequent sex. Orgasm alone can elevate a man's desire for having sex again. And don't be afraid to recommend phone sex services, professional escort services, sexual surrogates, and legal adult entertainment such as strip clubs. A visit to one of these places may give his libido a tremendous boost.

INSIDE STORY: PAUL AND THE NO-T COUNT

Paul called me with a fairly typical complaint: He was in a sexless marriage. (Approximately 15–20% of marriages are!) "I have no sexual desire at all," he claimed, his voice on the phone projecting despondency. I was a bit perplexed when he walked into my office. He was handsome, six feet tall, well built, happy, calm, sweet—and a sexy guy. "But I just don't feel the urge," he said. His wife was pressuring him to get help "or else." Coming to see me was, as he put it, "his last desperate act." Before addressing potential marital issues, I asked him if he'd had a test for T. Yes, he had, and he'd tested in the low normal range. Later I learned from the urologist I recommended for him that his free T count was in the basement.

Much of Paul's coaching involved encouraging him to do something about his situation. Discussing the test results with me helped push him in the right direction. That referral to a competent urologist was all he needed to start feeling sexually alive again. Once he boosted his T levels into the healthy range, he began to think more often about sex. He initiated sex with his wife on a vacation trip—a positive role reversal for Paul.

Low T was his problem, and it was easily addressed by taking a daily T supplement. His marital life improved, and he became interested in adding excitement and variety to their lovemaking. His wife, he reported in his last session, was "relieved and happy." He was smiling when he left.

This client's needs were met by: Using the PLISSIC approach, addressing the mental zone of informational/educational coaching for referrals and interpretations of results, and encouraging him to take that first positive step.

Concern 2. Early Ejaculation

Early ejaculation (EE) was, and in some circles still is, known as PE or *premature ejaculation*. This is another pejorative term I don't use with my clients. Instead, I label the concern as either early or rapid ejaculation. *Premature ejaculation* is a judgment call, sending the message: You've come too soon and disappointed your partner. A man internalizes that message and feels like a failure in his sexual performance. That's the last thing he needs. *Early* or *rapid* ejaculation sounds more neutral.

EE the most common sexual complaint of men under 40. Statistics from a variety of sources put the number of men with this concern ranging from a low of 30% to a high of 70%.

CAUSES

The causes of EE can range from something as subtle as a slight anxiety about performance to something more obvious such as a type-A personality with self-pressuring characteristics. This list begins with the prevailing cause of EE, the boyhood pattern that sets a man up for life.

Masturbation style. In my experience with clients, the single most common cause of EE is habituation from furtive masturbation where quick release was desired—maybe even necessary—if a boy didn't want to get caught by his parents. This style of achieving quick release, learned at an early age, is unconsciously replicated in adult partner sex. The man feels pressured to hurry without understanding why and releases his ejaculate before he and his partner would like.

Shyness or overexcitement. Sexual shyness or shame about being sexual causes many men to feel overwhelmed or conflicted about sex. A man may ejaculate too quickly out of the hidden desire to end sex. Men who haven't been sexually active for very long or men who have infrequent sex with their partners may be shy or overly excited at the very idea of intimacy. Some have told me that the sensation of being inside a woman (or a man) after a long time of wanting to be there turned them into the stereotypical one-minute wonders.

Performance anxiety. Anxiety about performance, specifically anxiety caused by past EE experiences, can lead to the very result the man most fears: early ejaculation. He needs to improve his sex technique, including becoming adept at bringing a woman to orgasm orally and manually. If he is confident in his ability to please her, he will feel less anxiety—and be able to control his ejaculation more effectively.

Type-A personality. Some men do everything fast. They gulp drinks, swallow barely chewed food, drive too fast, and rush headlong into life. Not surprisingly, they ejaculate quickly too. Motivational speaker T. Harv Eker of Peak Potentials Trainings says, "How you do anything is how you do everything!" I agree. But a man in a hurry can learn how to slow down in bed.

INSIDE STORY: MARCO AND THE EE DEMONS

Marco was a delightful client who suffered dramatically from his shame of EE. Newly married, he couldn't sustain his ability to control ejaculation with her, perhaps because of their infrequent sexual activity. Perplexingly, despite a past history of excellent performance and self-control with other women, this woman—whom he loved dearly—was the only one with whom he couldn't perform adequately.

After months of occasional visits to see me, he benefitted from rehearsing the traditional EE behavioral techniques and from my helping him to reframe his negative self-talk. "I'm going to lose it" was his mantra. Over 2 years he had tried everything: regular masturbation exercises at home, mental reframing, numbing creams, Viagra, and even Prozac.

Eventually he agreed with my repeated, loving coaching message: "If you have infrequent sex with your wife, you're never going to be able to control yourself. You're just too excited when you feel your penis inside her vagina, right?"

The realization that infrequent sexual intercourse was the real culprit eventually led Marco to addressing his needs with his wife. On our last session he happily reported that her understanding—and willingness—to be more sexually available were the keys to resurrecting sexual happiness for them both. After time, his EE subsided and he regained his former sexual confidence.

OPTIONS FOR RESOLUTION

For the EE man, resolution can occur in a variety of ways. He can learn to control his urges to release, especially through a calculated self-training module, which is discussed in this section. Some men benefit most from prescription drugs, whereas others do well with devices or practices they can do with a partner.

Use medical intervention. Surprisingly, the SSRI medications, such as Prozac, Paxil, and Zoloft, whose negative side effects include decreased sexual desire and less intense orgasm, can be a good treatment for EE. Viagra and other sildenifil-based drugs, including Levitra and Cialis, help a man sustain his erection even after the orgasmic release, making these medications also useful in assisting men with EE.

Employ mechanical devices. A penile ring (cock ring) or a vibrating penile ring device, which adds sensation to the testes and to the partner's genitalia, can also stop the urge to ejaculate too soon. Some men with EE who do not have a partner practice masturbating without ejaculating by using personal lube along with a realistic silicon replica of the female sexual anatomy. Sexual surrogates also can be very helpful.

Encourage the client to try other products. Some men get help from creams that numb the penis and assist in maintaining arousal. However, these can reverse new trends to get EE men to sustain increasing levels of physical pleasure. Self-help videos are also useful. Have your own video lending library for clients. You may also want to sell products on your Web site or provide links to adult-oriented online stores or local sex shops that carry self-help videos and DVDs.

> **MORE ABOUT THAT**
> A few good videos address EE directly; others help by teaching masturbation skills. My picks are:
> 1. *You Can Last Longer* (Sinclair Institute; www.bettersex.com)
> 2. *The Lover's Guide to Ejaculatory Control: The Desjardins Method* (Pacific Media Entertainment; www.loveandintimacy.com)
> 3. Videos from Dr. Joseph Kramer (The New School of Erotic Touch in Oakland, CA; www.eroticmassage.com)

Teach control. Ejaculation is a matter of control. Not surprisingly, the most common method for treating EE is the behavioral approach. He must learn to recognize what's happening in his head and his body before ejaculation. For some men this is a great challenge because it demands slowing down and paying great attention.

Self-training. The six behavioral process steps practiced during masturbation are as follows:

1. *Learn mental focus.* He needs to stop worrying about what's going to happen next and focus on his physical sensations of the moment. I train men to listen for thoughts such as: "Am I going to come too soon?" or "Will I lose this erection?" If he can learn to hear the self-deprecating messages distracting him from his own pleasure, he can learn to silence them. Then he can shift the focus to experience his own erotic sensations.

2. *Recognize ejaculatory inevitability (EI).* Once a man reaches this point, he will ejaculate. Nothing he thinks, feels, or does will stop it. He needs to recognize that point of inevitability so he can stop himself from getting there before he's ready.

3. *Read* the *pre-EI signs.* This is perhaps the single most difficult part of the learning curve. Some men go from zero to sixty in a minute and ejaculate. Patience!

4. *Get in touch with the arousal phase.* He probably doesn't pay attention to how his body changes during arousal. Once he really experiences (rather than ignores) the sensations of increased breathing, chest heaving, pelvic thrusting, and tension in different parts of his body (like the thighs or buttocks), he can decrease his arousal in a process I call *Back It Up*, the key to ejaculatory control. Use something concrete to help men visualize their arousal. When I teach men how to *Back It Up*, I use an Oriental carpet in the studio room. One end represents the beginning of the process and the other end is their EI. That helps most clients see their arousal continuum.

5. *Learn the squeeze technique.* When a man can read the signs and slow down his arousal somewhat but still feels the urge to ejaculate, he is ready for the *squeeze technique*, developed by William Masters and Virginia Johnson. He holds the base of his (erect) penis with his hand tightly to stop the urge to release or he can apply pressure to the frenulum (the sensitive spot on the underside of the head of the penis). Another squeeze method involves clenching or holding the PC muscles until the urge to ejaculate subsides. Remember: EE clients must practice solo before trying out their new skills with a partner. Some men need days, weeks, or even months for mastery.

6. *Practice with a partner.* This entails following the same steps, except that man's partner can use his (or her) own hand to

MORE ABOUT THAT

Back It Up requires a man to notice, recognize, and (ideally) to feel his bodily sensations associated with approaching but avoiding the point of EI. The Back It Up Process works like this:

1. Tell the male to notice when he reaches EI—how it feels, what bodily changes occur and especially to observe the physical sensations, such as pelvic thrusting, perspiration, changes in breathing, erectile fullness, and the urge to realse.

2. Instruct him to notice himself, during a masturbation session alone, as he approaches the point *just before* EI; at that point, tell him to stop.

3. Tell him to rest for several moments (or breaths) and to resume masturbation when the urge to release has subsided.

4. Have him continue to masturbate and allow himself to continue to notice what is occurring within his body in the stages that lead up to EI, stage by stage.

5. Assure him that the more astute he becomes at noticing, then responding to signs and sensations during his arousal cycle up to EI, the better his chances for ejaculatory self control.

6. Remind him that when he practices this technique with a partner, there will be heightened sensations and distractions; advise him to practice alone first, until he feels a level of self mastery has been achieved.

employ the squeeze technique. The man can also slow arousal and delay ejaculation by:

- Stopping any movement inside of his partner
- Resting his penis inside of his partner
- Removing his penis from inside his partner and using the partner's hand (or a penile ring) to stop the urge to reach EI
- Pressing firmly against the frenulum, or what I call the *male clitoris* (that spot on the underside of the penis where the foreskin or coronal head comes to a point—the most sensitive part of the sexual anatomy for most men)

Concern 3. Erectile Dysfunction

When a man is not able to get or sustain an erection long enough to penetrate a vagina or other orifice, he suffers from erectile dysfunction (ED). One in ten men and over 50% of men over age 50 have experienced ED. Viagra has radically changed the sexual landscape, especially for older men. But young men also use Viagra and other sildenafil drugs to prolong their erections. However, the drug may not be the answer to every man's prayers. There are two types of ED sufferers: those who cannot produce an erection, and those who cannot keep one. This section addresses both types.

CAUSES

Like LD, ED has various causes. Some of them are purely physical; others are truly psychogenic in origin.

Blood flow issues. Some aging men experience venous leakage, meaning that the blood leaks out of the vein in the penis. An erection is entirely dependent on engorged blood vessels.

Medications. Heart and blood pressure medications, and even over-the-counter cold and sinus remedies, can alter the body's blood flow capacities, affecting erections.

> **MORE ABOUT THAT**
> As noted earlier, be careful about the words you use to define sexual concerns. One of my pet peeves is the term *impotent*. The *I word*, as I call it when I talk with clients, is one of those judgmental terms that, in my opinion, diminish authentic male sexual power. A man may lose or be unable to produce an erection yet still be a potent, vital male. Gerval (see Chapter 6) was one such example. By creating a good-bye ritual in the woods, Gerval transcended his MD's diagnosis of impotency and rediscovered the sexual male inside of himself.

Diseases. Diabetes and other diseases can affect erections, especially in older men.

Psychological issues. Sexual shyness, inhibitions, guilt, depression, anxiety, repressed anger, and insecurity about masculinity and sexuality can render a man incapable of getting or sustaining an erection.

Relationship issues. Unresolved issues and anger in a relationship can make a man lose his erection with his partner, if not with others.

OPTIONS FOR RESOLUTION

There is a broad range of options for the ED man.

Medication. Prescription drugs include Viagra, Levitra, and Cialis, with more potent varieties probably on the way. Of the many herbs and other alternative medicines, yohimbe, a sexual stimulant made from an African tree bark, was prescribed frequently by urologists before Viagra and is still used successfully by many men. For men who experience severe side effects from Viagra, doctors also still prescribe self-injected medicines, such as Prostaglandin E and other solutions created to produce and sustain erections.

Mechanical devices. Relatively inexpensive (and adequate) penis pumps and penis rings are available online and in adult stores. High-quality pumps with better-fitting penis rings are available by prescription. Some manufacturers claim that their pumps can enlarge a man's penis permanently. They can't. A good pump can produce a firm erection via suction that lasts through a lovemaking session. The pump is a good choice for a man with situational ED caused by insecurity with a new partner. Sexual stimulants and pumps are most effective for men who can't produce an erection, whereas pills work better for men who can't sustain one.

Behavioral training. The same steps for treating EE can be used to help sustain an erection.

Couple coaching. If the problem is the relationship, bring the partner into the coaching process.

INSIDE STORY: THE 80-YEAR-OLD WITH THE WEAK
ERECTION COMPLAINT

One of my very favorite clients was a man I only saw once. In town for a convention in his field, he was fit, trim, and handsome, though noticeably aging. "I want to get checked out by an expert," he said. When I asked why he felt the need for a check-up, he said he was a bit disappointed in his sexual performance lately. "I just turned 80 years old," he said, "and my erections aren't as strong as they used to be." I laughed. He explained further.

He had a new lover (who was 25 years old!) and he feared he wasn't keeping up his end of the bargain in providing nightlong pleasure. Apparently he found great delight in dating younger lovers and expected a lot of himself and his 80-year-old penis. Once we discussed and reframed his idealistic expectations for his erections (their speed, hardness, and duration—all of this before the days of Viagra) I helped him to realize how good things were for him providing assurance that this was a natural result of his aging, which assuaged his concerns. He thanked me. I told him he was inspiring to me at his age. He promised he would come back after his ninetieth birthday for a little more coaching.

He left, smiling a broad toothy grin, looking as confident as a young buck. I never saw him again. But I won't ever forget him.

Concern 4. Delayed Ejaculation

Occurring in less than 10% of men, delayed ejaculation (DE) is easy to identify yet the most difficult concern to treat. The man can often feel an orgasm but cannot release his ejaculate. Orgasm in men actually occurs in two phases. The feeling of orgasm is experienced when the penis is disgorged of the blood that created the erection. The subsequent release of seminal fluids is the ejaculatory phase of orgasm. Although biologically one occurs right after the other, some men can train themselves to stall ejaculation and experience authentic multiple orgasmic contractions of the penis and surrounding genital area. Most men ejaculate immediately as the blood vessels in the penis drain.

CAUSES

I've identified three major factors that relate to this concern.

Medical conditions. Some men suffer from a condition known as *retrograde ejaculation,* in which their ejaculate reverses back into the abdominal cavity, not out the urethra. Delayed ejaculation is also one of the negative sexual side effects of some antidepressants.

The man's intimacy issues. Failing to release ejaculate can be an indicator of distrust of a partner or the relationship. Sometimes it only occurs at the start of a new sexual relationship; other times it is an ongoing problem within the relationship.

His partner's issues. Partners of DE men often try to take on responsibility for his problem, blaming themselves. In trying harder to make him reach orgasm, they may exacerbate the situation.

OPTIONS FOR RESOLUTION

The DE client may best be served by first ruling out the physical and then focusing on the inner self.

Medical intervention. Often the solution is in asking their doctor to change the medications that are contributing to retrograde ejaculation.

Prescription evaluation. Coach the client to talk to his doctor about the prescriptions he's taking. Encourage him to explore other medications or dosages that minimize negative sexual side effects.

Explore his safety issues. Men who don't feel safe enough to let go with a partner are not unlike women who haven't been orgasmic with a partner. The DE client needs positive encouragement and nurturing support—a safe space. The coaching process gives him that space where he can contemplate risking some of his safety for the sake of his pleasure. Some men have never felt secure enough emotionally, and perhaps even physically, to experience the intimate bond that orgasm and ejaculation often provoke during the sexual act.

Sex coaching may not be enough. In the MEBES model (Chapter 6) the E stands for emotional blockages. The PLISSIC approach with intensive coaching (Chapter 2) also may need to be redefined for the client. Make a referral to a psychotherapist for in-depth counseling or therapy on trust and relationship issues. Distrust of women and issues with parental figures, especially the mother, may be stifling the client's ability to feel pleasure and let his orgasm go in the presence of a woman. Unless you are professionally trained as a therapist or counselor to deal with these deep-seated emotional and psychological issues, get outside help.

INSIDE STORY: ROMAN, THE ENERGIZER BUNNY

I have rarely seen DE cases that weren't directly related to fear of intimacy with men or women or lack of trust in women, especially the current partner. Those clients need your help in talking through their trust and fear issues. The Love Letter process works beautifully in these cases. If the problem is severe, the client will need therapy.

One such client, Roman, laughed when he told me, "Call me the Energizer bunny. I can last and last!" I did laugh at the metaphor. We then discussed the pain he felt at not being able to share the beauty of simultaneous orgasms with his partner. I coached him to let his girlfriend know it wasn't her fault, a common mistake that partners make. We spent time on acknowledging his fears of intimacy and I provided specific guidance on alternate ways he could use sex coaching, to create more intense arousal patterns to propel his orgasm, helping Roman to resolve his concern.

Concern 5: Sexual Inhibitions

Almost anything can cause sexual inhibitions (SI). One traumatic incident, such as a boy catching a parent having sex with an extramarital lover, can inculcate the same inhibitions as a childhood imbued with strong antipleasure values and messages.

CAUSES

Three basic causes are responsible for most repression. They stem from how a client feels about himself and the influences from his past experiences, along with current relationship messages, good or bad.

Sex-negative messages. Often these are words or phrases heard as a boy is growing up. They are learned in childhood from religious, social, cultural, and family sources.

Long-term virginity. Being a virgin at age 30, for example, or marrying as a virgin or with little sexual experience can provoke deep shame or even a guilt-laden desire to explore with partners other than the man's mate.

Negative sexual experiences. These may occur early in sexual development or later in life, and they usually cause an impaired sense of self. The man may suffer from memories of incidents in which he was shamed, ridiculed, or belittled. For example, having a woman ask, "Is that it?" regarding his penis or his sexual skills can wreak havoc.

OPTIONS FOR RESOLUTION

The SI male may need anything from light sex coaching to a more intensive regimen of self-development.

Give permission. The P from the PLISSIC model, granting permission to be sexual, may be enough. Some clients require only one or two sessions to get the permission they never received.

Redirect his thinking. Clients with sexual inhibitions often respond well to suggestions for thinking in new ways about their own sexual history and sexual expression. These redirective messages may be as simple as saying, "All men are smaller when not erect—did you know that?" For another client, you may have to initiate an intense and ongoing discussion about, for example, growing up a Roman Catholic and feeling shame about the so-called *sin* of masturbating. Help him realize how healthy and natural masturbation really is. Other times SI men are simply uninformed about women. In these cases the coaching work involves educating them about female anatomy and sexual response and their role in communicating with a partner about sexual wants, needs, and desires.

Expose him to new forms of sexual expression. Men with sexual inhibitions typically have poor social and dating skills. Get him out into the world. Show him a wide range of sexual expression and help him learn how to navigate personally in those settings. You may even escort him to an erotic museum or a nude beach. Be sure that SI is not a smoke screen for intimacy issues, in which case refer out for therapy.

INSIDE STORY: RAJ

A sexless marriage prompted Raj to schedule an appointment with me. Raj attributed his unhappy situation to his own lack of sexual experience before marriage. He admitted he had a ravenous hunger to explore his own sexuality. As we discussed the dynamics in his marriage, I learned that he was a virgin before he married a much more sexually sophisticated lady. Her work life was depleting her of her sexual energy, he complained.

I suggested options for his personal sexual self-growth. He was a brave and eager sexplorer! Some of his field trips included a tantric massage and a visit to my favorite sex shop to purchase some pleasure toys. Raj browsed many websites on sex, signed up for the Playboy *channel at home, and became a seasoned solo practitioner. He even joined the mailing list of a local nudist resort community. Being exposed to different forms of sexual expression, including the different worlds of erotic spirituality, nudism, swinging, triple-X Web sites, and a sex boutique, made him feel more sexually alive. Although too much individual sexual growth can boomerang, leaving the existing relationship behind, Raj began having more frequent sex with his wife and was happier with his own sexuality. He blossomed under sex coaching and still visits me now and then to tap into the freedom of being in the sex coaching studio and to talk about his sexual dreams. Aside from these visits, our work was complete after several months of occasional sessions.*

Concern 6. Body Dysphoria Issues

I've observed two basic categories of body dysphoric (BD) concerns among male clients. The most common complaint among men of all ages, backgrounds, and socioeconomic groups is: "Am I big enough?" The penis size question still ranks number one in my online forum, too. The second category is more generic and usually accompanies worries about sexual performance, masculinity, sexual adequacy, obesity, and other vanity issues. He wants to know: "Am I handsome enough to attract women?"

CAUSES

Often the cause of BD is misplaced thinking and a warped self-view especially about penis size.

No basis for comparison or testing their attractiveness. Men who are concerned over penis size or attractiveness are often in the first and only sexual relationship of their lives. They often have been married for many years. Creeping self-doubt pulls them into sex coaching. They are longing to get an answer to their burning question: "Am I big enough?" or "Could I attract another woman?"

Uneven sexual desire in the relationship. If she doesn't want him as often as he wants her, he wonders if his penis is inadequate or his body unappealing.

Being single and sexually inexperienced. Perhaps his penis size or other body concerns have kept him from forming sexual relationships. He probably has low self-esteem and poor social and dating skills.

OPTIONS FOR RESOLUTION

Helping the BD to reframe and teaching him new skills is often the course of action.

Reframing session. I always do a reframing session with men who have penis size concerns. I use a variety of penis models, which you can find listed in the online stores in Appendix E. They include hard plastic models designed for use as a condom demonstrator, an elegant, six-inch-long carved wooden penis that is an art object, and a selection of carved penis likenesses made of fine crystal quartz from Brazil that are part of my personal art collection. Some are small and others are within the normal (but small) range of human penis size. Given the healing nature of quartz crystal, I am not surprised that it calms men to hold one of these pieces rather than a rubber dildo!

I often use a small measuring tape to show the average length of an erect penis: 5.5 to 6 inches. I also explain that most partners are more interested in girth (circumference) than in length, with the average girth of an erect penis being slightly more than 4 inches. The scientific approach to penis size helps to depersonalize their concerns.

Home assignments with measurements. I usually have BD men take their own measurements at home. They report back to me at the next session. Usually this is a happy session. Most clients put to rest their lifelong concerns about being too small. If, on the other hand, he does have a very small penis (a microphallus condition is quite rare), teach him about sex toys and penis enhancers (see Appendix E).

Personalized education session. A personalized education session encompasses most of the coaching work for the typical client with penis size concern. Clarify the difference in size between a flaccid penis and an erect penis. Many men measure themselves sexually by the size of their flaccid penis! And point out that a partner views their penis from in front or the side or eye level—not from the position of looking down on it as they do. Realizing that their penis looks smaller to them than anyone else because of their perspective is a breakthrough discovery.

Teach sexual skills. Help BD men understand the value of being a skilled lover. The amount of time spent on penetration during the sexual act is a small percentage of lovemaking if he's a good lover. Reinforce the importance of having manual and oral skills for his partner's pleasure. Putting the emphasis on erotic technique helps deflect some of the concern he has about penis size or his looks in general.

The lesson that porn is not real life. Correct the misconceptions the client has gotten from watching porn. X-rated star Ron Jeremy has an incredible 13.5-inch erect member—not your average Joe. Male porn actors are selected because they have big penises, which are exploited by crafty camera angles and close-ups. There's a reason that a penis on screen appears larger than real life: It is!

Help him toward self-acceptance. Your client may be overweight or underweight, have hair on his back and shoulders, or have noticeable scars, bad skin, or acne scarring on his face and neck. First, address his need for self-acceptance. Have an adequate list of referral sources for treatment, including skin care specialists, laser hair removal centers, cosmetic surgeons, trainers, and weight loss clinics. Help him commit to weight management and exercise programs.

Understand his perspective. In sex coaching, you must put your own personal values aside. You may disagree with a client who thinks he is too thin or too fat. Let the client guide you. Don't succomb to your own biases. If he wants help finding a plastic surgeon or other specialist, provide that assistance. "The client will always set you straight" is a good mantra.

Another wise option is to send the client to a urologist with whom you have a good enough working relationship for you to say, "Please let my client know his penis size is normal." As discussed in Chapter 6, you may want to do observational sex coaching. Or you may decide to work with a sexual surrogate, who can tell him he's fine just the way he is. Always encourage his self-esteem.

INSIDE STORY: THE MAN WITH THE GORGEOUS LARGE PENIS

I once worked with a witty, charming, intelligent man in his early thirties. He had a way with words. Though he was a chubby guy, he was still cute. I really liked coaching him because he learned quickly, picked up on my suggestions, and implemented them immediately. He was so committed to meeting the right woman and having great sex that he verged on being obsessive about it. We didn't address his obsessive tendencies. Instead we got right down to work each session on his learning goals for that week and his accomplishments.

After several weeks of sporadic dates going nowhere, especially not to the bedroom, he admitted that he was ashamed of his penis size. "I know this is stopping me from meeting and then being sexual with the right woman," he said. Yes, he admitted, he had a string of women interested in him socially and sexually but he never got past a casual drink or dinner date.

"Okay," I said, "let's get out the ruler!" Without hesitation, he showed me his erect penis. It was huge! I gasped in surprise. Then I laughed out loud, which was something we did a lot in session. Pointing to his erect penis, I shouted, "You have a gorgeous penis!"

Gorgeous was a word he used often as praise. Then, sitting very stiffly in my chair, with him still sitting on the floor next to the couch, I leaned in and told him: "I never want to hear you say you have a small penis again! I want you repeat after me: 'I have a gorgeous large penis. I have a gorgeous large penis. I have a gorgeous large penis.'"

He began to chant the words right there in the studio, escalating the volume with each repetition. Finally I told him to get up and get dressed. He hugged me for about 2 minutes. "This has changed my life. How can I thank you?" he asked.

"Keep chanting," I told him. We had a few more good laughs and that was the last time I saw him.

Concern 7. Social/Dating Skills Deficit

Why is a social and dating skills deficit (SDSD) included as a sexual concern? If a man can't get a date (or a second date), he has no context for his sexuality. Men who seek sex coaching often are clumsy with women, both in and out of the bedroom. Their lack of social skills creates a corresponding lack of sexual experience. Often they are homely (or clueless about what they could do to look more attractive), poor communicators, and generally lacking in self-confidence.

CAUSES

There are many possible causes for this concern.

Shyness. Shyness can cause late blooming into sexual activity or an avoidance of sex altogether.

Inexperience with sex and with women (or men). Unlike shy men, men lacking in sexual experience may seek sex coaching to help bolster their courage to attempt to be a better lover. These men may have dropped out of the social scene due to feelings of inadequacy.

Social awkwardness. Socially awkward men often have careers and lifestyles that keep them isolated.

Inability to communicate verbally. These men typically are incapable of making small talk and have no useful pick-up lines or conversation starters. Few women will take the time to draw these men out.

Emotional immaturity. These men may have a low EQ (emotional intelligence quotient), are unable express/process feelings.

Attractiveness issues. They may be unattractive and have poor grooming or unappealing hygiene habits.

Lackluster personalities. Clients with SDSD are often introverts.

OPTIONS FOR RESOLUTION

Many SDSD men respond well to directed discussions about dating and a personalized focus on communication.

Personalized education. Because these men have fragile egos, they are slower to open up to the coaching process than other clients. Many of them are at the "desperate" stage when they choose to face their sexual issues. Your initial sessions will probably be informational, focusing on educating the client on grooming, hygiene, skin care, exercise, and clothing choices. You may recommend a manicure or haircut, even coloring the hair, or suggest a dermatologist. In the most delicate fashion, take on breath and body odor if necessary. A makeover will make him more confident in his interactions with women.

Communication and conversation skills coaching. I practice role playing with SDSD clients to help them learn how to talk to women in social settings. Playing the prospective date, I coach them on nonverbal communication as well as conversation. Then I send them home with an assignment: Stand in front of a mirror and practice talking and flirting with a woman you want to date. Rehearsals help them feel more comfortable and confident when they take their show on the road.

Field assignments. Assign the client a place or event for practicing his new social skills. Many of these men live in front of the television or computer screen and don't know where to find a singles' bar, book cafe, or adult education class that appeals to women. No wonder they're isolated! Provide a menu of local options that might include: a singles' event (such as a dance or club—a hiking club, for example, if he likes hiking), online dating services, and personals ads. Be sure to coach him on how to use them! Include listings of art openings, book signings, lectures, and other events that will probably draw single women who share some of his interests.

INSIDE STORY: THE BOOK CAFE BROWSER

Jerry was a dedicated client who absorbed every bit of coaching advice and worked it to the max. A single man with minimal social skills and sexual experience, he presented a wide range of concerns when he came to me. I addressed his lack of social and dating skills first.

A self-described desperate guy, Jerry browsed bookstores, sitting for hours in the cafe area, hoping that a woman would discover his presence. It never happened. After a series of coaching sessions, I sent him to a book cafe in the neighborhood where single women hung around hoping to meet single men. (You thought bookstores were for readers?)

Per instruction, he would select a few books meant to provide food for a conversation. Using one of the discussion starter lines we'd practiced, he would approach an appealing woman, regardless of whether she had indicated interest in him. The goal: Practice conversational skills with desirable women. He kept a scorecard and pencil in his shirt pocket and afterward recorded what he said and to how many women.

Some of the women brushed him off; others talked to him. Regardless, Jerry was proud of his tally: He gave himself points for effort. That's how Jerry honed his social skills. In short time, he learned to talk easily with strangers and boosted his confidence to begin dating.

Concern 8. Desire for Enhanced Pleasure

You'd think almost everyone would want to make sex better! But you will be surprised at how few people actually seek sex coaching for help in becoming a better lover. Like therapists, coaches see people with problems, not good lovers aspiring to be great lovers. That makes desire for enhanced pleasure (EP) an unusual concern.

EP men do not have erectile or ejaculatory difficulties or suffer from low desire or body image issues. In fact, you will probably want to ask this client: "Why are you here?" And he will proudly roar: "I love sex. I have no problems, but I want to be a better lover." These men are going to show you the real joy of coaching and may even teach you a few new tricks.

Typically these clients are single and not in a sexual relationship but are dating—they are between relationships. They want to show the next woman in their bed the time of her erotic life. Their goals include increasing pleasure for themselves and their partners, enhancing their technical skills, and perhaps finding the holy erotic grail: the male *multiple orgasm.*

CAUSES

EP men are usually driven by a high sex drive, a desire to be better than other men, and, for men over age 40, the realization that they need to upgrade their oral and manual techniques in case their penis falters. Theirs is a noble pursuit. Coach them.

INSIDE STORY: ENHANCING PLEASURE MAY BE ENOUGH

Occasionally a man will call me to ask for EP coaching. Joel, a young man in his early thirties, showed up at my studio with a wide grin as he stated his goal: "Dr. Patti, I don't really have any sex problems. I just want to learn how to masturbate better!" I agreed to coach him.

We talked about his usual masturbatory pattern and speculated on new ways that he could build more intensity into his orgasmic release. I introduced plenty of new information, with targeted suggestions for enhancing his masturbatory pattern: sustaining the erection, pelvic lifts, PC exercises, whole-body self-caress, and erotic fantasies. He left a happy camper!

OPTIONS FOR RESOLUTION

This type of client may need a slight adjustment in current sexual patterns. Often this is a call for body coaching.

Find out how he does it and help him figure out a new approach. Get a detailed and accurate description of the client's current sexual style and patterns. Use this as a sexual skills baseline for helping him develop his goals. For example, if can masturbate for 10 minutes, give him weekly time goals to extend masturbation and prolong his pleasure. You may also suggest that he switch from KY Jelly (dries quickly) to a more sophisticated product such as Astroglide or Liquid Silk. He may be open to trying new sexual devices, including an electrical stimulator, a penile ring, or sexual aids that promote sensation during masturbation (e.g., a rubber or silicone sleeve).

Body coaching. EP clients are often candidates for body coaching. Body coach specialist Joe Kramer shows men a variety of exercises and techniques for reaching ecstatic heights through masturbation. You also may want to observe your client's masturbatory patterns to help him find ways for increasing his solo sexual pleasure and satisfaction.

Teach him how to strive for multiple orgasms. As noted earlier in this chapter, multiple orgasms occur when a man is able to have the rhythmic contractions of orgasm without ejaculating. There are some wonderful books on the subject, including *The Multi-Orgasmic Man: Sexual Secrets Every Man Should Know* by Mantak Chia and *How to Make Love All Night (and Drive Your Woman Wild)* by Barbara Keesling. Add them to your lending library. (See Appendix E for suggested reading lists and other resources, including videos and DVDs.) If a client is interested, you can recommend qualified tantra teachers and other specialists.

> **MORE ABOUT THAT**
> Body coaching is the most common method for treating EP, but you can be an excellent sex coach without ever watching a client masturbate. You may be shocked. Don't castigate yourself for having those feelings. If you can handle body coaching, you will learn to think of yourself as the football coach on the sidelines shouting directions. If you choose not to body coach, you might suggest that the client review Kramer's materials on his own. Guide your client through the process and provide feedback as he tells you about his masturbatory experiences using recommended techniques.

In most sex coaching sessions, I offer the basics, including focused breathing, PC muscle exercises (Appendix D), sensate, and other self-focus techniques for heightening pleasure.

Concern 9. Sexual Trauma

Sexual trauma (ST) is usually a woman's issue, but some men also suffer from it.

CAUSES

ST clients are often highly sensitive or emotionally shut down.

Sex abuse, even rape, during childhood. The beginning of sexual trauma in males can be as subtle as a brush against the leg of a relative that felt yucky or awkward feelings from being shamed by a parent about having a skinny body, or the severe reality of a childhood filled with years of molestation. Children of both genders suffer from

MORE ABOUT THAT
I met John Gray, author of the Mars/
Venus books, in the 1980s when he
taught seminars on emotional healing. One particular seminar, *Men,
Women and Relationships,* was the
nucleus of the Mars/Venus work. I
often recommend Gray's book *What
You Can Feel You Can Heal* to ST
clients as they begin their healing
journeys.

family-based violence, sexual exploitation, and even rape. These are always tougher cases to resolve.

An emotionally scarring sexual incident. I had one client whose sister pulled down his pants, shamed him by yelling "You've got a tiny dick," and teased him about it in front of her girlfriends for years. Sexual trauma can leave deep scars that shut down a man's pleasure, leaving him incapable of sharing his body and his feelings with a lover. ST clients typically need to be referred to a competent psychologist, therapist, psychiatrist, or social worker who specializes in this area.

OPTIONS FOR RESOLUTION

Helping this type of client to open up will require your most delicate skills and powerful techniques.

The MEBES model. The five steps:
1. *Mental.* Help the client stop giving himself negative messages. In 12-step programs, this is called "stinking thinking." Examples: "It was my fault." "I deserved it." "I am no good."
2. *Emotional.* Focus intensely on the emotional pain that he holds in his body. This is often the place for a therapy referral. I also use guided imagery techniques to soften the pain such as the one in Appendix A. Have the client construct a forgiveness letter. When he can forgive the perpetrator (and also himself), he can move on. Some men can work through ST issues by: (1) disclosing the traumatizing incident, (2) reviewing it, (3) experiencing the feelings, and (4) doing forgiveness work. Others may require months or years of therapy.
3. *Body.* Blocked emotions live in the body until they are released through deliberate bodywork. Reiki, the Feldenkreis method, Rolfing, Trager, and even therapeutic massage can be helpful. In *The Complete Idiot's Guide to Sensual Massage* I teach ways of integrating sensual touch into a person's lifestyle for healing and other benefits.
4. *Energy.* Energy is everything. That is one of my teaching principles. Help your client allow energy to flow into the blocked

regions of his body, especially those areas where the prior abuse or trauma occurred. A simple ritual may help. Have him create a place that he feels is sacred in his bedroom. He should put objects that promote his healing and self-acceptance in that place. These may include pictures of him as a happy boy, his parents (unless one was the perpetrator), a baseball, an award, a love letter from a girlfriend, his wedding vows—whatever allows him to connect with feelings of love. He should sit or stand in front of those images, while perhaps lighting a candle each night. Then he should allow for a moment of thanks for being a healthy, mature, adult male with the power to love or be touched again, saying those words aloud in some format that resonates with his own style (such as "I, John, am a happy, healthy man, ready to love again" or "I, Samuel, am willing to share my body and experience pleasure").

5. *Spirit.* Some men are very open to spirituality, whereas others shy away from exploring this side of life. Ask your client if he has a spiritual belief system or follows a spiritual or religious path. His response will guide you. If he is a spiritual man, suggest that he turn to his higher power, to God, or to the Universe— whatever he views as a spiritual force—for assistance in his healing process. That force may be his anchor as he lets go of the past, moves forward to self-acceptance, and allows sexual pleasure to return to his life. Some trauma survivors (I never use the word *victim*) can use spiritual books or audio programs to facilitate healing.

INSIDE STORY: THE NUNS IN THE SHOWER

A recently divorced client came to see me with a body dysphoria concern. He hated his scrotum, which was peppered with white cysts, saying that he found it repulsively ugly. An M.D. with whom I had a good working relationship agreed to let me view the client's genitalia at the exam. When I saw his scrotum, I was sure the cysts were stopping him from being sexually open with women.

In our next session I began a dialogue about his sexual past to see how his condition had affected his partners. After a few sessions, he began recalling past abuse. I suggested he keep a journal. Each morning he wrote down something he remembered about his childhood. He was born into a wealthy family, lost his father at age 5 to a sudden heart

attack, and was sent to a Roman Catholic orphanage. After 6 years, he
was reunited with his mother and her new husband.

I thought his trauma was losing both parents, though one was alive.
Then he described the abuse he suffered from the nuns. They required
all the boys to shower in their bathing suits. For this pretty little boy,
they took extra care. They removed his bathing suit after each shower,
fondling his penis as they did. Other nuns also shamed and brutalized
him with beatings over those critical years of early development.

I cried with him when I listened to his story. His experience caused
him to shut down sexually. And I believe his ugly bumps (i.e., hardened
cysts) were his way of denying his masculinity. I referred him to a ther-
apist to work more intensely on his issues while I coached him to believe
in his male beauty and to restore his sexuality.

The range of male sexual concerns is enormous. Don't panic. You
will learn how to deal with the whole range as you develop increased
knowledge and skills and have confidence-building experiences.

Get It!

1. List three options you might recommend to a client with Early Ejaculation.
   (medically based)
   (behavioral)
   (mind-focusing)
2. What might you say to a married man with small penis size concerns
   (body dysphoria)? Include information on what makes a man a
   good lover, how to do a reality check, and positive encouragement
   for self-acceptance.
3. Now ask yourself these same questions for each of the nine male sexual concerns.

CHAPTER EIGHT

Women
Common Sexual
Concerns and Resolutions

FEMALE SEXUAL CONCERNS are often more openly discussed and written about than those of men—a dialogue partly facilitated by the self-help culture fueled by women's books and magazines and daytime talk shows aimed at women viewers. Women in general may not have more sexual concerns than men, but they have been more open in reporting them to doctors, therapists, researchers, and writers of behavioral surveys. For example, in 1999 a major survey on female sexual behavior reported in *JAMA* claimed that 43% of women suffer some form of sexual dysfunction. That's an astonishing number!

Women and men today face many overlapping concerns about their sexuality, with some notable exceptions. Low or no sexual desire leads nearly every published list of women's sexual concerns, with inability to reach orgasm in most or all of their partner sex encounters ranking a close second. In my practice, I also see a lot of women with dyspareunia—pain associated with sex. Although dyspareunia may not be widespread among women, it is common among clients of therapists and sex coaches.

Emerging drug therapies to treat women are under investigation, including female versions of sildenafil/Viagra and testosterone therapies. Non-prescription topical ointments (some of questionable merit) to stimulate clitoral sensation abound in the marketplace, and do devices to pump up the female genitals. But the range of options available to women is not as wide as that for men.

A complex web of concerns often interferes with a woman's sexual pleasure. First, many women still need permission to feel erotic pleasure. (Dr. Ruth Westheimer has often said that "giving permission to enjoy sex" is her primary job as a therapist.) The women who come to me for sex coaching may require instruction on how to have an orgasm as well as help in healing the relationship wounds caused by this concern and in freeing their own inhibited sexual desire. Sometimes you may feel like you are teasing apart intertwining strands as you coach a female client. And often you will find that the last strand is that primary concern: Permission. She never learned how to say "yes" to herself about sex.

THE TEN CONCERNS

As I did in the last chapter, I will present the concern, discuss the underlying causes, and outline options for resolution, using case examples to illustrate actual application. See Appendix C for intake and assessment forms for women.

The ten most common sexual concerns for women are:
• Low or no sexual desire (LD)
• Preorgasmic primary
• Preorgasmic secondary
• Dyspareunia (painful sex)
• Vaginismus
• Sexual inhibitions (SI)
• Body dysphoria issues (BD)
• Social/dating skills deficit (SDSD)
• Desire for enhanced pleasure (EP)
• Sexual trauma (ST)

Concern 1. Low or No Sexual Desire

Peruse a stack of women's magazines in the waiting room of a doctor's office and you may conclude that women are always thinking about how to have better, hotter sex by making all the right moves in bed. That may be true for *some* women. But be prepared to focus most of your coaching with women on one sexual concern: low or no desire, the eye of the hurricane in my profession.

Labeled *inhibited or hypoactive sexual desire* (ISD) by medical professionals, low desire (LD) is the leading sociosexual trend among women (and to a somewhat lesser extent among men, too). That lack of desire leads to endless complaints about no time or no energy for sex. The sexless relationship, even among couples under 40, is a phenomenon of our time—one that I will cover in greater detail in the following chapter.

For 2 years I taught an online course about unlocking sexual desire at iVillage.com, a site with over 18 million users, 80% of whom are women of all ages and socioeconomic backgrounds. Thousands of people have signed up and paid for this course, and many have written testimonials about how this nonmedical approach has improved their life. I call this course their *journey to awaken the sexual self.* Online courses and teleclasses can be a sound adjunct to your sex coaching business.

Not surprisingly, many factors can play a role in shutting down sexual desire. LD is often the tail that wags the dog—the dog being one of the other female sexual concerns. The sex isn't working. Logically, she has stopped wanting to have sex.

> **MORE ABOUT THAT**
> My online course on unlocking sexual desire (either again or for the very first time) also included an active online discussion board for students. Every week I answered a handful of their newest questions. For only $39.95 iVillage offered a life-altering event for women who may not otherwise ever find the time or money for a sex coach or therapist. I am always touched by these women's stories about how they improved their self-image, let go of their painful past, became willing to explore pleasure, increased their sexual knowledge, and improved their erotic skills.

The following list of basic causal factors may seem redundant because they are similar to the list for men.

CAUSES

The list of possible causes is extremely lengthy, because there are many contributing factors to today's epidemic of low desire.

Aging. Perimenopause, the period before the onset of actual menopause (defined as one year following the last menstrual period), plays havoc with a woman's sex drive. A decline in estrogen production can suppress a healthy sexual appetite in some women, whereas a decrease in testosterone production from both the ovaries and the adrenals (an effect of stress, not just aging) has the same effect in other women. Hot flashes, night sweats, weight gain, bloating, and being ignored by men can make a woman feel as desirable as cold toast. (I've also noticed in my practice that increasingly younger women show symptoms of perimenopause, a condition often misdiagnosed by their primary care physicians.)

Hormonal soup. Dealing with the symptoms of aging, including loss of desire, is confusing enough. Add the ongoing controversy about hormone replacement therapy to that, and many women feel like they're in the hormonal soup without a life raft. Taking a hormonal supplement may alleviate LD symptoms, but at what cost? Women with medical conditions from hysterectomy to depression (antidepressants often dampen libido) may believe they have nowhere to go for help, even though such help exists. No sex, they fear, may be the cost of health.

Relationship conflicts and power struggle issues. Anger and resentment fester in many relationships. That infection inhibits desire. Conflicts about daily life issues from money to childrearing can have the same effect. Some women lose interest in sex due to conflicts over disparate desire. Remember that famous split-screen scene in the film *Annie Hall?* Woody Allen says to his shrink, "We *never* have sex . . . only three times a week" while Diane Keaton says to her own therapist, "We *always* have sex . . . three times a week!"

Body image issues. Feeling embarrassed or ashamed of her body (even hating the figure she sees in the mirror) can annihilate a woman's sexual desire.

Fatigue. She's a working mother, a driven single professional, a high achiever who keeps her mind, body, and money in excellent shape, a caretaker caught between aging parents and growing children—today's woman is exhausted!

History of sexual abuse or an abusive/coercive relationship. A woman can't give herself permission to enjoy sex until she exorcises her demons and heals her wounds.

Unskilled lover or partner. I am always amazed at how many people believe the phrase "no sex is much better than bad sex." Women with poor lovers—especially women who are not orgasmic with a partner (preorgasmic secondary)—often lose desire. Subconsciously they are avoiding another erotic disappointment.

OPTIONS FOR RESOLUTION

Be prepared to work on all levels to address this concern: physical, intellectual, emotional, and spiritual.

Rule out the physical/organic reasons for LD. Does your client have regular medical care? Has she had a recent and comprehensive physical? What was her most recent sexual health assessment outcome? Know your community well. You should have a network of professional referral contacts, including gynecologists, obstetricians, specialists in the diagnosis and treatment of sexually transmitted infections (STIs), vulvar pain specialists, therapists, and Planned Parenthood and other sexual health clinics. Help her decide on the best course of medical treatment if necessary.

Advocate for hormonal balancing. Know the facts about birth control and STI prevention, including the possible negative sexual side effects of treatments. You must be savvy about the range of treatments for aging or prematurely perimenopausal women, including prescription medications (usually synthetic hormones), bioidentical hormonal preparations (and the doctors willing to prescribe this option), and natural herbs in health food stores or online. Be familiar with alternative and New Age resources like acupuncture centers. Knowing what's safe and what's not is a challenge. But you must provide the most complete and reliably accurate information available in your community.

Teach her how to have better sex. Women with unskilled lovers are prone to developing LD. Nothing turns off a woman faster than a poor lover—a partner who doesn't help her reach orgasm, for example, or a lover with a clumsy or rough touch. (Many women choose to stay with these men for other reasons.) Your sex coaching must be artful because you are teaching her how to teach him without making him feel he's in remedial training.

Try:

• *Redirecting information.* Help her learn what she can about her own sexual response cycle. Coach her to use masturbation as a way to take charge of her own body and explore her capacity for pleasure. You may decide to use body coaching, the single best method for encouraging a successful masturbation technique, or you may choose other resources (e.g., videos, DVDs, books).

- *Showing her how to redirect him.* Give her books, videos, and other educational resources (including some from your lending library) that give her explicit directions for teaching him what she's learned about her own body.
- *Educating her.* Most women require direct or indirect clitoral stimulation to reach orgasm, with cunnilingus being the surest path. Many women can reach orgasm through stimulating the G-spot with a hand, penis, or sex toy. Fewer reach orgasm via anal stimulation. Teach her the skills she and her lover will need to turn knowledge into erotic action. The more you empower your client about her options for greater sexual pleasure and how to get there, the more likely it is that she will share her lessons with her lover. You may have to do some rehearsal role playing to coach her in how to approach her partner.

Inside Story: Andie and the Wolf

Of the many women I've coached who suffered from LD, caused by everything from inept lovers to early hysterectomies, Andie particularly stands out in my memory. She had absolutely no sexual desire. She and her partner came in together on the initial visit. He was jittery and angry, she was repressed and sad. I interviewed them intensively on their personal sexual history as a couple. They both had active careers and traveled extensively, though not together. Couples in that kind of relationship will either pant at the sight of one another or find themselves longing for the sound of the next airplane boarding call.

After I assessed them and suggested an action plan, Andie's partner stood up, headed for the studio door, and said, "She's the problem. Let her work it out!"

Andie and I got down to work. I used a guided imagery session to elicit what Native Americans call an animal totem. Andie's totem was the wolf. She then had a personal revelation: She realized that she derived her sexual hunger from her inner wolf. That part of her, the wolf spirit, was hiding back in the cave and didn't want to come out. I coached her to invite that wolf out to play. Suddenly things at home began to change. Letting her wolf spirit out gave her permission to confront her own truth about her low desire. She'd lost her urge to hunt because her prey was too eager for sex. Without the thrill of the hunt, she had to create a new paradigm for meeting her inner sexual needs.

By tapping into the energy of her huntress self, she reawakened her sexual energy.

As part of the coaching plan, she agreed to take time each day to acknowledge the wolf in her. She created a space to perform morning rituals honoring her wolf. Two weeks later she reported that she had seduced her (very satisfied) husband not once but twice since our previous session. Andie was brave enough to go inside the delicate fabric of her inner reality. That can sometimes be all that's necessary to kick-start the libido.

Concern 2. Preorgasmic Primary

Preorgasmic primary women cannot reach orgasm—either alone or with a partner. This is a difficult concern to treat, but not a common one. Most women who seek coaching for an orgasm concern are preorgasmic secondary, (unable to reach orgasm with a partner). The preorgasmic primary client typically doesn't masturbate.

Notice that I say *preorgasmic*, not *anorgasmic*, the term used in medical literature. Like the old-fashioned word *frigid*, anorgasmic carries judgment and condemnation and doesn't leave much room for hope. I believe that every woman can find her path to orgasm.

CAUSES

The causes for this concern often stem from the past.

Rigid and sexually repressive upbringing. Preorgasmic primary women may have received and internalized sex-negative messages from parents, other family members, or religious authorities.

Childhood sexual abuse or shaming experiences. Consistent negative criticism about her developing body or overt molestation can be predictors for this client. Even being shamed by a parent or sibling for nudity can inhibit sexual development.

Ignorance about her own body and sex in general. Some girls grow up in isolated cocoons. They may have normal adolescent feelings of desire, but not know how to translate those feelings into a personal erotic quest for pleasure.

Lack of privacy and no or poor boundaries in the family of origin. Preorgasmic primary women may have grown up in a crowded home or have been smothered by a parent who denied her time to explore her sexuality.

OPTIONS FOR RESOLUTION

As you review the client's history, use your creativity to recommend self-help resources, and body coach her if you are willing.

Carefully review her sex history. You will probably discover that the client had a difficult sexual evolution—an incident of sexual abuse by a stepfather, for example, an early boyfriend whose awkward groping embarrassed and confused her, or a fearful nudity experience. Some preorgasmic primary clients have been told that touching herself "down there" is dirty, bad, or sinful. In these situations, your main job as a sex coach is to teach her that masturbation is a healthy, natural part of human sexuality—and give her permission to discover and enjoy her own pleasure. Then address her past to learn exactly what held her back from childhood exploration with masturbation. Give her masturbation sessions as home assignments.

Give her the best self-help resources for learning how to masturbate. Two books top my required reading list for women with this sexual concern: Betty Dodson's *Sex For One* and Lonnie Barbach's *For Yourself.* These are the best books in the field of sexology about solo sex for women. Your lending library should include both books as well as others, along with videos and DVDs, including Dodson's video of her women's masturbation training workshops, *SelfLoving.* Another wonderful self-help resource is the Sinclair Institute's book and corresponding video program *Becoming Orgasmic,* in which the woman discovers her own anatomy and masturbation patterns and becomes orgasmic with her loving husband.

Use body coaching. I find that women who are brave enough to undergo body coaching for masturbation have powerful breakthrough experiences that lead to good results in their private masturbation sessions. A sex coach can teach her the right moves to go beyond her old restrictive boundaries. For some women, body coaching makes a critical difference. Having a bedside coach to help her sustain the process can be the element that lets her break free to her orgasm.

INSIDE STORY: MARLA AND HER FIRST O

Marla, a 45-year-old client, had never touched herself below the belt, much less masturbated. Not surprisingly, she was preorgasmic with men. After I did her history and learned that she was preorgasmic primary, we began the masturbation training.

She was a bit shy at first about taking down the assignments for home practice. As the weeks went by, she achieved some success at touching herself on her genitals and playing with her new sex toys. Initially her progress delighted her. But she didn't progress to the point of orgasm.

We both felt that she was stuck. When I suggested body coaching, she barely hesitated, so great was her desire to find release. In person I instructed Marla to undress and lie down on the towel-covered settee with personal lubricant, her Hitachi Magic Wand, and other toys at her side.

"Take deep breaths," I said. "Let go of any anxiety you feel about being viewed by me." After stroking her genitals for several minutes with her lubricated fingers to warm up, she buzzed her wand over a washcloth on her pubic mound. Then she picked up her curled acrylic vaginal dildo and used that for a while. Alternating between buzzing and thrusting, she hovered at the level of high arousal.

"Keep going," I said. ("Keep going" is the sex coach's most useful mantra.) "Keep going," I repeated, and I could see her begin to push through the barriers that had prevented her from experiencing release. She lifted her pelvis into the air, shuddered and shook, and, yes, finally achieved her first orgasm! Afterward, she lay on the settee for quite a while as tears rolled quietly down her face. She looked me in the eye. "How can I ever thank you?" she asked. "You have given me my sexuality."

I moved close to her, held her hands, and put a blanket over her. I was honored to have been her guide on one of the most special events of her life. Even if you only become the voice inside a woman's head helping her reach that first orgasm (not sitting by her side as she gets there) you will play a powerful role in another person's sexual journey.

Concern 3. Preorgasmic Secondary

Preorgasmic secondary women are able to reach orgasm via masturbation but not with their partner. Unfortunately, we will probably see more and more women with this concern as the use of antidepressants proliferates. When medications are not the culprit, there are other causes.

CAUSES

Logically, this concern relates to the relationship as the context for sexuality.

Lack of trust. She may not trust a particular partner—or men in general.

Fear of intimacy. Yes, women have intimacy fears too. They just express them in different ways.

Inability to let go. She may need to be in charge or feel in control of everything. In fact, she may energetically hold herself back, even stop breathing during sex.

An unskilled partner. She may be with a lover who provides insufficient physical stimulation for her release.

Insufficient mental arousal. She may need more mental or fantasy stimulation for arousal before or during the actual physical act.

Lack of permission to be sexual with a partner. Often the trio of shame, fear, or guilt about partner sex, especially intercourse, can diminish a woman's orgasmic ability with a partner.

A pattern of faking orgasm. Any woman may do this to avoid displeasing her partner or hurting his feelings.

Sexual ignorance. She and her partner may not know exactly what they can do to bring her to orgasm.

Poor communication skills with a partner. She may know what she needs him to do but feel unable to tell or show him.

Some of these causal factors are also discussed in the next chapter (on couples) because they are intimacy issues. You need to help your client figure out what's holding her back with her partner. If she can't do that with your help, refer her to a trained psychotherapist or counselor. Sex coaching may not be enough for a client who has deeply rooted emotional or psychological blocks to orgasm with a partner, such as a history of serious intimacy issues or lack of trust from a traumatized childhood.

OPTIONS FOR RESOLUTION

The more you can help her see what is and is not working in her relationship, the better!

Help her identify her pleasure blocks. She reaches orgasm through masturbation. What is stopping her from having that experience in partner sex? Explore her causal factors. Correct any technical misinformation she might have—for example, that she should be able to reach orgasm via intercourse alone. The vagina is not the primary site of female pleasure for every woman. For the overwhelming majority of women, it is the clitoris.

Reframe her right to experience pleasure with a partner. Help her construct a list of personalized affirmations that apply to her orgasms in partner sex. For example, suggest she say each morning, "I, Sallie Jo, will have stupendous orgasms with John." Or, "I, Macy, am easily orgasmic with Joe." These daily positive affirmations can strengthen a client's belief system and help her move into a mental/emotional place where she is more likely to have orgasms.

Help her face the truth about her current sexual relationship. Sometimes a client feels unsafe in a relationship because she *is* unsafe there! Tell her what you think and feel about her relationship based on what you have heard her say. Encourage her to look at her options—both within and outside the relationship. Maybe her difficulty in reaching orgasm is an indicator of serious relationship problems that have nothing to do with sex.

Teach her the Three Doors technique. With new clients I often use a technique based on the *Three Doors* metaphor. First, I have her (or him) list the questions she must answer before the concern can be resolved. Then we discuss each option. The result is an informed choice by her, as part of her empowerment process.

For example, a woman who is not orgasmic with her partner may have to face an unpleasant reality: The problem is the relationship, not her sexuality. She has to ask herself critical questions: *Is the relationship a healthy one? If there are difficulties, can they ever be resolved? Can I improve the relationship by working on myself? What can I realistically expect to accomplish with (or without) my partner involved in the sex coaching process? It this relationship too far gone for a resurrection? Is it time to move on?*

To help her answer those questions and make her decisions, I say: "You have three choices. Envision three doors opening to your choices. You have to pick one door."

• *Door 1: Do nothing.* Let things remain as they are. Accept that you will continue to live with the sexual concern that bothered you so

much that you sought help from a sex coach. (I also call this "the choice to keep suffering.")
- *Door 2: Work to change the relationship.* Engage your partner in the process of change. If he or she is not willing to change, you must change, especially in your perception of the relationship.
- *Door 3: End or leave the relationship.* "You get to choose," I tell her. "No one can make the choice for you."

I have seen it happen time and time again. Helping the client learn how to tap into her (or his) power to choose—and then to act based on that choice—becomes the single greatest lesson you can give her as a sex coach.

Empower her. This is a familiar catch phrase to any woman who was sexually active or learning about sex in the 1970s and 1980s: "*You* are responsible for your own orgasm!" When a woman is not orgasmic with her partner but does reach orgasm via masturbation, I always begin with this empowering message. *She* must take responsibility for learning her own sexual response patterns, asking for (or telling and showing) what she wants/needs for sexual stimulation and then letting go. Role play with her if she has difficulty communicating with him.

I also teach: "You cannot make yourself have an orgasm. You have to let it happen." Magical thinking? You bet it is! An essential element of orgasm is the ability to relax into the sensations and let them lead to release.

Suggest individual or couples counseling. If the problem is *this* relationship with *this* man, she may need therapy to help her sort out the issues that are coming between them in bed.

Provide educational and erotic books, videos, and DVDs. Erotic videos that show a man satisfying his partner via cunnilingus and manual stroking will both arouse and teach her and her partner. An excellent example is *The Complete Guide to Oral Lovemaking* from Pacific Media Entertainment.

Teach my nine steps to orgasm. You can use this as a model for body coaching or as directions for her to practice at home.
  1. *Breathing.* Use concentrated breathing to open up her body and feel alive. Slow, deep breathing can help her transition from workday

stress to sexual feelings. Breathing is the first step in relaxing into the sexual moment. I call it the "egg breath"; I coach women (and men who have difficulty relaxing) to form an "energetic egg" around their body and breathe deeply with that in mind.

2. *Mind control.* Use erotica to generate fantasy if she cannot fantasize actively inside her own head. Fantasies help quell anxiety about orgasm. Never *try* to have an orgasm!

3. *Foreplay.* Focus on pleasurable sensations as she is being kissed, stroked, touched, and fondled. Do whatever is arousing for her at this stage, whether it is kissing and breast fondling or watching triple-X movies and talking dirty.

4. *Sustain the arousal.* Usually intermittent kissing and fondling of nongenital regions alternated with genital touch keeps a woman aroused. Use elements of sensual massage. (See *The Complete Idiot's Guide to Sensual Massage.*)

5. *Apply clitoral stimulation.* Most women require direct or indirect clitoral stimulation with a finger, penis, sex toy, or mouth to reach orgasm. Never forget that.

6. *Add containment sensations.* Insert his penis or a sex toy (dildo or vaginal vibrator) into the vagina (or anus) while receiving clitoral stimulation to provide the sensations of vaginal containment.

7. *Mimic signs of an orgasm.* When she's near orgasm, she should moan, arch her back, lift her pelvis, thrust it up and down, curl her toes and fingers, and squeeze the vaginal muscles (or use PC contractions)—all activities that will encourage orgasm.

8. *Practice PC exercises daily to keep PC muscles in orgasm shape.* (See Appendix D for my model.)

9. *Renew permission for pleasure on a regular basis.* Teach her to say yes to her orgasms, whether she's busy, tired, stressed, feeling fat, or even annoyed with her partner. She always has the right to pleasure.

INSIDE STORY: THE LADY ON THE RED FOX STOLE

A client session that makes my list of most amazing was the last of nine intensive orgasm coaching sessions for a very tough lady in her late fifties. She was a glamorous, sexy, sophisticated, and worldly woman—who couldn't reach orgasm with any male partner, much to her dismay. This woman could wrap any man of any age around her pinkie finger, but she couldn't get what she most wanted from him in bed. She attended one of my seminars and sneaked me a note to ask if I would coach her in private. Like everyone else, I was charmed by her.

"I've been through self-awareness therapy and personal erotic growth seminars—and I can't reach an orgasm," she said, but she was determined to break through her resistance and experience what she had come to regard as the ultimate pleasure.

On that final day she walked to the studio with her red fox stole slung over her shoulders and a big grin on her face. "I know I'm so close," she said, flinging the stole into the air as she swirled herself down on the couch. Suddenly she got up, marched to the bathroom, and minutes later paraded out, a Hitachi Magic Wand in hand, wearing nothing but makeup and a triple strand of pearls. She picked up the stole, draped it across the carpet in front of the fireplace, and lay down. I closed the drapes, put a hot flick in the VCR, and said, "Okay. Show me your progress."

Like a perfect student, she flawlessly performed every single step I'd taught her in orgasm coaching. But she was stuck on that precipice of high plateau before orgasm. I began cooing at her, softly but audibly, "Come on now, you can do it." She sighed and continued. I increased the volume. "You can do anything. . . . Keep going, sweetie. . . ."

Then, like a starship entering hyperspace, varoom—she came. Shrieking, moaning, and laughing to the point of exhaustion, she said after she could finally speak, "I did it! I'm there! And on a red fox stole, no less!"

"Just like the princess you are," I said.

As my last piece of coaching advice, I told her to ask her partner to say these same things I'd just said to her, first in a whisper, then louder and louder, whenever she reached that plateau. It must have worked, because I never saw her again.

Concern 4. Dyspareunia (Painful Sex)

Medical professionals report an increasing number of cases of painful sex, known as dyspareunia. The three most common forms of dyspareunia are pelvic pain disorders, vulvar pain issues, and pain caused from extreme vaginal dryness, a condition that can result from aging or as a side effect of medication, unnecessary surgeries, or even late childbearing—as well as relationship issues. These painful conditions make intercourse difficult, impair sexual pleasure, and, if left untreated, stifle desire as well.

CAUSES

The causes of pelvic and vulvar pain disorders may be physical but they can also be psychological, often requiring extensive therapy.

OPTIONS FOR RESOLUTION

Treating this concern is often a matter of addressing the purely physical aspects of sex.

Refer a client with serious pelvic or vulvar pain disorder first to a medical doctor and then to a therapist. Painful sex disorders are usually resolved medically. Send the client to a gynecologist, sexual health center, or a urologist specializing in the treatment of female sexual conditions. She needs more than a sex coach—though coaching later will help her to restore confidence and revive libido.

If the client's concern is caused by simple vaginal dryness, find out why she isn't lubricating during sex. The single most common complaint among women who are aging or taking certain prescription drugs (even over-the-counter medicines can dry mucosal membranes) is vaginal dryness. In perimenopausal or postmenopausal women, hormonal imbalance is the culprit. Many aging women have insufficient levels of estrogen, which leads to little or no lubrication from natural responses. They are aroused, but they don't get wet.

Refer the client to a competent medical professional who can prescribe products such as prescription hormonal creams or suppositories that can be inserted into the vagina for sexual enhancement. She may need to take hormone replacement therapy, estrogen replacement therapy, or use herbs to stimulate both her libido and her capacity for lubrication.

Teach her arousal techniques, including ones she can use on herself and others she can teach her partner. Younger women who suffer from this concern and aren't on medications may not be lubricating because they aren't aroused before they have intercourse. Particularly if she's inexperienced, she may not know what arousal mental and physical techniques work for her. She may also have a poorly skilled lover and need help in communicating her arousal needs to him.

If physiological (and deeper psychological) causes have been ruled out, explore her feelings about her partner. The client may be ambivalent about her partner, which suppress her arousal. She may have some emotional issues surrounding the relationship that are keeping her from getting aroused. Sometimes women stay in relationships for reasons other than sex (he's a good provider, her family loves him, he's her best friend) and then find they can't get aroused sexually.

Suggest lubricants. I always recommend a personal lubricant for women with dryness. Good choices are: Astroglide, Eros, Liquid Silk, Probe, and Replens (the latter is designed exclusively for vaginal dryness). Sexual stimulants, including homeopathic compounds or herbs that enhance sexual feelings, include brand names such as Allurex or Vigorex. My personal pick for a lube is ID Pleasure, which contains L-arginine, improving a woman's ability to sustain arousal in the clitoral region.

INSIDE STORY: ROY AND AMANDA—OOPS, WE'RE
OVER 50 NOW!

I coached Roy and Amanda only briefly—they didn't need much more than a simple opportunity to express their fears about aging in a safe setting and learn about products that would help them remain sexual in this new phase of life. Amanda was perimenopausal. Roy was terrified that their sex life was all but over. Her sex drive was already significantly reduced when they came to see me.

"I'm not turned on to sex," she admitted. With a little coaxing, I got her to admit she was avoiding sex because it hurt. "I feel sore afterward."

"She isn't as juicy as she used to be," Roy added defensively.

They'd tried to address the issue with good old spit (which didn't do the job it once did), KY jelly (which dried too quickly), and some fancy lubricants that, according to Roy, were too sticky, too gooey, or too perfumed. In one session I taught the couple about a new sexual stimulant that produced increased vaginal lubrication without hormones. That product is sold as Allurex for Women, a homeopathic drug that is a safe alternative to the controversial hormonal options. Within week Amanda's vaginal dryness was over. She grew wet with arousal, and that wetness made them both ecstatic. The couple called me later to say thanks and laughed about stocking up on the product.

Pain caused by vaginal dryness is an easy concern to treat as long as you have good information with which to educate the client about all the products on the market, including natural ones.

Concern 5. Vaginismus

Vaginismus, a painful spasmodic contraction of the vagina, is relatively rare. If you do see it, you'll have the opportunity to transform the client's life in a miraculous way. A woman who suffers from this concern really *suffers*. Vaginismus leaves her truly unable to tolerate any vaginal penetration. Intercourse is not possible. Obviously the situation can ruin a relationship. I have seen cases of women who were virgins on their wedding day and discovered intercourse was absolutely out of the question on their wedding night.

Many vaginismus sufferers have been dismissed by medical doctors who told them the problem was "all in their head." Although there are psychological components, this appears primarily as a physical concern for the female client and must be treated like one.

CAUSES

Usually the cause is psychological or emotional, but sometimes it can stem from an intact hymen.

OPTIONS FOR RESOLUTION

After exploring the possible causes, encourage the client to do the necessary self-touching to break through.

Rule out the most simple explanation: an intact hymen. Ask the client if she knows whether her hymen is still intact. (Virginity does not guarantee an intact hymen—it can be torn during athletic activity.) Occasionally a woman with a very tough hymen must have it surgically removed. Also ask the client if she has regular periods. If she does, there is probably not another obstruction inside of her vagina.

Probe her sexual history. Look for a history of molestation (even a single event) that perhaps caused her to shut down her vagina. Work with her to heal those wounds, and refer her to a therapist who specializes in sexual abuse issues.

Refer her to a doctor or help her find a vaginal dilation kit. Send the client to a gynecologist who you know will work patiently with her to open up the vagina with a series of dilating rods, a process done under close supervision. Some sex shops also sell vaginal dilation devices. If she won't see a physician or you can't find one in your area who does this treatment, help her find a good product and coach her through the process of using it.

Teach her to touch herself. Teach her (and her partner if she has one) how to open herself up to vaginal touch in the privacy of her own home. One technique: Gently insert an oiled Q-tip (recommand vitamin E oil), followed by an oiled finger, then two fingers, and so forth until the opening is wide enough for penile penetration.

Body coaching. I generally do not advocate touching a client during body coaching. You may want to have her show you the depth of touch she can tolerate inside her vagina. If that seems necessary and acceptable to both of you, use an oiled Q-tip or finger. Always use latex gloves if you decide to do a probe as her sex coach, and be sensitive to possible homophobic fears.

Inside Story: Overcoming Vaginismus

I've encountered only one female client with vaginismus. Margot was a "technical" virgin who had never had vaginal penetration by a penis. Although she had occasional bisexual fantasies, Margot longed for sexual penetration by a man. ("I don't want to live the rest of my life as a freak!" she once exclaimed.) I supported her quest to explore all of her sexual longings.

Her action plan included working with a male surrogate (a rare find) who gently coaxed her into sexual penetration with his finger in 2 sessions. She terminated surrogacy work as we approached the climactic session for penile penetration. "It's just too scary—I can't," she wept in my studio. The course of her work with the surrogate was powerfully transforming for her, despite the lack of sexual intercourse.

"I feel like a real woman—I let a guy in!", she grinned on our debriefing session.

She did, though, continue to explore sexual touch with women. Having used the sex coaching method of inserting different widths of objects into her vagina, from a Q-tip to her own finger to the surrogate's finger, she had overcome her vaginismus.

Concern 6. Sexual Inhibitions

Sexual inhibition (SI) in women is common and often signals other concerns—inability to reach orgasm; shame, guilt, or fear of sex; body image issues; even a history of sexual trauma or abuse. Many SI women have a problem with drinking or using recreational drugs, which reduce inhibition but also impair judgment and may send the woman down a toxic path to self-destruction.

Like men, women often suffer their sexual inhibition in silence until a partner they love pushes them to open up. SI women differ from women with orgasm or painful sex concerns in that they usually will either ask outright for help in overcoming their sexual shyness or, more commonly, plead for help in appeasing a disappointed boyfriend who is begging for erotic variety. The SI woman wants to release her inner siren. However, helping her do that isn't quite as easy as waving your magic wand!

CAUSES

The causes of SI in women mirror those for SI men: Sexually repressive childhoods, incidents in which they were shamed or ridiculed, or long-term virginity. Whether the sexual inhibition results from a childhood filled with negative or repressive messages about sexuality, a history of self-loathing regarding her body, or a simple lack of experience, this can be a wonderful type of client for sex coaching.

INSIDE STORY: SKIP TO M'LOU

M'Lou was a classic SI client. "My boyfriend sent me here," she sadly shared when we first met. "He wants me to be less inhibited about sex."

M'Lou and I created an action plan that included her taking tango lessons, striptease classes, reading erotica, watching the sexy movies of Candida Royalle (see Appendix E), and even browsing an online fetish/lingerie catalogue. One evening we met at a local sex boutique to buy her a vibrator, a dildo, lubricants, a sex game, books, DVDs, crotchless panties, a whip and handcuffs (soft-core), and a few other goodies. Her credit card was smoking at the register when she rang up her purchases!

M'Lou was a real trooper. Whatever I suggested, she did. Her fiancé even sent me a thank you note by email, acknowledging her hard work and her transformation. That kind of feedback makes sex coaching feel even more worthwhile.

OPTIONS FOR RESOLUTION

Helping this type of client will give you a great sense of accomplishment. Use some or all of the following possible options for resolution.

Check her history. First excavate the roots of her inhibition. Using the sexual history discussed in Chapter 6, dig into her past to discover if a traumatic sexual situation occurred during childhood, adolescence, or young adulthood—for example, losing her virginity in defiance of her family's church-based values or feeling shame about parts of her body. (Shame and body image development are discussed in the next section on body dysphoria issues.) Identifying the cause and helping her to reframe the issue may be all she needs to overcome inhibition.

Emphasize permission. Emphasize the P word: *Permission.* Sexually inhibited women either haven't resolved old issues of shame, fear, or guilt from their upbringing or past experiences or don't feel worthy of being sexual and receiving pleasure. They haven't been given permission by anyone, especially themselves.

Teach her erotic skills. This is where the real coaching work begins, both in sessions and in her home assignments. Help her create a new sexual persona. You can coach her to unblock her inhibitions by helping her see the lover she wants to become—and by giving her the skills to do that.

Provide resources. Encourage her to read books, such as *Exhibitionism for the Shy,* by avowed exhibitionist Carol Queen. Give her erotica and porn books, movies, and DVDs that contain positive images of sexually assertive women as inspiration. Suggest belly dancing or stripping classes—any activity that will sexually liberate her physically, mentally, and emotionally.

Concern 7. Body Dysphoria Issues (BD)

Perhaps the single greatest block to sexual self-acceptance and fulfillment for many women is body dysphoria (BD). Hating the shape of your body reflected in the mirror, feeling too thin or too fat, wishing you looked like anyone other than you, and never wanting to slide between the sheets with your partner with the lights on are not only damaging to one's self-esteem but also to sexual functioning.

BD is a major cause of LD, because a woman who does see herself as sexually desirable quickly loses her desire for sex.

CAUSES

The causes for BD are similar to many of those already presented, including a childhood filled with shame, guilt, or fear related to sexuality. The BD woman may hold a misguided idealized image of the female body or feel plagued by one or more particular areas of her body.

OPTIONS FOR RESOLUTION

Watch for signs of BD even when the client does not explicitly mention it as a concern, and use your intuition to guide you on how to help her let go.

Give her a reality check. Whereas men's BD issues generally focus on penis size (and can be alleviated by showing the client models of normal-sized penises), women's BD issues tend to be more far-reaching, focusing on breasts, hips, weight, legs, and buttocks. As a sex coach you will even eventually encounter a woman who thinks her clitoris is too small or her vulva lips too big. To help her understand how varied women are, I use the book *Femalia*, which has color photos of female genitals, and Betty Dodson's video, *Viva La Vulva*, which shows real women in one of her workshops displaying their genitalia in full splendor. You can give women who are concerned about breasts, body fat, and other BD issues the same kind of reality check by showing them photos of nude women in all sizes, shapes, ages, and colors. Seeing other women naked can be the beginning of healing.

Encourage her to get therapy. Women (presenting with any sexual concern) who have been traumatized, abused, coerced, shamed, and devalued in their sexual development often require therapy to overcome their sexual past. If you are a therapist, you can combine coaching and therapy for deeply rooted emotional concerns. If not, refer out.

Use guided imagery and other self-acceptance techniques. Guided imagery is a powerful technique for encouraging a client to accept—and eventually love—herself as she is. Through exercises she learns how to change her thinking about the offensive body parts. (For a sample guided imagery exercise, see Appendix A.) The *Mirror Activity*, described in the following inside story, is another technique that can have spectacular results.

INSIDE STORY: THE WOMAN WITH THE
STUPENDOUS BREASTS

Janet, a particularly brave client, and her husband sought coaching help in rekindling their sexual passion. I saw them for several sessions, scheduled sporadically over a few years. I used the Mirror Activity *in the most memorable session of our work together. I began by explaining the exercise to her and suggesting she do it as a home assignment. She gave me a puzzled expression. Suddenly it was clear to me: She needed me to do it with her.*

I began by demonstrating the exercise. While she watched in silent absorption, I took off my clothes and stood naked in front of the full-length mirror in the studio. "Starting with the top of your head," I said "and then going down your whole body, look into the mirror and tell yourself what you see and how it makes you feel." Then I did the process on myself, body part by body part, saying aloud what I saw in my reflection and how I felt about it. This is not as easy as it may seem. Looking in the mirror and speaking about your own body is a powerful activity, the words acting like a Roto-Rooter for whatever emotional baggage you carry about your body. As I worked my way down my body, I shared with Janet a tear and a laugh, and I expressed my vulnerabilities, especially about my small chest. Initially stunned, she gradually opened up. I read the tenderness in her face.

"Your turn," I said.

Naked, she stood with gigantic breasts that seemed to cascade down to her navel. She cried when she got to her breasts. "These breasts cause me so much pain and shame her for being so huge. They are such burdens." Then she chuckled. "But he *loves them!" She sort of twirled herself around in girlish glee.*

I brought her focus back to the deep, painful feelings she was trying to push back beneath the surface. Sobbing, she poured out her emotions until she was spent. At the closure of the activity, we hugged, robes on.

"Dr. Patti, I've never allowed myself to tell the truth about my body. Nobody but my husband has ever seen me naked. You make me feel whole—like a beautiful woman." That session was her turning point. Soon she began to make amazing changes in her sex life. I will always honor that day with Janet. I sent her home beaming and ready to let go of her inhibitions with her husband.

Concern 8. Social/Dating Skills Deficit

John Gray was right: Most women do not rely on the *Yellow Pages* to find professional help in becoming socially active. Men are more likely to seek coaching with this concern than women. Although Internet dating services have helped alleviate this concern somewhat, most women with SDSD remain isolated, perhaps complaining to their girlfriends about not being able to meet men. Often SDSD women have other concerns in addition to the social/dating skills deficit, with the SDSD hidden beneath the others.

CAUSES

Like women with body dysphoria, women with SDSD often feel vulnerable in public. They lack the social skills for easy conversation and may avoid social circulation altogether. A single incident, lack of opportunity, or even simple naivete or innocence can be the causal factors for SDSD.

OPTIONS FOR RESOLUTION

For these clients you may have to pull out all the stops!

Send her out into the world. She may not know where to go to meet men (or women, if she is a lesbian). You must have a database of dating services, singles activities, and social training opportunities in your community. Remember that the venues constantly change. You have to stay current to be savvy.

Here in Los Angeles I've recommended dating workshops and singles groups—some generic, others tailored to lifestyles, religious affiliations, hobbies, and other interests. Often you'll find that you have to prepare her for handling relationships and developing comfort with herself before she'll move out into social or sexually-charged circles.

Ask her about her specific goals and give her recommendations tailored to meet them. Does she want to meet a Jewish husband or find a surfing buddy?

Prepare her for socializing and dating. Use role playing to help her develop and hone conversational skills. Teach her to find her safety radar about appropriate settings and safe men. Unfortunately, we do need to coach women on taking precautions when meeting strangers, especially when they are meeting men they have spoken to online and *think* they know well. Stress the importance of meeting in neutral public places. Coffee houses are the best. Tell her to schedule meetings that involve little time and little money and take place in *very public venues.*

Be a beauty and fashion consultant. Delicately—with as much tact as you use for men—address hygiene and grooming issues, including unpleasant body odors. Have sound information for women concerned about maintaining a sweet-smelling vulvar area. For example, you might suggest that they avoid perfumed douches, nylon (non-cotton crotch) pantyhose, smoking, excessive drinking, very spicy foods or condiments, and, of course, not bathing. It may seem obvious to you, for example, that an overweight woman needs to take special care with cleansing, but it may not have occurred to her. Advise her on hair, makeup, and clothing, and know where to send her for makeovers, cosmetic surgery, and other treatments, including facials, hair coloring, and pedicures.

Concern 9. Desire for Enhanced Pleasure

Occasionally you will have a female client who says: "My sexual relationship is good, but I want to make it better." These women are sexually empowered. They know who they are, what they want, and what they like. They set goals and go all out to reach them.

The EP woman may want to expand any aspect of her sex life from masturbation to intercourse. She'll set the course for your work together. In short, she is a sex coach's dream client.

CAUSES

The EP woman is free of the baggage that sends other types of clients to your practice. She is devoted to personally expanding her sexual experiences. Let her bloom!

OPTIONS FOR RESOLUTION

These clients will be among the most enjoyable you work with. Let yourself get inventive about possible recommended activities to allow her to grow her pleasure.

Teach her new tricks. Recommend books, videos, and DVDs on sex techniques. Teach her how to use (or maximize the use of) sex toys in enhancing both her and her partner's pleasure. Plan a field trip to a sex toy store with her. Introduce her to fantasy sex products, like masks and costumes. Teach her role playing games to use with her partner.

Body coaching. She may want body coaching for techniques, such as increasing her capacity for multiple orgasms with a vibrator. Again, you make your own call here. Always feel free to say, "No, I don't do that." But also be prepared with an alternative if you turn her away. Rehearse a few responses, such as "I'm sorry, I don't do that type of work, but I'm happy to refer you to Sally Boston, who's an expert at that." Having those responses ready will keep you from falling into the trap of doing something outside your professional comfort zone.

Suggest advanced resources. If she wants more than what books, videos, and DVDs can provide, send her to advanced workshops (on tantra, for example) to study under the best practitioners. [See Appendix E.] Suggest that she take some courses at the Institute for the Advanced Study of Human Sexuality in person or through the extensive in-home certificate programs. She may even want information on a possible career path in sex education, counseling, or coaching—or even dream of making erotic movies.

Explore her bi or lesbian side. She may be vacillating about her sexual identity or orientation and seeking your help in exploring those options. Because our current cultural climate is more permissive of the discussion of lesbianism or gayness, women will seek you out to get help in determining if they are lesbian or bi. (This is true of your male clients as well.) They also may want to have you guide them in how to explore this bisexual pull they feel inside. You can steer her in the direction of local groups, reading materials or online support if she requests it. Many women in the EP category may be in a relationship with a partner who insists she have another woman sexually involved. You can help her to explore this option.

Concern 10. Sexual Trauma

Sexual trauma (ST) in women is not much different than it is in men. Sexual trauma leaves scars in both genders. Like men, women say they feel dirty and shameful. ST often results in sexual shutdown and, if not addressed, eventually destroys people and relationships.

Some ST clients, like Sarah, who felt she had a glacier for a chest, can work through this sexual concern with the help of a sex coach. Others will need to be referred to a therapist (or, if have one, put on your therapist hat) who can help them resolve their deep-seated emotional issues. Just as with any client who presents deep emotional pains or complex psychological reasons for their present sexual concern, you may want to refer to an outside source for handling these aspects of her spectrum of needs.

CAUSES

The causes for ST in women are the same as those for men.

OPTIONS FOR RESOLUTION

Review the possible resolutions for ST in men. If you feel that the client is not responding to your coaching, let your instincts guide you and change directions. This client type may be your greatest challenge.

Take an in-depth history. If you know or suspect you're treating a client with ST, take an expanded history, especially if her issues are deeply rooted. Has she sought therapy or counseling for this concern in the past? Learn everything you can about how she's coped with ST in the past. She may already have taken the steps you're prepared to suggest. I once began to dig into the sex history of a new client with a background of terrible ST—only to be told that she'd been in therapy for years and did *not* need to spend any more time on it with me. Quickly, she set me straight!

Help her face the truth. If your ST client is unwilling to face the truth about how she's been affected by sex abuse, you won't get anywhere sex coaching her. Try to get her to acknowledge the ST incident and its effect on her. If she won't, insist that she must at some point during coaching be willing to acknowledge the traumatic event, either with you or with a therapist. Realize too, that some ST clients are not deeply scarred or traumatized by their past. Work with your clients based on how the ST affected them and help them move quickly in the present.

Find group support. I also usually insist that ST clients find a group for peer support. The group can be a 12-step program or other support group. You can find them through a women's rape center or crisis counseling service, a local mental health agency, or Planned Parenthood, among other sources.

Get her to keep a journal. In all my work with women—in groups, through my online courses, or in personal sex coaching—I tell them that achieving their sexual goals is a journey, not an event. That process (which often involves healing, especially in the case of ST clients) deserves to be recorded. A woman can observe her own progress through her journal.

Some women love the idea of keeping a daily journal of their sexual journey. Others tighten up and say, "I don't have time" or "I hate to write." Do your best to get the reluctant journalist to write down at least one feeling or thought each day in her sexual healing journal. Writing in a journal helps her to accept, forgive, and eventually love herself—and others in her life, too. When she can love herself, she can share love or intimacy with another person. The habit of journal writing is often her breakthrough to feel sexual again—or for the very first time, alone or with a partner. Push it!

Be an advocate for pleasure. Encourage her to feel sensual as well as sexual pleasure in her body. I tell women to take a bubble bath, get a massage with warm oils from a partner or a professional, get a pedicure, wear furry slippersocks, or buy silk pajamas. Encourage her to do anything that provokes pleasurable sensations—it will help her restore her sexuality. Even patting her cat or brushing the dog may put her in touch with sensual pleasure. *The Complete Idiot's Guide to Sensual Massage* is filled with suggestions for enhancing sensual pleasure.

And, of course, give her permission to masturbate when she's ready.

You may feel overwhelmed by the enormous range of concerns that both women and men will come to you to resolve. Take heart. As one great counseling professor once said, "Fifty percent of the therapeutic process is showing up." Although as sex coaches we are not therapists, our work *is* therapeutic—don't forget that. Along with a few toys in your sack or tricks in your basket, your personhood—your ability to be there for clients as an anchoring presence—is what helps them to heal.

Get It!

Name three of the most common female sexual concerns:

1.

2.

3.

Describe two things you can do to treat clients with one of those three most common concerns.

1.

2.

What is the single greatest insight you are taking away from this chapter? How can that benefit you as a sex coach?

CHAPTER NINE

Couples
Common Sexual Concerns and Resolutions

THE COUPLE IS a three-part challenge for a sex coach: the two partners and the relationship itself. Couple clients often have overlapping concerns that contribute to the one big concern they initially present as "our" sex problem. In sex coaching individuals, you'll rarely see a person who needs help for only one concern; usually a complex of concerns is hiding behind their opening complaint. That's also true for couples—and often even more so. Couple power dynamics add a unique twist that makes coaching more than simply a matter of sorting out the individuals' overlapping sexual concerns. Typically one partner says his or her partner has a problem with sex. That may or (more likely) may not be an accurate assessment of the relationship. You need to figure out their power dynamics in the first session. You also need to have them paint an accurate picture of what's happening (or lacking) in the sexual relationship right off the bat.

As you take their sex histories and determine their outcome goals, identify which concerns belong to which person before you construct an action plan and begin the coaching process. I always start with a joint session and then schedule a separate session for each partner. I firmly believe that individual sessions are key to coaching couples successfully. This private time—often the only personal attention given to one partner—gives each person a place to tell you his or her truth and establishes rapport between you and them. You may never discuss a client's individual session with the other partner, but you will have a better understanding of them and the relationship, which makes it possible for you to coach them through their difficulties.

WATCH OUT FOR SECRETS

Be wary of getting caught in the trap of keeping secrets when you coach a couple! Here's how it works: One partner tells you a secret, insisting that you cannot reveal it to the other. The secret, however, is a pivotal part of the concerns that brought the couple to you. You're trapped: You can't reveal the secret, and you can't help them either.

For example, after one of my initial sessions with a couple, I saw the husband in a private session. When he told me he was having an affair, I encouraged him to tell his wife the truth (or let me tell her), but he remained steadfast in refusing to let that truth be told. I was caught in his web of deceit. I had the critical piece of information that informed his sexual behavior in the marriage. His obstinate refusal to let his wife know why he was avoiding sexual contact with her polluted my working relationship with him as well as his intimate relationship with her.

I told him I couldn't work with them as a couple and referred him to a therapist I knew was qualified to handle his withholding issues about his nefarious ways. But I continued coaching the wife to empower her sexually and provide her with a soothing foundation of support.

After this experience I vowed that I would never again become the container for a secret in couples work. "Don't tell me information critical to the coaching process and ask me to keep it a secret," I say to couple clients at the beginning of their private sessions.

THE FIRST THING YOUR COUPLE CLIENTS WILL PROBABLY SAY

Most couples present their problems in this basic way: "Let me tell you what's *not* happening in our bedroom." The sex, they insist, is lacking something. That laundry list of lacks includes:
• Lack of time for sex at all
• Lack of foreplay
• Lack of female lubrication

• Lack of interest in sex
• Lack of transition time from a busy day into the mood for sex
• Lack of touch
• Lack of communication
• Lack of the negotiation skills or communication abilities to work out sexual compromises

Be sensitive to the hidden message behind your clients' focus on *lack*. They probably also have a lot of complaints about their partner outside the bedroom. Help them shift their thinking away from what they don't have to what they do have—increase their gratitude and perception of abundance. If you get them to look at their relationship as a glass half full rather than half empty, you improve their chances of a positive outcome.

THE EIGHT COMMON COUPLES' CONCERNS

The eight most common sexual concerns for couples are:
• Little or no sex in the relationship
• Aversion to touch or misplaced touch communication
• Conflicts about desire/uneven desire (UD)
• Conflicting values about monogamy/affairs
• Performance skills deficit (PSD)
• Body image issues (BI)
• Communication style conflicts (CS)
• Negotiation skills deficit (NSD)

Concern 1. Little or No Sex in the Relationship

This is the single most common complaint in both sex coaching and sex and couples therapy today. The sexless relationship is a modern phenomenon, the subject of books, newspaper and magazine articles, and jokes by comedians everywhere.

Relationship conflicts are often to blame for sexless relationships, but the problem can also be caused by other sexual problems. Review all the sexual concerns presented in Chapters 7 and 8 in order to understand how EE, SI, touch aversion, or even LD, for example, can dampen interest in sex, allowing it to wane to a distant memory.

CAUSES

Because this is such a rampant concern, you should study it in detail. You will find a fairly exhaustive list of possible causes—practically anything can propel a couple into a sexless relationship.

Repressed or unexpressed emotions, past or present. Buried anger and resentment eventually strangle desire.

Low or declining hormonal output. Low estrogen production in women can make sex painful. Low testosterone in both men and women reduces sex drive.

Side effects from medications. These may include blood pressure medications and antidepressants among others discussed in earlier chapters.

Aging. Function is hampered by aging, especially in men. ED is a problem for over 30 million men. As humans age, things slow down, dry up, and sag.

Relationship issues. Often these are subtle causes seemingly unrelated to sex, including discord over money and children or disappointment in a mate's career, financial earnings, or level of physical fitness. Continuing power struggles aren't sexy.

Apathy. Not making sex (or sexual attractiveness) a priority will surely result in a relationship with little or no sex.

Physical disabilities. If a person cannot move his or her limbs, has chronic pain (such as lower back pain, the most common medical complaint), or suffers from a chronic disease (such as clinical depression or diabetes), he or she will probably lose interest in sex.

No time, no energy. With dual career families on the rise, increasing overscheduling of children, and couples caught between the needs of growing families and aging parents—who *isn't* busy today?

MORE ABOUT THAT

I get email letters every day at iVillage from women (and sometimes men) trapped in sexless relationships. Statistics show that about 20% of all married couples are in sexless marriages. Add to that number married couples who seldom make love, as well as couples who aren't married but live together in sexless relationships, and you get the picture: You can make ice cubes in American bedrooms.

I advise my iVillage readers to have quickies; share sensual touch (and find pleasure for themselves, even if it's only a bubble bath); explore sexual playgrounds, read erotic books (like my book, *The Adventures of Her in France*), and seek sex coaching or counseling as soon as possible.

OPTIONS FOR RESOLUTION

There are many choices when it comes to sex coaching the sexless couple.

Make medical referrals. You need to rule out medical problems leading to repressed desire, ejaculatory and orgasm concerns, and other issues. Help clients decide on safe and effective hormone replacement treatments, including natural options, and possible alternatives to antidepressants, including exercise programs. Some ongoing medical conditions require treatments or medications that interfere with desire or sexual functioning. Your challenge is to help those clients find erotic ways around their limitations.

Examine the relationship—and refer out if necessary. Many couples don't realize that something as small as procrastinating about discussing something that bothers one of them can adversely affect their sex life. Unexpressed feelings fester or get stuck. Find out what they haven't been telling each other. Help them clear the air without resorting to harsh accusations.

What else is going on in the relationship that keeps this couple from connecting sexually? If they have issues such as money problems, childrearing arguments, or conflicts with in-laws, you may want to refer them to a couples counselor who specializes in conflict resolution. Deep-seated unresolved anger may require therapy.

Encourage the couple to identify all their relationship issues and get help when needed.

Suggest individual and mutual masturbation and sensual touch. Sometimes a good orgasm is the antidote for pain and suffering. Suggest they masturbate alone or side-by-side. Provide recommendations for stimulating erotica. Mutual masturbation may jumpstart their libidos.

Sensual touch can be the salve for sexual aches and pains and can also support the intimate bond. Again, provide recommendations, including *The Complete Idiot's Guide to Sensual Massage.* Some couples find it easier to put sex gradually back into the relationship the same way beginners learn how to swim—by dipping a toe into the shallow end before diving off the high board. "No pressure, no intercourse" touching often leads to unexpected hot sex.

Insist that aging clients "use it." As your clients enter middle age, the old cliche "use it or lose it" takes on real meaning, becoming more true with every passing year. Like other muscles in the body, sexual muscles must be exercised to remain fit and ready for action. Affecting millions of men and women, sexual atrophy leads to performance problems.

Prescribe sex dates. I tell clients that they must make sex (shared sensual touch) a priority in their busy schedules. Many people won't have sex if they don't put it in their date books! Suggest lunchtime or Sunday afternoon quickies. Carole Pasahow's *Sexy Encounters* is filled with ideas for hot sex when time and sometimes energy are in short supply.

Encourage them to explore their wild sides. Not every couple will want to visit a sex club or nude beach or experiment with bondage, erotic spanking, or other adventurous games—but some will. Go through your resource list with them and make suggestions. Even watching a porn movie or going to a high-end strip club together can make a couple excited about sex again.

Don't accept "I can't" as an answer. They have to do something sensual or sexual together at least once a week. No excuses.

Concern 2. Aversion to Touch or Misplaced Touch Communication

I am surprised when couples who turn to coaching for help with a sexless relationship admit that they don't touch each other. "We never touch," one will say while the other nods with a blank expression. Or maybe they touch like friends, not lovers. They exchange hugs and quick kisses and maybe an occasional affectionate pat on the backside. Then there are couples where he thinks he is clearly sending signals of affectionate touch, and his partner reads it as pressure for sex. Or vice versa. Misplaced signals through touch can lead a couple into confusion or conflict.

CAUSES

This is becoming another very familiar concern in sex coaching. Once touch subsides for a couple, avoiding it altogether can become a pattern. Sometimes it is a red flag indicating their need to address intimacy issues.

They've become too familiar. "She is my best friend," he'll say. Sometimes they relate to each other more like affectionate siblings or good friends.

They've stopped all touch. Couples of any nature can fall out of the habit of touching. Whether they are too focused on the to-do lists or the kids, these couples have lost their original way of relating through touch.

They fear the intentions behind the touch. I've found that many clients are afraid to be touched because they don't know what their partner means to convey by the touch. Many men and women are confused about what "touch message" they are receiving or how they can use touch to send a message to their partner without being misread.

For example, a man comes home tired and stressed. His wife reaches out to him in an affectionate touch. But he reads her move as an invitation to be sexual—the last thing on his fatigued mind. Another example: A woman avoids her partner's touch altogether, fearing that it is a demand for sex, when she's barely able to handle the baby or has tomorrow's final exams on her mind. Instead of receiving comfort from his caring, tender, and even muscle-relaxing touches and caresses, she pulls away. He's really saying, "Honey, I love you so much and I know what you're going through," but she won't accept his touch message. It's no surprise that he stops touching her that way.

They've stopped touching with passion. Rekindling passion is tough for these couples, but that is their assignment. They must shift the way they touch each other from the best friends or siblings model to steamy touch.

One partner has a past history of abuse and touch triggers aversion. Aversion to certain types of touch, especially sexual touch, can be a sign of past abuse or subjection to coercive sexual behavior.

OPTIONS FOR RESOLUTION

You can get into some intensive sex coaching with these clients. The models that follow will help you move the client to a higher level of touching.

Teach them the Touch Continuum model. The Touch Continuum (Figure 9.1) maps out the five different types of touch.

Figure 9.1 The Touch Continuum

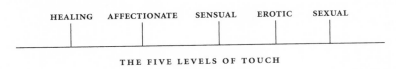

Help the couple use the Touch Continuum to identify the intentions behind each act of touch. Coach the couple to discuss what type of touch they are seeking and how to communicate that need or desire without words. A pat on the back for helping with the dishes or a pinch on the behind to show erotic interest can be enough to show intention. Once a couple is able to acknowledge their gap in understanding each other's intentions, they begin touching each other more often.

In learning to let all kinds of touch messages come through, the couple moves easily from the left side of the continuum, where sex isn't on the radar screen, to the right side, where they desire sex. Sex coaching with the Touch Continuum helps couples to restore touch, a vital step in becoming sexual again.

INSIDE STORY: GETTING BACK TO TOUCH

Marissa was a classic case of aversion to touch. I felt so sad for her and her failing relationship. Her intimacy fears created a wall that neither she nor her previous therapist could tear down. I suggested she review the Touch Continuum with her partner and then practice identifying intentions for each of the five levels of touch. Previously, when her partner extended a hand in affection, Marissa shut down, thinking it was a demand for sex. Once they clarified her misinterpretation of those gestures, they relearned how to speak to each other through their bodies. Suddenly things improved at home. Eventually, by not feeling that she was "on demand all the time," Marissa and her lover were able to become more intimate and sex became a favorite way of sealing their bond.

Teach them the hand caress. One of my favorite nonthreatening touch activities is the hand caress, which I first learned during my doctoral training at IASHS. It's a caring touch that helps couples to reestablish intimate touch without getting overtly sexual—unless, of course, they're both naked.

Here's how it's done: They take turns, allowing at least 10 to 20 minutes to give the other a sensual hand caress. Using oils, lotions, or warm liquids, she first soaks her partner's hand. Then she rubs, presses, and gently pulls the hand while expressing an intention of caring or loving. (Think: "I care about you" or "I love you.") Then they switch roles.

Both the giving and the receiving of the hand caress are done in silence. Sometimes pure intention is more easily felt without dialogue. Giving love through touch is scary for some couples. That simple activity provokes their fears about intimacy or commitment. It may push buttons for undecided new lovers or for seasoned couples who are in a touch-avoidance rut. Help these couples feel your coaching when they do the hand caress at home by giving them "what if" responses they can recall when they leave your studio. Help them prepare for unexpected outcomes, such as "What if he gets an erection during the hand caress?"

Refer the couple to therapy. In some cases, outside therapy may be necessary.

As with all other concerns, if the couple appears to be trapped in deeply rooted emotional conflict (especially if emotional outbursts occur repeatedly in sessions), use your judgment as to whether to refer them for therapy first, before going much further with your sex coaching. Or use your own therapeutic skills to address emotionally disabling issues.

Concern 3. Conflicts About Desire/Uneven Desire

One of the most easily diagnosed complaints presented by client couples is uneven desire UD. Imbalanced or uneven desires can be the underlying cause for continuing battles about sexual frequency, with one partner's "not enough" being the other partner's "too much." "A sexual shutdown can result. You'll usually discover this breakdown area during joint coaching sessions.

Every couple has a pattern of intimate behavior. Whatever the sexual concern, but especially with UD, this intimacy pattern can often predict the couple's willingness and ability to relate sexually more accurately than any other factor in their relationship history. How close or how distant do they say they feel toward each other? How do they behave together?

To get a sense of how the couple relates—their model of intimacy—listen to them, read their histories, and tease out the causal factors. You will become more skilled at this with each assessment.

CAUSES

The causes of UD can be anything from hormones to daily relationship conflicts. Even poor communication or negotiation skills can impede the desire of one partner in the couple. Unhealthy patterns of intimacy, which will be discussed next, often are the most significant contributors to low desire for one and higher for the other. How a person handles intimacy can be a predictor for erotic attraction in the long-term relationship.

OPTIONS FOR RESOLUTION

The options for resolution of UD are as far-reaching as the causes of the concern. If you suspect a medical or hormonal problem, refer to a specialist. If there are problems in the relationship, such as unresolved anger or power dynamics that are beyond your skill level, refer to a therapist or qualified couples counselor. However, you may find that teaching communication exercises or negotiation skills is all that is needed to resolve this issue.

Identify the intimacy pattern. Intimacy patterns may create uneven desire for some couples. I developed a three-part model for use with clients in my practice. At some point I share the information about their pattern with the couple (or individual if I never get to meet the partner). I use hand gestures or a handwritten diagram to show them how their pattern for intimacy in the relationship is working.

The three patterns are:
- *S: suffocating or overly fused* (indicated by two overlapping circles, with little space left in the two individual circles). Example: He wants more sex. The more he insists on sex, the less she wants it. Why? She feels like she is suffocating in the relationship. The S pattern is often described as fused, merged, or codependent, where the individual sacrifices his or her needs for what he or she perceives are the other's needs. That lack of breathing space leaves little room for desire to build.
- *D: distant or overly separate* (indicated by two very slightly overlapping circles, or two circles that do not overlap at all). Example: She

wishes they had more sex, but he's always too busy, either working late at the office, bringing work home, or traveling. She keeps busy with her own job, the kids, the house, and her social life. They are the classic "no time for sex" couple. She has an active fantasy life and masturbates frequently. He suppresses his sexual desires.

- B: *balanced, integrated and whole* (indicated by two comfortably overlapping circles, allowing space for togetherness as well as separate lives). Example: The couple has a strong intimate connection balanced by rich individual lives. But they may not be having sex as frequently as one partner would like. On the plus side, they are open to discussion and negotiation about making more time for sex. This is the healthy pattern.

INSIDE STORY: THE LITTLE RED CAR

When Beth and Todd came to see me they said they felt hopelessly trapped in their uneven desire. The more he pursued her, the more pressured she felt and the less willing she was to let him win. They rarely had sex. Eventually he stopped petitioning for sex. She was, she said, "too busy to think about sex."

As I did the intake, I initially thought they were a D couple, but I quickly realized they were a B. Their concern was uneven desire but changing their pattern of intimacy wasn't the immediate action plan. He felt left out—and he needed to vent his anger and frustration about that. "She has affection for the children, her family, and her friends, but nothing left for me," he said.

After he had his say, they both agreed to set aside adult time away from the demands of the children and his job. I encouraged them to be resourceful in sending cues to one another that they were feeling sexual. They created the following signal during a coaching session.

Their sports car (which he kept locked in the garage most of the time) was dubbed the "Little Red Car." "The car makes us both feel sexy," she said. He nodded in agreement. "When we were first dating, we'd take long rides in the car and make out till dawn." As his signal, he left a sweet note under Beth's pillow, asking her to go for a ride in the Little Red Car. Occasionally he would just scribble "LRC?" on a notepad to get her attention in the kitchen or family room. She started using the same device to give him sex cues. After a month, they reported that they'd put some miles on the car. The smiles on their faces told me more strongly than their words that they'd found a solution that worked for their particular concern.

Help your clients find a way to signal desire for sex without putting pressure on a partner. Reframing sex as a fun opportunity, not a relationship duty, may provide the shift in gears your couple needs.

Concern 4. Conflicting Values About Monogamy/Affairs

Coping with the aftermath of an affair is one of the most challenging tasks facing sex coaches and clients. With time, forgiveness, and a little forgetting, couples can get past the betrayal, disappointment, and loss of trust that are the aftermath of affairs.

Affairs are common. Statistics vary wildly depending on the source, with some surveys and studies putting the number as low as 20% of all married couples and others as high as 50%. Sooner or later—and probably sooner—you will deal with affairs in sex coaching.

The impact of affairs varies among couples. One couple may describe the heartbreak of a tattered marital bond, while another reports that the affair was a small blip in the timeline of their relationship. For some, an affair is a wake-up call leading them to address their neglected intimate relationship.

There are no honorable reasons for having an affair that breaks a marital or committed relationship bond, just a long list of excuses. I'm a big proponent of helping couples keep their agreements regarding integrity and trust. The reasons a partner cheats on another, if that is what the couple determines an affair to be, are practically endless.

INSIDE STORY: THE PITFALLS OF TIT FOR TAT

George had cheated on Olivia 2 weeks before she came in for help— an angry, betrayed, emotionally desperate woman. Our work occurred over 2 years, regularly at first, then sporadically. To me, this affair was a mistake she had to forgive for the marriage to thrive. A devoted husband and father of their two young children, George never came in for a session, despite my invitations through Olivia. She saw no option but to stay with him and "grin and bear it." "I guess one day I'll be able to let it go," she said over tissues on our second session.

George continued to seek Olivia's forgiveness, which eventually occurred through her dedication to heal the emotional wound. However, midway through our sex coaching process Olivia had an affair. She revealed that sex at home was sterile, infrequent, and mechanical, and that she had longings to feel more sexual pleasure. Finding pleasure outside the marriage was, to her, the sole option. That may have been part it—the rest was, well, pure revenge.

"It's only fair," she chortled when she blurted out that she'd had the affair. I don't think that tit for tat is a good path to healing, but I always support my clients in their choices about the paths they must travel to find the turning point for healing. Some clients will sense your judgment and hide the truth. Giving Olivia a safe, nonjudgmental space to tell her story was critical to letting her go through her process of recovery from George's affair. Eventually she stopped seeing the other man.

When I asked why she had discontinued the affair, she replied, "I've seen the light. Two wrongs don't make a right." She finally reconnected with the man she married and who was a father to her two daughters.

CAUSES

Almost anything can trigger the urge to stray. Regardless of whether the tempted person acts on the impulse or not, that impulse itself is normal. Often partners who consider themselves too moral to have sex outside marriage have emotional affairs that take a greater toll on their relationships than a purely sexual fling would have. At the other end of the spectrum, some couples build sanctioned affairs into their marriages. (See chapter 12 on swinging.)

Conflicting values about monogamy are going to crop up in many relationships. The reasons are a vast as why people get together in the first place. This is a list of some of the more common causes.

Lack of satisfying sex or no sex at home. When sex isn't happening at home, it can become a reason to drift.

Insecurity about masculinity or femininity. Couples often report that having an affair is a way to affirm their sexual identity, masculinity, or femininity.

Power dynamics. Sometimes a couple is trapped in a power struggle. One partner may feel the need to express her power outside of the primary relationship, which leads to an affair.

Misplaced anger. There are times in a relationship when a partner may feel anger or resentment and act this out by being sexual with someone else.

Acting out. Another form of acting out can occur when one partner's adolescence was aborted or never lived out. Affairs during a midlife crisis are often this type of delayed adolescent reaction.

Emotional immaturity. People who are emotionally underdeveloped are more likely to become lured to the world of affairs.

Naivete. Sometimes a person is just ignorant about the lure of an affair, or makes a very poor choice under special circumstances, such as while he's away at a trade show or as the victim of a workplace seduction.

Effects of drinking or drugging. Recreational drugging and social drinking impair judgment—period. Men or women who use drinking or drugging to engage in extramarital affairs are not making good decisions.

Real love. If a client is, for example, in an arranged marriage or is married to the guy who got her pregnant, there may never have been real love between them. People in relationships can fall in true love with someone else. It happens. Healthy relationships require setting boundaries and sticking to them, regardless. However, sometimes an affair leads to divorce and perhaps remarriage.

A true midlife crisis. Just like the real love situation, a client may be undergoing a real midlife crisis. That can sometimes be the ramp onto their freeway of an affair.

OPTIONS FOR RESOLUTION

Work with your client to get to the root of the affair. Be sure to address the impact on the relationship and home life, along with several options for forgiving and moving back into a trust bond.

Listen in a nonjudgmental and supportive way. Listen without criticism. Be a nonjudgmental supportive force for both partners as the story unfolds.

Help the client reframe the language. Don't refer to the other partner as the "victim." Instead, use phrases like "overcoming the affair."

Enable forgiveness. Help the other partner to experience his or her power in overcoming the betrayal or breach of trust. Explain that both parties need to forgive themselves and the other.

Help them see their options. Review the *Three Doors* technique discussed in Chapter 8. They have three choices. What do they want to do?

Be a reality check. Ask the hard questions: Does this appear to be a permanent affair? What was your client's role in causing it, if any? What does your client expect after the affair? Tell them your views about how long you predict before things might return to normal, including posing the question: "Will there ever be a 'normal' again?"

Help rebuild the trust. The foundation for an enduring intimate relationship, trust must be reestablished unless the couple chooses to divorce. Repeat the message that trust is earned over time and with trustworthy behavior. I use the metaphor of a train wreck with postaffair couples. Initially, the knowledge of the affair feels like a train wreck. Afterward, they have to get their cars back on the track. Rebuilding their own love train will require intention, time, work, skill, and patience—and love.

Give your real opinion. A sex coach often makes observations, offers opinions, and gives advice. Couples coping with an affair (a relationship hot topic) may require more input from you than other couples do. You may want to share your insights, saying, for example, "This seems like a silly mistake" or "This affair was part of a pattern of betrayals." Whatever you say, be sure you're helping your client look forward, not backward. If you detect alcohol or drug abuse, speak up and help them get into a treatment program.

Help the wronged client avoid payback. Payback is retaliatory sex— the tit-for-tat affair. For many people, payback is the natural first choice for balancing the books of the relationship. Help your client avoid this pitfall.

Help them minimize the family damage. Panic, rage, and distrust leak from the marriage into the family system. Suggest ways for minimizing that damage, for example, by avoiding sarcasm during mealtime, allowing for affectionate touch, or being alert for the escape instinct, taking time away from the family to avert emotional pain.

Help them own the truth. Help each of them focus on the missed warning signs and the cues that indicate whether the affair is unforgivable, part of a lifelong pattern for the betrayer, a one-time fling, or a symptom of a relationship dead or damaged beyond repair.

If the affair is a flashing signal to leave the marriage, guide your client to the safest exit.

Concern 5. Performance Skills Deficit

Don't downplay the importance of erotic skills. A performance skills deficit (PSD) on the part of one partner can cause a breakdown in the relationship. Inability to reach orgasm or satisfy the other partner is often a PSD marker. PSD will usually show up on the intake forms in the sections on current sexual concerns and on problem sexual patterns over time. If the intake forms don't reveal it, you will probably hear it in the first coaching session.

CAUSES

Causes for PSD may seem obvious, but sometimes there are hidden reasons behind this concern, such as undisclosed illness, unexpressed fears, shame stemming from inexperience or even a secret affair.

Sexual ignorance. A client may just not know how to please a partner. How the female or male sexual response works may remain a mystery until you take the lead as teacher.

Inexperience. People may enter into short- or long-term sexual relationships without any prior experience. Not understanding the right moves or words is an obvious cause of PSD.

Laziness. Some people are born lazy! They either chronically act tired or they simply expect others to pleasure them.

Masked anger or resentment. Sometimes a lingering anger turned to resentment is misinterpreted as a lack of skill. In fact, the resentful partner is withholding.

OPTIONS FOR RESOLUTION

Resolution of PSD is often the heart of sex coaching—teaching clients skills, helping their communication, shifting the patterns of the relationship toward sexual fulfillment.

Help them identify the real causes of PSD. Refer to the concerns for men and women in Chapters 7 and 8.

Encourage medical intervention if necessary. Again, refer to Chapters 7 and 8 for medical causes of and treatments for individual sexual performance concerns.

Bridge their communication gaps. In sex coaching sessions, help the partners learn communication skills.

Teach skills. Use self-help books, videos, and DVDs to educate clients on sex techniques, including the use of sex toys.

Reject the laziness excuse. Let the client know that laziness is not attractive. Tell them that being active and giving may help save their relationship.

Dispel the angry undercurrents. If you determine that anger or festering resentment is a causal factor, help the couple to resolve their anger conflicts, using the Love Letter process or other anger-reduction techniques.

INSIDE STORY: THE MAN WITH THE JAGGED NAILS

Josie was married to a man who became violent if she declined his sexual advances. I had no success in my efforts to get him into the office. In fact, I was lucky to persuade her to make the 90-minute train ride to my studio. "I'm so afraid of him," Josie sobbed. "And I've never had an orgasm." I began orgasm-directed coaching with her.

Jerome was a hardworking construction worker who—in spite of her first description of their marriage—really loved his wife and kids. Her failure to reach orgasm in response to his "good lovin'" was eroding his masculinity, Josie said he had blurted out one night. In that same session she also casually remarked, "I wish I could get him to stop hurting me with those jagged nails on my privates."

"What?" I almost shrieked with joy at this new revelation. Every time he used manual touch, his favorite form of foreplay, he scratched her vulva, including the inner lips. Obviously, his inadvertent scratching on her privates, as she called them, was slamming the door on her pleasurable sensations. I let her connect the dots as we talked: Jagged nails equals no orgasm. Josie left my office that day with a new game plan.

After they put the kids to bed that night, she clipped, filed, and smoothed those hands. Later, she had an orgasm. She stopped her work with me 2 weeks after that.

I cannot overemphasize this: Your coaching depends on vigilant attention to details. Sex coaching can be much like doing detective work, where you are searching for that pivotal clue to what is causing the concern. Asking Josie how Jerome's fingers on her labia felt led her to change her sex life with one simple grooming act. Simple answers and small miracles can lead to big changes in your clients' lives.

Concern 6. Body Image Issues

Couples, like individuals, have body image concerns (BI). I've coached clients who have never been able to be naked with each other or cannot have sex with the lights on. Sometimes that behavior is rooted in shame; other times BI concerns develop following weight gain, scarring from an accident, or a medical condition or treatment. One partner's appearance may have altered to the point where the other cannot adjust to the new image. Such extreme situations are addressed in the next chapter, especially with regard to pregnancy, postpartum, and recovery from serious illness or surgeries.

Even something as small as a C-section scar or the lines from a breast implant can raise BI issues. Self-loathing creates a negative response in others, including sex partners. Sexy is a feeling that emanates from inside the person. The BI partner projects negative feelings on the other because she doesn't feel sexy inside.

In some cases in which couples present with other complaints, BI is actually the underlying, unexpressed concern, and it must be treated before the other issues are addressed. For example, bad acne scarring, a birth defect, severe weight gain, or genital size issues may need to be addressed in coaching before anything else can be done.

CAUSES

Refer to the sections on BI in Chapters 7 and 8.

OPTIONS FOR RESOLUTION

Body image issues can be resolved by action. Experiment with the following activities.

The Mirror Activity. Review the Mirror Activity in Chapter 8. You can explain the technique verbally to the couple or model it during a body coaching session.

Use teaching tools. Recommend videos and DVDs that show people of various sizes and body types in sexual situations.

Have them vocalize their feelings about their bodies. In a couples session ask each partner to say what he or she likes, does not like, loves, or hates about his or her body. Negative feelings often dissipate after they have been shared.

Help them fix what can be fixed. If weight, for example, is the concern, direct the client to a suitable gym, health club, or weight loss program—and help him or her commit to it. Act as a life coach by helping clients design and maintain exercise and other programs.

Encourage self-empowerment techniques. I often send clients home with written assignments on index cards or handouts that encourage positive self-talk and affirmations. Sometimes I instruct them to record their own voice on a machine or computer so they can act as their own self-improvement coach!

Debunk their myths. Use realistic models of male and female genitalia and other images to show sexual anatomy. Have the couple cut images of their ideal body image or type from magazines and keep a scrapbook of their progress in moving toward their idealized body shape. However, it is essential that their goals are realistic, especially if they are younger clients or extreme type-A personalities.

Encourage a team approach. Suggest ways the couple can overcome the BI concern (his or hers) together as a team. This approach reinforces their intimate connection, assuming they have one.

Watch for signs of intimacy avoidance. For some couples the body issue—she feels she's too fat, he thinks his penis is too small—is a carefully constructed intimacy block. If you believe intimacy avoidance is behind the BI concern, you may need to refer the clients to a therapist (or shift your work from coaching to therapy.)

Point out their overlapping perceptions. Most BI couples have disparate views of their bodies. She, for example, may think he hates her body because she's fat when he doesn't hate her body at all. That disparity between self-image and the partner's perspective can be a contributing factor to a sexless relationship.

Assign the Partner Drawings activity. One of my favorite coaching activities, especially for BI couples, is Partner Drawings. Assemble materials including:

• Construction paper or plain white paper (preferably with some texture, not copy paper)

- An assortment of drawing utensils, including pastels, pencils, drawing pens, ink, and erasers
- Glue sticks, scissors, and, if you want to get fancy, buttons, spangles, feathers, and so on

Seat your clients at a table with the materials spread in front of them. They should have plenty of room to work. Allow about 30 minutes for the drawings and another 30 minutes for discussion—in other words, one sex coaching session.

Tell the couple something like this: "Make two drawings: one of yourself and one of your partner. How well you draw is not the issue. What matters is what your picture shows. The drawings don't have to be elaborate, but, if you want, you can dress them up, using the materials on the table. Have fun! I'll let you know when the time is almost up."

When the couple finishes the drawings, begin processing them by following these steps:

- One partner begins describing the drawing of himself, and then of his partner, while showing the drawings to you and the partner.
- The other partner then does the same.
- You facilitate a discussion about their drawings, helping them find the similarities and discrepancies. Help the couple see and discuss what is not meshing in their images of themselves and the other partner. With your guidance, they can feel relief, sadness, elation, or clarity. Some couples I've coached found the key to understanding why they were blocked and then made positive changes. For example, the first partner might say, "I see a beautiful face, a thin body, great breasts, nice skin, and a big smile. That's my wife!" The second partner responds by saying, "Here's me. I'm too fat here, and I could use a nose job, see?" Elicit the honest feelings expressed in their drawings. Verbally note where they have drawn something they're not saying in words. This is a revealing activity!

Concern 7. Communication Style Conflicts

In a segment of A&E's *Biography*, Dr. Phil McGraw said that women use 5,000 words per day whereas men use only 1,500 words. These figures seem to support John Gray's theory that, in an emotional crunch, men run screaming into their caves and women grab their phones. Your couple's communication style (CS) may be the critical factor in determining what does or doesn't happen for them sexually. In helping them improve communication skills, you teach them how to say what they want, need, and feel—and maybe what they won't tolerate anymore.

In Chapter 2 I discussed neurolinguistic programming (NLP) and the three modes everyone uses for encoding their world: visual, auditory, or kinesthetic. Find the dominant mode in couples with conflicting communication styles and you will turn on a light in their darkness. "He never listens," she says. "She never stops jabbering at me when I get home," he complains. Differing communicating approaches stop some couples from having sex as often or in the ways they want.

Couples' communication conflicts often are influenced by inattention or deficiencies. There are many factors that affect communication styles and lead to a breakdown in a couple's ability to relate.

CAUSES

If there is anything that can stop a sexual relationship in its tracks, it is the inability to communicate. Causes vary, with poor listening skills at the top of the list.

INSIDE STORY: CAN YOU HEAR ME NOW?

Fred and Mara were highly educated "personal growth junkies," their favorite expression. They knew they had a sexual breakdown because they didn't communicate well. Despite their eloquence and articulateness, I saw the pattern right away. Fred would finish Mara's every sentence and then she would clam up. We worked with a "talking stick" process, getting him to listen and allowing her to feel heard. Just shifting him out of his style of parroting back to her what he heard—instead of rephrasing her messages—helped a lot. His previous rote repetition made her feel like he wasn't really listening before. Putting her words into his own made her feel heard. Finally, when they realized that their communication style patterns were literally disrupting their flow, they relearned how to speak to each other, especially when emotions ran thick. Over three intense sessions, their practice of talking, listening, repeating messages, feeling heard, feeling understood, and acknowledging the messages opened up their deeply held feelings of love.

Adjusting the process of communication with Fred and Mara restored the foundation for their relationship. Of course, once the communication blocks were removed and love was expressed, sex resumed.

Poor or inadequate listening skills. Listening is an art. However, you can train someone to become a better listener by, for example, teaching him not to talk while his partner is speaking or by encouraging him to nod affirmatively while speaking is taking place. Other signs of a poor listener include not hearing what the other person is really saying or aborting dialogue before the point is completed. Misinterpreting what is heard can have a major negative impact. Being distracted during important conversations is a no-no for couples. Not knowing what exactly to say to express a thought or feeling is the most common culprit in the CS concern.

Bad timing for important talks. Using in-between moments to talk about important things, while distractions are rampant, is a common cause of CS breakdown.

Emotional explosions/emotional pollution. Speaking out of anger instead of love, blaming, and complaining can pollute communication.

Focus on problems, not solutions. Couples often get stuck in talking about what's not working, or they rely on a steady diet of to-do lists as their constant dialogue.

Substance abuse. Drinking or drugging impairs judgment and good decision making, allowing hurtful communication to occur without careful thought. Often fear of communication is masked by use of alcohol, drugs, or food.

OPTIONS FOR RESOLUTION

There is a range of actions that you can take in your own practice with this type of client. This is one concern that relies heavily on home assignments.

Refer out. You may decide this couple's communication concern is best handled as a therapy issue. CS may be red flag for much deeper intimacy issues, festering resentments, or past history (for example, as the "wounded child" from a dysfunctional family).

Recommend advanced education. Send them to seminars or workshops such as Imago therapy training or active listening workshops, or suggest self-help books, tapes, or DVDs.

Teach skills. Teach or suggest one or more of the following, depending on cause of the CS concern:

- Listening skills such as maintaining eye contact, hearing the partner while being quiet, echoing back what they hear, acknowledging the positives, and taking equal time to speak without interruption.
- Playful note communication, like posting little signs on the refrigerator that say, "I want your body!"; "Meet me at 8 in our bed?"; or "I love you darling."
- Weekly or monthly communication meetings. I often tell clients to schedule regular meetings to make sure the business of their relationship is running smoothly. At that suggestion, they take out their planning calendars.
- Abstaining from drinking or drugging so they can talk. No substance abuse! Stop sex coaching until this problem is handled.
- *Private sessions* at home, without kids, pets, pagers, or cell phone interruptions. Help them identify how to minimize distractions and maximize adult time or time alone as a couple.
- Setting of healthy boundaries for acceptable communication, such as a ban on sarcasm, the rule in my own household.
- Spotting the warning signs of an impending *emotional earthquake.* Help them develop a mechanism for stopping the pattern, such as a 10-minute *time out* from being together or changing the subject to the weather, sports, or movies. Frequent or intense emotional outbreaks may require therapy.

Concern 8. Negotiation Skills Deficit

Couples with a negotiation skills deficit (NSD) do not know how to negotiate their sexual needs. They may be adept negotiators in their professional lives, and even in other areas of their personal lives, but they can't employ those skills in the bedroom. Negotiation is the single skill that can upgrade their sex life. The causes for reticence vary from couple to couple.

CAUSES

Negotiation skills are closely related to communication skills. Causes of NSD frequently evolve out of past shame or discomfort.

Discomfort with sexual language. Not being comfortable speaking about sex can be a barrier to a satisfactory sex life. This may encompass asking for the type of sexual behaviors you want to give or receive, or using erotic language.

The belief that a loving partner should how to please the other. It's a myth to think that a sexual partner, even after years of marriage, can read your mind or body. A couple may need to be coached out of expectations.

Embarrassment about admitting needs and desires. Some partners feel too embarrassed to use frank sexual language to ask for what they want. Others may not feel they deserve to ask for what they want for sexual pleasure. I find that clients aren't always able to admit to their needs.

Inability to connect sexuality patterns to the rest of life. Couples may not be able to relate how they are in the bedroom to the rest of their lifestyle. Failure to recognize partners of their sexual relationship—such as the lack of compromise or overly demanding expectations—may reflect the overall relationship dynamics.

OPTIONS FOR RESOLUTION

The suggestions below will help the couple to resolve conflicts about what each wants and doesn't want from sex. Teach them the broad range of actions they can take together to improve not only their sexual relating, but their lives as a whole.

The Red/Yellow/Green Light exercise. I've had success in using a common exercise, Red/Yellow/Green Light, with these couples. It teaches them how to become explicit about their sexual wants, dislikes, and unexpressed desires. It's a good sexual boundary setting activity.

Here's how it works: Each partner prepares a chart with Red, Yellow, and Green at the top of three columns. Provide the couple with a list of sexual activities for their consideration or ask them to write their own list. The couple then categorizes the activities under Red (no: sexual activities they will not do or allow), Yellow (possible: those activities they will consider with caution); and Green (Yes: activities they will do or want to do).

For example, both partners may list kissing, sexual intercourse, and phone sex in the Green column, but one partner enters anal intercourse in the Red column whereas the other lists it under Yellow. Or, one partner may categorize outside sexual relationships under

Red, whereas the partner puts them under Yellow. Encourage the couple to save the list as a way of evaluating the progress of their sexual evolution. Over time some couples find that sexual activities once in the Yellow zone have moved comfortably to the Green. This exercise can help them develop the confidence to explore even after they've completed sex coaching.

Explain the five negotiating areas, help the couple identify their weaknesses within the five areas, and make suggestions for improvement. There are five areas where couples must have adequate skills for negotiating a dynamic sexual relationship.

- *Asking (not demanding, not begging) for what you want/need.* In my clinical experience, women have more difficulty asking for what they want than men do which may partly explain why they report more sexual dissatisfaction. If a couple (or partner) cannot tell or show, they are not likely to get what they need and want. Teach them to use nonverbal communication, such as her putting his hand lower on her genitals. Suggest she pay attention to her own sexual response cycle during masturbation so she can convey her need, for example, for deeper, faster thrusting by using her hands on his hips. Assign them mutual masturbation sessions for homework. That way each can see what the other needs to become aroused and reach orgasm.
- *Setting realistic expectations.* Direct your clients away from media images of perfect bodies and instant hot sex and toward their reality. Help them set attainable sexual goals. Expecting oneself to perform again without a refractory period (and no medication) is not a realistic goal at age 40 or over. Having sex three times a day on the weekend may not be feasible given their lifestyle. Help them see what's really possible versus what looks inviting on the page or screen.
- *Going outside your comfort zone.* Empower the couple to take risks. Their risks may be emotional (saying "I love you" for the first time), physical (fellatio, cunnilingus), or esoteric (exploring tantric chanting during sexual union). Trying out "dirty talk," for example, is a classic way to get the couple to explore new territory. Send more adventurous couples to a swing party or suggest they explore light forms of S&M. For other couples, having sex with the lights on may be a radical change. Anything that takes a couple outside their comfort zone is a good move!

- *Overcoming power struggles.* The next chapter discusses the three elements of an S&M encounter. There is much that "regular" couples can learn from players in the realm of S&M or B&D (bondage and discipline). Power dynamics exist in all relationships at one time or another. These dynamics come into play in issues such as childcare, money, religious values, and, of course, sex. I find that couples with severe power dynamic issues often end up in sexless marriages, with one or both partners using the power of sexual withholding as a power chip. You may have to spend some time with a couple to see how the dynamic works. Ask questions about how they handle power conflicts in other parts of their life, such as finances, vacation planning, decorating the home, selecting a car—and, finally, their sexual life. Simply learning how they choose a restaurant or a movie clues you into how they handle power. Help them see their patterns and suggest ways of modifying them.
- *Compromising.* Sexual compromise is truly an art. Meeting in the happy middle takes skill—like a ballet performance. We all want our own way, don't we? I coach couples to see their relationship as a corporation and make decisions for the good of that entity, not for one partner alone. Getting a couple to focus on *us* not *me versus you* is the key to a successful, lasting relationship, especially if there is tension and insecurity about giving up control. A couple with NSD may save their relationship by learning how to compromise artfully.

INSIDE STORY: THE EROTIC PHOTO SHOOT

Jenny and Raymond were a client couple that benefited from being encouraged to move outside their comfort zone. A childless married couple in their early thirties, both partners were very career-oriented and impressed me with their willingness and bravery to make a change. "After only 2 years of marriage, sex is a distant memory," they joked, but their story made me sad. How could two such attractive and vibrant people not be sexual together?

I detected some clues to their situation in Jenny's intake history and assessment, including a repressive family background and intense sexual guilt rooted in her Catholic upbringing. She confided that she feared being a bad girl. Jenny carried the burden of those attitudes into the marriage. Ray thought marriage would free her, but it didn't. As a way of coping with his frustration, he masturbated to porn magazines he kept hidden in the bathroom late at night while she slept.

After 2 weeks of delicate coaching with little progress, I recommended a self-help video program to inspire sexual activity. That suggestion moved her out of her comfort zone and into his arms. Then I said: "I have an idea. Are you ready?"

"Sure, we're game," they both smiled, a little nervously.

"Why not do an erotic photo shoot, Jenny? I know just the right guy for you."

They agreed. I knew a lovely man who did such photography. More importantly, I knew his warm, easygoing personality would soothe any qualms she had. It did! She posed in teddies (and less) while Raymond watched ("and drooled," he reported) behind the screen. "I adored the attention!" she said. Jenny delighted in her newfound naughty side as she showed me the photos at our next session. He was grinning when he added, "Our sex life is on fire!"

Thanks to their willingness to try together and her ability to transcend the old boundaries of her comfort zone, they captured the brass ring. I loved them for it.

Sex coaching with couples is deep and intense. The complexity of the issues that couples face can take you into realms that you wouldn't go with an individual. Remind yourself that you are literally working with three clients—the two partners and the relationship itself. It can be the most frustrating or the most rewarding sex coaching you will ever do.

Get It!

Name at least three couples' concerns and how you would address them:
1.
2.
3.

What concern from this chapter seems most challenging for you? Why do you think that is? Write down your resistance or fears about the concern and what you can do to overcome them:

CHAPTER TEN

Gay, Lesbian, Bisexual, and Transgendered Clients
Concerns and Resolutions

YOU DON'T JUST hang out a shingle as a sex coach to attract GLBT clients. This chapter will give you the insights you need to address these special populations. Many GLBT clients will seek out their GLBT peers for sex (or other) coaching and therapy. Others will realize that regardless of your sexual orientation or identity you will bring them the special talents it takes for you to meet their unique—and yet similar—needs compared with your other non-GLBT clients.

THE RANGE OF POSSIBLE CLIENTS

I make a distinction between sexual orientation and sexual or gender identity. The sexual orientation categories are: heterosexual (i.e., straight), homosexual (i.e., gay), lesbian, and bisexual. Many people shift in orientation over the course of a lifetime. The term *transsexual* (TS) is sometimes mistakenly associated with sexual orientation. A true TS is coping with issues related to sexual or gender identity, not orientation.

Gay/Lesbian/Bi

Same-sex attraction is an adolescent developmental phase. Many young people experiment sexually with the same gender without being homosexual. Others may have a lifelong bisexual orientation. Still others may engage exclusively in sex with partners of the same gender throughout their lives. Following are some ways of measuring sexual orientation.

KINSEY SCALE

On the 7-point Kinsey scale (1948/1998) there are two extremes—pure homosexual (6) and pure heterosexual (0). A zero is a pure heterosexual; a six is a pure homosexual. Few people occupy the extremes. As we grow sexually, we will probably occupy different places on the scale at different times of our lives. But most of us do have a number that is more or less our own.

KLEIN SCALE

The Klein scale takes the concept to another level by adding measurement factors such as: how we identify ourselves sexually, our choices of social companions, and our self-described level of social connection with people of various sexual orientations (Klein, Sepckoff, & Watt, 1985). Klein also differentiates between *attraction* to genders versus actual *sexual encounters* with genders. For example, we may fantasize about one gender while having sex with another. This allows for a more fluctuating sexual orientation identity.

The assumption in our culture is that 10% of the population is gay/lesbian with another 10% being bisexual. Fact or myth? No one knows. Depending on your definition of homosexuality—an occasional or exclusive same sex encounter or attraction or self-identification—the figures vary. Kinsey's 10% for males became 4.4% for women and 6.3% of men for same sex attraction in the landmark University of Chicago NHSLS study (Laumann, Gagon, Michael, & Michael, 1994). Someday we will probably discover that sexual orientation is too fluid to be measured and fix in such a determinate way.

The Transgender Spectrum: Transvestites to Transsexuals

Gender identity occurs on a continuum. On one side are the heterosexual cross-dressers (90% of them married men) and the homosexual cross-dressing *drag queens*. The second group is made up of possibly your most fun clients!

Although the term *transvestite* (TV) is reserved for men who dress in women's clothing, some women cross-dress as well, passing as men when they go out in public (often known as *drag kings*).

On the other side are transsexuals (TS)—males who are born male and transition via a sex change to a female (male to female, MTF), and the females who are born female and transitioning to male (female to male, FTM). The current vogue is to use the term *transgender* (TG) to address the full gender spectrum.

TSs may be in the early pre-op stages, taking hormones and undergoing counseling, or in the post-op stages, with their surgery complete. Between these two extremes (TVs and TSs) is a broad range of gender identity. You may encounter—though it's a rare condition—an *intersexed* person or *hermaphrodite*. They have ambiguous genitalia or the sexual anatomy and sometimes sexual functioning of both genders. In certain Native American cultures TGs are revered as "two spirited" and often considered the healers of their tribe.

SEX COACHING GLBT CLIENTS

As a sex coach, you will encounter clients at various stages of their sexual orientation and identity development. Some may be confused about their orientation and identity. Some will be in denial—to themselves, family, or friends. Some clients may be in transition, moving from one identity into another. And some will be comfortable with and sure of their sexual orientation and identity.

Your client's stage of orientation and identity development will play a role in your sex coaching plan. A heterosexual cross-dressing man, for example, may be best served by a simple granting of permission on your part to indulge his feminine side (like Charles in Chapter 1). A lesbian couple in a long-term relationship and comfortable with their sexual orientation may be suffering from the same sexual concerns that face many heterosexual couples—uneven desire, for instance, or body image issues. A pre-op transsexual client may seek your help in understanding how the surgery will affect his or her sexual functioning and performance. As with all clients, you must collaborate to create a sex coaching plan.

Gay, Lesbian, and Bisexual Clients

What distinguishes your work with GLB clients will be the additional issues that surface during the course of your time together. Because heterosexism prevails in U.S. culture, social stigma, prejudice, even violent hateful acts occur because of one's sexual orientation and identity. The resulting homophobia—both external and internalized—may become a cloud over the lives of your GLB clients, even when they are not in touch with its effect. Your sex coaching action plans will mirror those of your non-GLB clients, yet require an extra sensitivity for the social and political concerns of GLB sexuality.

Common concerns include
• Questioning sexual orientation and identity
• Attempting to overcome issues related to homophobia (internal or external), social stigma, or personal shame
• Wanting to meet a GLB partner
• Having the same concerns as Chapters 7 and 8 for all men/women
• Coping with pressures from a partner to engage in sex with a third or more partners of the same gender

OPTIONS FOR RESOLUTION

Sex coaching for your GLB clients is going to echo everything you do for all clients. These are some of the extras you'll want to offer, too.

Redirect your client away from his or her fears and other damaging emotions. Work with these clients to help them reframe negative self-talk or pejorative dialogue about their sexual orientation/identity. Teach them creative strategies for combating homophobia, such as political action, support groups, or even art projects that transform such energy.

Be a label buster. When used pejoratively, terms like *straight, butch,* or *queer* don't belong in your vocabulary. As a sex coach part of your job is to help your gay/lesbian/bisexual client find peace with that orientation and to stay away from labels. This is particularly true with bisexuals, who may feel like misfits—unable to fully belong in either gay/lesbian or or heterosexual communities.

Help your clients make real (and nonjudgmental) distinctions between heterosexuality and homosexuality. We're all seeking better sex, happier relationships, and a positive sense of self. The differences lie in sexual styles and techniques. Two women, for example, may not have sex in the same way that a man and a woman do. If you use your logic, you quickly will learn quickly how to help non-heterosexual clients achieve more pleasure in their sexual behaviors and personal choices.

Deflect pressures for bi-exploration. You may have to take an active role to uncover the truth about a client's (or partner's) desire for bisexual exploration. Remind your clients that fantasy doesn't equal reality. Provide a safe haven for discussing the pros and cons of breaking the barrier for inviting another person into their bed. Always take a stand for setting healthy boundaries and for your clients' self-acceptance.

Be a resource. As always, know your community resources, and refer out if you can't help. Add to your roster of client resources some valid options for socializing and meeting sexual partners, including online GLB dating services.

Be an advocate. In politically charged climates, your clients may seek your help in coping with their fear, guilt, rage, or desire to take political action. Know your politics. Take a stand and advocate for rights that you believe in, especially ones that support your clients' needs.

Transgendered Clients

The single most challenging—and probably most rewarding—clients you are likely to meet are your TG clients. Why? Because not only are you handling sex coaching issues, but also addressing the core of a person's identity. You may become their sole beacon of hope as they shape how they are perceived by the world. It doesn't go much deeper than this. I've found a lasting bond with my TG clients, despite my close connections with many other types, that transcends description. It is something profoundly personal. The sheer complexity and multi-dimensionality of your work with a TG client will affect you—and them—forever.

The assessment process for the transgendered client is complex. The options for resolving transgendered concerns vary, but generally the coaching process is lengthy and complicated. Don't try to play the role of a transition coach for TSs unless you are trained for it.

You will want to use the intake and assessment form for transgendered persons (use Appendix C as a guide). As with all materials you use, you may restyle it according to your own coaching approach or based on emerging treatments, laws, and changing social norms. Assessment includes the usual facts, but also seeks to capture a more in-depth history than you would for your other sex coaching clients, especially if you opt to do transition coaching. I always focus on a more holistic accounting with the TS client—i.e., social, medical, sexual, vocational, legal, spiritual issues and anything that appears to be relevant to their TS journey.

> **MORE ABOUT THAT**
>
> I had the opportunity to work with Miss Vera, who runs the Manhattan cross-dressing academy Miss Vera's School for Boys Who Want to Be Girls. Her school motto is *Cherchez La Femme!* She and her faculty teach male students (mostly heterosexual) how to dress, walk, talk, and fix their hair and makeup like real women.
>
> The running joke about cross-dressers is: If she looks too good to be true (as a woman) she probably *is* too good to be true! The TV or TS often is a hyperfeminine creature, an image that most regular gals will never pull off—too much work!

Determining whether a person is a true TS can be a challenge for your client and you. Teasing out the true gender identity is a special process which, as I have said, requires intensive training, time, and experience. You will meet clients who worry they are a true TS. Your role is to help them sort out myth from fact, guiding them to a resolution of their concern. Randall, who became a sex coaching client for about a year, warmed my heart with his initial story of what he termed his "dark secret."

INSIDE STORY: RANDALL, THE LAUNDROMAT THIEF

Randall worried that he might be a true TS. He would discreetly pull out the bras left in the machines from laundromats and, back home, masturbate while holding them. "Does this mean I want to wear women's underwear?" he asked.

He almost cried, sighing in deep relief, when I told him: "Not even close, Randall." But he wasn't convinced.

Pulling nervously at his sweater and turning his head away from me as he spoke, he said, "But Dr. Patti, I m-a-s-t-u-r-b-a-t-e with women's bras! Doesn't that make me a transsexual?"

"What you have is a sexual fetish," I said. "The bra is a fetish, an object that turns you on. I've been working with true transsexuals for several years now and I just don't sense that you are one of them. Can you believe me?"

After a few coaching sessions, he began to accept himself as a man with a fetish and let go of his shame and fear. Instead of gender-identity-based sex coaching, we worked at getting him back into social dating. Eventually he found a wonderful sexual partner!

On the other side of the spectrum was Jed/Aurora a true MTF transsexual, who found me through my work with the TS community, and startled me with his sudden changes.

INSIDE STORY: THE GIRLY GIRL, JED/AURORA

Jed, one of my first transgender clients, showed up for his first visit in unisex clothes with a hidden ponytail and no makeup. A pretty but buff boy, he was obviously seeking permission. On the second visit Aurora appeared. She was full-tilt girly, with curly hair, Tammy Faye makeup, micro-miniskirt, shaved legs in high open-toed sandals, and a shockingly sassy walk.

I put to Jed/Aurora through the usual set of critical assessment questions: Was she a true transsexual? What about the old gender life needed to shift before transition could begin? Was the current support system working? Was she working a job as the new or old gender? What paperwork needed to be done? (At the time permission letters from professionals with Ph.D.s and special training were required—and are still recommended—for a TS to receive hormonal/surgical sex changes and identity changes, including a driver's license and passport.) Jed/Aurora was clearly a true TS but faced a lot of work and social problems with no support system. Without a good support system, most transgendered persons crash and burn. We addressed her conflicts with her family, her radical appearance, including mannerisms, dress, and even her diet. Eventually, we got her into a supportive environment—with a new job as a female, and a good social network of other TS in transition, and she thrived. Most TS need to be with peers to cope with the enormous strain of this process. She was a delight and a great student of my sex coaching for her transition. I'll always remember those ponytails and miniskirts!

COMMON CONCERNS

The transgendered clients who come to you for pure sex coaching (not transition coaching) will be seeking help for six basic reasons:
• Impact of gender identity conflict/confusion on family and lover(s).
• Concerns about dating—in the old or new gender identity.
• Performance issues. A common question: Is orgasm possible for the post-op TS?

- Body changes concerns—including worrying about *passing* as the other gender.
- Emotional turmoil surrounding the new sexual orientation identity.
- Mental confusion—concerns about how to move into new gender lifestyle.
- Social isolation—not having the social skills or the daring to reveal a new gender identity or feeling shame about it.

One of my all-time most lovable TS clients ran the gamut in our sex coaching over the years—from needing transition coaching to dating tips, with concerns about his new body, confusion and doubts about his true gender identity, and constant social challenges he faced as a new man. His story is not unlike that of many other TS you will meet, even though this FTM is a unique person.

INSIDE STORY: LORI THE FUNNY GUY

Lori was a true FTM, knowing he had, as he put it, "a male brain," despite being born female. When he first met me, he'd gone through a series of therapists. "They all mishandled and traumatized me," he said, with contempt. At that first session in walked a unisexual person who appeared agitated, distrustful, and hostile. Three months later, on massive doses of testosterone, this short woman he had morphed into a guy with beard, hairy arms, deep voice, and beefed up muscles. It was amazing that he sought out my help. (But, frankly, just as with Jed/Aurora, at that time a TS required letters from qualified professionals to get identity change papers, hormones and surgeries.) Over the many weeks and months I learned how to work with his resistance and began to earn his trust. We truly bonded deeply, thanks to my genuine caring for him, tolerating the hostility, and accepting him for what he was. Lori was not easy! Maybe it was our blended senses of humor, more than anything, that let us keep moving forward. We laughed a lot at his wit and charm. We worked together regularly for 3 years, then continued by phone, emails, and an occasional personal meeting.

My initial coaching consisted of redirecting his recurring guilt, fears and doubts about transitioning. As a team we confirmed his true TS identity, and I provided a stable platform when he had work concerns, drug reactions, hormonal side effects and even sat on the phone for hours with him before and after his "downstairs" surgery. I went the distance with Lori—sending him a stuffed toy after the surgery, being a vehicle for unconditional acceptance, letting him express his full range of emotions, and never shying away from sharing his quest to become the best man he could be. His lack of success in dating after the transition, and his recurrent questions about sex, shifted our work from transition to sex coach. From a former lesbian to a hetero Don Juan, Lori wanted it all—work, love, and success as a guy. The journey to dating and finding love (or just sex) can be a daunting one for a TS. To this day he sends me cheery emails and knows that the lines of communication between us are always open.

OPTIONS FOR RESOLUTION

Your role will to shift and change as your client's needs evolve.

Encourage partner and/or family discussion out in the open. Hiding a gender identity issue leads to increased confusion and turmoil. Becoming a sex coach for both (or all) parties in a family or existing relationship may be your greatest service to the TV/TS client. Be sure to locate and refer to appropriate TV/TS support groups.

Be a tolerant listener. You must be an unconditional container for them to spill their confused feelings. Encourage their self-acceptance. Hold the bar high for their TG success regardless of whether they are just a weekend crossdresser or bound for a full sex change.

Help them find community resources and social outlets. Recommend Web sites, books, magazines, and groups and individuals who can provide information, including IFGE (International Foundation for Gender Education), AASECT (which offers Gender Attitude Reassessments, or GARs), Tapestry, CDI (Cross-Dressers International), and others. Help clients find local or global advocacy groups, including The Transgender Menace and The Harry Benjamin society. Be able to refer clients to reputable surgeons, affordable hormonal treatments, annual conferences, and resources such as the Gender Identity project and its remarkable clinical system. They may need your help in finding dating and social outlets in the new gender.

Work with their particular performance issues. You will have to handle a variety of concerns, including giving a man advice on how to perform sexually while wearing a dress, enhancing the clitoral response for an early pre-op FTM, helping an MTF overcome hatred of his penis, and more.

Help them deal with physical and emotional adjustments. One moment the client may be expressing emotional turmoil, asking, "Who am I now, and who will ever love me?" The next moment she might be concerned about physical appearance. Imagine a FTM who was a lesbian, now wants to date women as a man, and identifies herself as heterosexual but has no penis. Confusing?

Help them develop a plan for moving into the new gender lifestyle. Get specific—down to such details as determining which bathroom to use at the restaurant on their first date in the new gender. Be sure they don't become socially isolated. Get them into peer support groups and social activities that are gender-neutral.

The tapestry of work with the transgendered client is rich. Your sessions are sure to enlighten you as you direct these special clients along their path. Remember, that you're often a port in a very stormy sea. Whether or not you choose to address this type of client is up to you—your training, comfort zone, confidence and ability, your personality and your dreams for your sex coaching practice. Maybe these are the divers in a world of mostly skaters. Dare to go deep.

Get It

1. Describe the gender spectrum, identifying the two extremes. How would you handle these clients differently?
2. List what insights you have gained regarding working with GLB clients.
3. What characteristics (and additional training) would you need to become a sex coach for transitioning a true Transsexual?

CHAPTER ELEVEN

Pregnancy and Special Medical/Clinical Issues

Concerns and Resolutions

THE PRECEDING CHAPTERS focused on common sexual concerns for men, women, and couples. The bulk of your work as a sex coach will consist of cases involving those types of issues. You will also, however, encounter clients with special or atypical concerns. This chapter and the one following it present some of the situations you may face. These cases will be challenges beyond the ordinary. They will require more time and energy. And you may have to overcome some personal fears (of being with people in great pain or coping with disfigurement, for example) and lingering prejudices.

On the other hand, coaching these clients can also be more interesting because it stretches your skills and expands your definition of client services. But be forewarned. These will be the tough cases in your practice. Do what you can!

Physical concerns that impair sexual function or affect the sexuality of an individual or a couple run the gamut from pregnancy to a disabling accident or disease. The first part of this chapter investigates the physical, psychological, and emotional aspects of pregnancy (including childbirth, postpartum, and infertility) as they relate to sexual functioning and desire. The second part of the chapter discusses the physical, psychological, and emotional aspects of clinical/medical concerns (for example, breast cancer, hysterectomy, and chronic pain) as they relate to sexual functioning and desire.

PREGNANCY

Pregnancy concerns fall into four basic categories: TTC (trying to conceive), pregnancy prevention; pregnancy itself; and postpartum. Treating the complex sexual concerns surrounding these categories can be difficult. It is imperative that you have the latest factual information on (or at least a working knowledge of) related topics, including birth control, fertility treatments, and postpartum depression symptoms and treatments.

The most common complaints are: no (or infrequent) sex, unsatisfying sex, and fear of sex because of its negative consequences (including physical or emotional pain). Female clients with pregnancy concerns will often tell you that they have an aversion to sex altogether.

During pregnancy and after childbirth, couples may view their sex life as less a priority than the other aspects of their lives. But an unsatisfying sex life can negatively affect other aspects of the couple's life. Sexual concerns can also crop up for couples (or single women) trying to conceive, as well as for individuals dealing with the aftermath of an abortion.

The Range of Possible Clients

Be prepared to encounter the following types of clients in your work as a sex coach.

- A couple or single woman who is desperate to get pregnant. I call these clients TTCs.
- A couple or a partner who is desperate to reestablish a sex life after childbirth.
- A woman who has given birth within the past few months, perhaps to a second child, and is completely exhausted, with a partner intent on jumpstarting her libido and having a sex life again.
- A woman who has had a recent abortion and is haunted by her choice. Guilt and fear of another pregnancy have shut her down sexually.

Concern 1. Trying to Conceive

TTC couples may be young or old, rich or poor, childless or with children (sometimes adopted)—but they will almost always tell you in the initial assessment that their sexual problems are connected to fertility issues. Men feel they must perform on demand (and suffer terribly if they can't). Both partners say that having sex on the fertility clock deprives the act of intimacy, spontaneity, and pleasure. And the disappointment of repeatedly trying without getting pregnant makes it even harder to have or enjoy sex at the next medically prescribed opportunity.

OPTIONS FOR RESOLUTION

TTC cases require a lot of tenderness on your part. You also must keep abreast of the latest information and know how to keep the wheel of encouragement rolling.

Show compassion and encourage patience and understanding. Your job is to support their fertility efforts while encouraging them to lower their sexual expectations and to find solace through intimate caresses, touches, and kisses that are not part of their sex program.

INSIDE STORY: DAN, THE TTC MAN

Dan, a sweet man in his late twenties, was stressed about his TTC marriage when he came to see me. I never did meet the wife.

"I can't take it sometimes," he said, his voice nearly a scream. "I miss having the great sex we used to have. I am so worried about getting her pregnant that I keep losing my erection before we do anything." Holding his face in his hands, he almost cried as he sat forlorn. "I feel like such a failure," he whispered.

Added to that load of expectations, Dan felt compelled to be the perfect son to his critical father—who, of course, wanted that grandchild.

I sent him to a urologist to get help with his erectile functioning (pre-Viagra). The doctor suggested penile injections, which helped with the weak erections. I showed him ways he could break out of the performance anxiety loop. We spent three coaching sessions preparing him, including to tell his father, "Stop pushing me so hard!" Given the enormous pressures Dan felt to impregnate his wife, it's no wonder that he sought my help. Having a sex coach to guide

MORE ABOUT THAT

When a TTC couple consults you, don't assume they are already getting the best possible treatment. You need to be savvy about fertility treatments available in your community (and their success ratios) so you can make referrals. You also must understand that you can't *solve* their problem. Your job is to be part of their support team—a cheerleader and a sounding board for their concerns. If necessary, help the couple develop a plan for consulting fertility specialists and reporting back to you after each consultation. Being a good listener and giving them the tender loving care they currently aren't able to give each other is the best short-term coaching action plan.

him through the anxiety-laden process, assisted him in becoming, well, a dad.

Concern 2. Pregnancy Prevention

Clients seeking advice on pregnancy prevention are usually young couples or women, single or married. Some are women who are dating again after a divorce or a long, monogamous relationship. Some couples seek advice after experiencing a birth control method failure. Or the clients may be a new couple who needs help in assessing their options for birth control and STI prevention. Sometimes one partner, usually the woman, has an aversion to sex that stems from an unwanted pregnancy, a fear of pregnancy, or an STI experience.

OPTIONS FOR RESOLUTION

Have accurate, up-to-date information on birth control and STI prevention. Keep current. Information about contraception and STIs changes frequently. The birth control pill, for example, comes in many forms now, including a birth control patch. However, providing contraceptive expertise is not your primary function as a sex coach. Help your client establish her own resources, including doctors, clinics, and online sources.

Assess the couple's patterns for using contraception and STI protection. Are they avoiding sex because they fear pregnancy or disease? Is one of them tense during sex for the same reasons?

Analyze their current relationship pattern. Do they have multiple sexual partners? If so, suggest ways of minimizing their risks of pregnancy and STIs.

Help them choose the best contraceptive method. Give them information on pills, hormonal implants, IUDs, condoms, creams, gels, surgical contraception, and sterilization.

Advocate regular use of their contraceptive method of choice. If they have multiple partners, stress the importance of using condoms and spermicides every time. A good sex coach takes a stand on these issues, while understanding that clients must choose products that fit their unique needs.

Throughout the coaching process, check up on how well they're doing. An occasional call to them (or email check-in) to perfectly fire if both partners know you are working on their concern.

Concern 3. Pregnancy

I frequently receive email messages from women concerned about sex during pregnancy. A typical complaint is: "My husband wants sex, but I don't—and I'm scared he may find it somewhere else." I offer these women comfort and let them know how common their situation is. Remember: "Am I normal?" is the question many clients are really asking.

OPTIONS FOR RESOLUTION

Changing body image. She may not be feeling attractive or sexy, is getting fatter, rounder and looking odd in the mirror. Help her find her beauty. Encourage her to get facials, wear attractive clothing, do anything to feel better about her looks.

Low or no sexual desire. This may be especially true during the first trimester when many women suffer from morning sickness or late term when they are tired, truly heavy with child, and worried about harming the baby. Allow her to accept the reality of her physical state. Do a comforting reality check-fatigue, illness and anxiety are going to make her less interested in sex.

Body pain. Many women have aches and pains, especially backache. Guide her to resources for soothing her pain, including yoga, physical therapy, chiropractic or deep-heating rubs.

Painful or awkward sex. As her body changes, the couple may need to use different angles of penetration and adapt movements and positions. Lend her videos or send her out to buy self-help books, DVDs, and other tools for techniques.

Low or no energy for sex. Many women feel tired throughout a pregnancy, while some experience intermittent energy bursts. And then there is my aerobics teacher: *Pregnant with her third child, she actually led classes (a bit more slowly but no less intensively) until the day she gave birth!* Encourage your clients to rest. Sometimes just your acknowledgment and permission for greater self care can alleviate her anxiety about lack of energy.

Fear of harming the developing fetus. Some women must stop having sex to avert a miscarriage. You may meet a client who falls into that category, so be sure to ask about her physician's medical instructions to her about sexual activity, or coach her to ask for them.

Concern 4. Postpartum

The new mother (and her partner) will probably ask: "How can I get back to feeling (and acting) sexual again?" Your job as a sex coach is to help her and her partner find their way back to a satisfying sex life.

OPTIONS FOR RESOLUTION

Body image issues. Typically these include weight gain and slack muscle tone. Help her create a realistic diet/exercise program for getting back in shape.

Fear of hurting her if they have penetrative sex. (Men often wonder: "Is she really healed inside?") Coach her to find alternative sex play to sexual intercourse, to keep sex alive. Get her to dialogue with her OB/GYN about when she's ready to resume sex.

No desire for sex—either from hormonal imbalance or exhaustion. Encourage her partner to read about post-partum recovery and help him be nurturing and patient until she is ready for sex again. Suggest ways for her to have time alone to rest and relax.

Unable to make the transition from baby back to babe for her and sometimes for him, too. They need to set aside *couple time* to recreate the feelings they shared before the baby came. Be an anchor for their commitment to make "us" time and to let go of the pulls of parenting now and then.

Trauma from birth. Couples can suffer an emotional trauma if the birth doesn't go well or the partner witnesses too many details. Work at de-traumatizing them if you can get both partners into your studio for sex coaching. Or refer them out for therapy.

Physically painful sex—that can be caused by episiotomy or a healing C-section incision. Suggest forms of non-penetrative sex— and insist she report these problems to her doctor.

LILY AND THE HOSPITAL NO-NO

Lily came to see me when her second child was six months old. "I am ready for sex," she said, "but my husband isn't." She wanted to

know what she could do to turn him on again. "I'm so frustrated!"
she said.

In taking her history, I learned that she'd had an emergency
C-section. Her husband John had witnessed the entire bloody, gory
operation—something that should never have happened. He was so
traumatized that he couldn't have sex with her for months.

I worked with Lily alone to get him to see another professional to resolve
this trauma. We set up an action plan, in which she initiated some sexual
contact with John 2-3 times a week, even if they just cuddled or fondled.
Gradually, over time, he learned to re-associate her sexual anatomy with
pleasure, and they regained the closeness she so desperately craved. Adding
an inside lock to their bedroom door helped a lot, keeping their 3-year-old
out of their bed at night. Eventually their relationship healed.

MEDICAL/CLINICAL CONCERNS

This year more than 600,000 women will have hysterectomies, with
perhaps 15–20% of them unnecessary, especially for diagnoses of
heavy bleeding or fibroid tumors. You will almost surely see a few of
those women and their disillusioned partners in your sex coaching
practice. You'll also see clients with lingering pain or stiffness from
recent surgeries, (nonsexual) chronic pain disorders (with lower back
pain being the most common), and, of course, men with prostate
problems and people on medications that are causing negative sexual
side effects. Even a client on cold medications or over-the-counter
sinus preparations may have a sexual breakdown from taking what
seems like a benign product. All these conditions and many more
either repress desire or affect people's ability to act on their desires.

You are a sex coach, not a medical doctor. Nevertheless, you must
know enough about medicine to serve the needs of your clients. Sometimes you will learn from them. Clients are often the best teachers!

OPTIONS FOR RESOLUTION

Just as with the pregnancy concerns, clients in this category are
going to need for you to be up-to-date on information and offer a
soothing presence as they heal.

Learn as much as you can about the condition or disease and the typ-
ical courses of treatment before the client even comes to your studio.
Use the vast resources of both the Internet and your local library for

comprehensive coverage on medications, especially if you know the pharmaceutical company that manufactures the client's prescription drugs. The company's website will give you drug information, including side effects, and tell you a lot about the disease or condition requiring that medication.

Get specialized training through courses and workshops for those conditions you're most likely to see in your practice. If you spot a trend, for example, the burgeoning cases of clinical depression and vulvar pain disorders, learn as much as you can about the condition and how the medications affect sexual desire and functioning.

Be an advocate for better care with their current medical providers if necessary. Get permission from your clients to share information with their medical team. You won't always need to be an active participant in the medical process, but be ready and willing to so when the need arises.

Listen and respond. The client who tells you, "My medication is interfering with my sexual functioning [or affecting desire]," may not have shared that information with the doctor prescribing the drug. Coach them to renegotiate their medical treatments, even to the point of suggesting other drug options. Anti-depressants and anti-anxiety medications frequently inhibit sexual desire and orgasm. Review Chapters 7 and 8 for more on this subject.

Assist your clients in creating a plan. Help your client devise a workable plan for coping with his or concern, including step-by-step directions for finding another medical care provider, getting second opinions, and exploring other options for clinical care.

Refocus them on pleasure. This is your most valuable service! A client in pain may be defining pleasure as purely pain relief. She may not be focusing on sexual pleasure. That's where you come in. Begin by reminding them of the analgesic properties of orgasm.

MORE ABOUT THAT

Refocusing clients with physical pain issues is a two-fold process.

1. Help them to alleviate the physical pain, referring them if necessary. For example, I often coach clients to obtain arnica gel for minor aches and pains, whereas I might refer someone with chronic back pain to a pain management clinic that offers a range of options, including alternative medicine.

2. When the physical pain is controlled, help them get back to desiring and experiencing sensual and sexual pleasure. For example, if a client has difficulty getting his mind off lower back pain, give him fantasies or soothing music to keep him focused during masturbation.

Help them identify and locate options for sexual expression. Clients who have been avoiding sex—or finding sex painful or uncomfortable—need to find ways for giving and receiving physical love and affection. They need to get in touch with their sensual and erotic sides again. In fact, they probably need help with all forms of sensual/sexual communication. Review the Touch Continuum in Chapter 9—and use it with your client.

Some clients may benefit from adopting a pet, taking a massage class, or even studying martial arts to feel energy running through his or her body. Other clients respond to sensual massage in the areas of her body that are causing discomfort. If you can help a client think outside the box of pain that he is living inside, you elevate both his capacity for pleasure and his goals for a higher quality of living. The more you open a person to pleasure, the more you increase their capacity for living. I believe that.

For significant physical disabilities, consider referring out. In the referral listings in Appendix E you will find the few experts on sexuality and disability. This is an area of sex coaching requiring specialized training in most cases. One of the greatest gifts you can give a disabled client is treating him like anyone else, offering your full range of regular services. But, if this person is disabled to the degree where performing sexually is difficult if not possible, you may not be the person most qualified to help. Honor that person for his courage, strength, and determination to improve sexual pleasure.

One growing category of women (and men) who are undergoing surgeries and medications for cancer or other life-threatening illnesses will present some of your greatest challenges and rewards. Often their rigorous treatments have deeply scarred their emotions as well as their bodies. Their image of themselves as sexually attractive may be distorted.

MORE ABOUT THAT

PWAs (persons with HIV/AIDS) may seek sex coaching to find sexual pleasure postdiagnosis or during remission. Sometimes PWAs are coping with shame at being HIV positive. Partners of PWAs who are HIV negative may be coping with survivor guilt and feel unworthy of sexual pleasure.

Fortunately, the stigma that once surrounded HIV/AIDS is now a shadow of what it was. For many people, HIV/AIDS is a lifelong manageable disease like a heart condition or diabetes. However, some prejudice still remains. Keep that in mind when you coach PWAs.

You must advise and encourage safer sexual behaviors and offer creative sensual and erotic solutions, including masturbation. You must also empower your client to take full responsibility in not infecting others.

Breast cancer or cervical/endometrial cancer survivors, for example, have to cope with severe changes in how they look, feel and function. These women in particular who seek out my services (beyond the range of other supportive care) for rekindling sexual desire or pleasures have to overcome so much: Low energy; body shame; loss of hair on their head and pubic area; scars; misshapen anatomy; rejection by former lovers or current partners who may not be able to look at or touch them in those places; lowered self esteem; and fear of recurring illness. Some women report that they abhor their bodies themselves, especially the ravaged breasts or the vagina that was the entry to the formerly cancerous uterus.

These clients are quite special. They will require more of your time in devising a careful assessment and action plan for a realistic sexual recovery, given their limitations. They will respond to the love you give them as their sex coach. But if the connection between you and this client isn't strong—you won't be successful in coaching her to a positive transformation. Sex coaching clients in this area is no less than heroic. This is your chance to spin lead into gold!

And finally, you are not likely to provide useful services to clients with severe mental impairment, unless you have extensive training in that area.

Get It!

1. Name one pregnancy-related concern your client presents and how you would devise an action plan for that concern.
2. Cite some of the issues that arise for postillness or postsurgical clients and how you would address them.
3. How would you address the sexual concerns of an HIV-infected client? Name some of the prevailing issues that may surface and your solutions.
4. What are your reactions to this challenging group? Discuss the range of your emotional responses.

CHAPTER TWELVE

Non-Vanilla Sex
Concerns and Resolutions

CLIENTS WHO ENGAGE in non-vanilla sex present a different kind of challenge than those I've just discussed. Traditional therapists often fail in working with them, and the mental health establishment pathologizes their behavior, diagnosing it as a disease or disorder. They may prescribe medications or suggest intensive treatment, institutionalization, or, in rare cases, incarceration. As a sex coach you must know your state law, such as your duty to report child molestation, violent spousal abuse, or rape—but not husbands and wives who play with whips. Most of the sexual behaviors discussed in sex coaching are treated as acceptable behaviors, identified as forms of play, not pathology.

The field of sexology embraces sexual experience and behavior between two consensual adults who are not harming themselves or others. The two important words here are *adults* and *consensual*. Your clients may be doing something they consider an erotic ride into ecstasy but you would consider reason to call the cops if it happened in your private life. Your job as a coach is to support them on their erotic journey, not impose your views of right and wrong. That said, these clients will probably provoke some judgments on your part and help you set boundaries concerning whom you will coach in your practice.

You need to examine your own mind and heart carefully before you decide to coach a non-vanilla individual or couple. If you don't have the kind of background or training that elicits deep understanding and compassion for the broad (and I would say limitless) range of human sexual expression, these clients may have you searching for the nearest exit in your own office. Coaching the non-vanilla client may never be your style. That's okay. If you cannot sustain an open acceptance for a client, refer him or her to someone who can. Providing the right referral is a tremendous service. You can feel good about yourself for being able to do that.

If you do decide to coach a client whose sexual appetite differs radically from the mainstream, try to avoid the terms *normal* and *abnormal*. Instead, consider theese clients as more complex than others.

THE THREE MAJOR NON-VANILLA CATEGORIES

These categories are divided arbitrarily, to help you sort out the range of sexual expression found in this type of client. Although you may cling to one term over another, think of these are generic groupings, many of which seem to overlap and at times combine.
• Kink, fetish, and BDSM (bondage, discipline, sadomasochism)
• Swinging/group sex
• Erotic indulgences (including porn and compulsive sex)

Kink, Fetish, and BDSM

Kink is a broad term that actually encompasses all of the sexual practices addressed in this chapter. Everyone has their own very personal definition of *kinky sex*, usually defining it as "what *other* people do sexually that we don't do." For the purposes of this book, I will define kink as not only including the erotic behaviors in this chapter (fetish, B&D, S&M, swinging, and erotic indulgences) but also sex with animals, roleplaying without the erotic power exchange associated with BDSM scenes, sex in public places (very common), extrasensual/sexual experiences (thrills) that seem unrelated to sex but produce sexual arousal (such as rope climbing and bungee jumping), sensory deprivation or activities that heighten sensations (such as deep tissue massage), sex with fruits or vegetables inserted as dildos, and behaviors that cause arousal without being directly related to sex (such as sniffing a woman's soiled underwear). Sometimes thoughts are kinky because of their taboo quality, for example, fantasizing about sex with your parish priest.

A *fetish* is an object or body part that produces sexual excitement or arousal. Often the fetish object was anchored to arousal during childhood, for example, Auntie Betty's nylons brushing against a little boy's penis and causing an erection. The sensory memory of that experience is triggered when he's around nylons. There are four fetish categories:

- Visual (seeing women naked)
- Sensual (the feel or smell of latex, nylon, leather)
- Experiential (being tied up or hearing commands to do certain things)
- Fantasy, in which just the act of *imagining* seeing, sensing, or experiencing is arousing (thought of peeing on a partner's buttocks— the pee or the buttocks could be the fetish objects, whereas the act of peeing on a partner would be a B&D behavior.

MORE ABOUT THAT

Many women have sought sex coaching with me because their male partners want them to play dominatrix in the bedroom. "He wants me to dominate him sexually," they often say, with some degree of puzzlement. These women don't understand why their successful, aggressive mates want to be topped sexually. Often powerful men do crave playing the submissive role because it gives them a place to relax and let someone else be in charge.

BDSM includes games involving domination/submission, pain/pleasure, master/slave, or top/bottom—anything that incorporates an erotic power exchange that produces mental, emotional, and physical tension. These games are sometimes called "doing a scene." The sexual nature of the scene may not be obvious to anyone but the participants. Although some danger, risk, and pain may be involved, the activities are highly structured and consensual. The roles are carefully defined in advance. The key elements are trust, communication, and negotiation. Players use "safe words" such as *spaghetti* to stop the action, because saying *no* while meaning *yes* is often part of the play.

There are fine distinctions between B&D and S&M.

B&D—bondage and discipline—is a power dynamics game that always utilizes mental, psychological, or physical restraints such as blindfolds and handcuffs. Denial of pleasure is often a key component of the game, with the partner in power taking charge, for example, of the other's orgasm. The submissive partner relinquishes power willingly. S&M—sadomasochism, named in part after the Marquis de Sade—is also a power dynamics activity, but is defined by

a pain/pleasure continuum. More pain typically leads to greater pleasure. The sadist knows his partner's limits but occasionally may push
her a little past them. Implements can be fiendishly clever or simple
everyday items like kitchen spatulas. Some typical items for adminis-
tering pain include whips, paddles, ropes, floggers, clamps or clips,
piercing devices including needles, fire, and heavy restraints that
cause pain, such as metal leg cuffs raised with suspension devices or
scrotum/weighted ball stretchers. Again, the activities are consensual, the roles clearly are defined, and safe words are used to indicate
when the masochist can tolerate no more.

INSIDE STORY: BOBBY AND THE CHAMBER OF PAIN

*Bobby, one of my toughest clients, came to see me after a well-
respected dominatrix I knew referred him. I admired his intellect. He
and I had our first mind battle over his insistence that I become his
dominatrix while coaching him to wellness. He was skillfully persistent,
but I never compromised my boundaries with him.*

*"I am addicted to torture from smart, dominating women," Bobby
said. "I pay well and often." That was his problem. He was draining
thousands of dollars and hundreds of hours each month from his family
and business on professional domination and needed to stop.*

*Baffled, I tried various sex coaching approaches without success.
I tried to convince him to seek therapy or medication for his compulsion, but he refused. I even threatened to stop my work with him if he
wouldn't give up these damaging visits to dominatrices.*

*"I know you are the person who can heal me," he said. When I con-
fessed I'd run out of ideas, he begged me to try one more thing. "Come
see me with Mistress M in her dungeon," he pleaded. You'll understand
what I get there and maybe you'll know how to help me." Reluctantly,
I agreed.*

*That next week, wearing a dark outfit and with notebook and pen in
hand, I sat quietly under a shrouded makeshift hiding place in the dungeon torture chamber where I could watch without being seen. I did not
speak. Mistress M verbally degraded him, saying things like "You're a
piece of shit", "You're scum," and "You don't deserve to live, you rotten
imbecile." Bobby begged for abuse, both verbal and physical. She
whipped and spanked his body and pulled his hair so hard I thought she
would pull it out. The more cruel the treatment she administered,*

the more aroused and erect he became. She twisted his mind and body—turning his repentant words back to her commands and spinning around him as she administered more pain to his fleshy body—torso, thighs, buttocks, neck, and face. I felt as if I were watching a dark ballet or fencing match.

I watched in awe. She was a masterful dominatrix. He was a perfectly pliant slave. I scribbled notes, writing down my observations. When Bobby finished his session, we met in her back room to discuss my findings.

Ignoring my insights and suggestions, Bobby chose to remain addicted to torture. He didn't want advice—from a sex coach or a truly helpful dominatrix with his best interest at heart. He only wanted punishment—at the cost of ruining his life. I know that by not allowing the boundaries of the sex coaching process to become compromised, I did give him some form of healing, perhaps in ways he could not imagine at the time.

You may never find yourself inside a dungeon or a playroom designed for the administration of pain or what appear to be cruel acts. But you must be comfortable knowing that clients may find this to be the single most sexually fulfilling part of their life.

OPTIONS FOR RESOLUTION

You may have to stretch beyond your current limits as a sex coach to find the information and tools you need to resolve these client concerns.

Educate yourself about kinky sex. Watch the award-winning documentary *Beyond Vanilla* (which can be ordered from www.beyond-vanilla.net) or the video *Whipsmart* from Good Vibrations or Pacific Media Entertainment. Read a wide range of material by scene participants and commentators. Attend workshops and educational meetings of local S&M societies.

Experience the scene in person. If possible, visit a dungeon or an S&M club. Feel the equipment. Gently try it out. Open all your senses—sight, smell, sound, and touch. You may be amazed at how tactile it all is. Observe and absorb all you can from the environment, including the distinctly tense and erotic energy that fills an S&M playground.

Schedule an appointment with a professional dominatrix. You may even want to experience being dominated or watch a live demonstration of a scene.

Define your personal comfort zone. Review Chapters 3 and 4 about preparing to become a sex coach. Will this client stretch your personal limits too far? Remember that the "do no harm" motto applies to you as well as your clients.

Coach clients to maintain their boundaries. Help these clients set and maintain healthy, strong boundaries. Good boundaries are critical to their (and their partners') empowerment as well as necessary for maintaining your sanity working with them. Encourage safe play. Discuss how they can avert dangerous situations, including real injuries, arrests for indecent exposure, and emotional damage from taking unhealthy risks.

Be alert for clues to pathology. Some clients get into increasing levels of pain. Others may be acting out against authority figures rather than exploring pleasure. If necessary, refer them out for therapy or move into that mode if you are a therapist.

Teach communication and negotiation skills. Review Chapter 9 for information on communication and negotiation skills. Encourage the use of "safewords" by the couple, pre-designated terms that show a definite request to end an activity, S&M or not.

Provide resources. As you do with other clients, help these clients find resources for information, social activities, and partners (online or in the local community). Know about the range of materials, such as books, DVDs, videos, clubs, societies (sometimes secret), and classes. Help them learn better, more advanced techniques if this truly is a lifestyle for them. (See Appendix E for resources.)

Steer clients away from illegal or dangerous practices. Although your role is to empower and support your clients, there will be times when you are their guardian in another way. Direct your clients away from the two big no-no's: child-adult sexual activity and bestiality. Laws differ from state to state, but the bottom line is to help your client stay clear from self-destructive behaviors, fantasies or not, that will land them in jail. If your client discloses such activities, and if you are licensed in another profession that requires you to take legal action, do so. If not, keep a steady beat on ways to redirect their energies into legal and less potentially harmful activities.

Swinging/Group Sex

Swinging is hot once again—attracting younger urban couples in addition to the midlife suburban couples that have been swinging for decades. According to Lifestyles, the prominent swinging organization, over one million Americans participate. Swinging, group sex, and menages (threesomes) have been practiced since ancient times. These practices may be titillating and exciting to some clients who will come to you for permission to do it. I have identified five "levels" of swinging:

• Voyeurism (watching another person/persons being sexual)
• Exhibitionism (acting sexual in front of others)
• Shared touch/shared sex with one person outside the couple (threesomes)
• Group sex with more than three people
• Fantasy swinging (using the idea of swinging as a fantasy, not acted upon)

You will have clients who participate at one or more of these levels. Help clients, especially couples, clarify what level they wish to participate in.

OPTIONS FOR RESOLUTION

Often this type of client is looking for your permission to try swinging. Some will seek your help in trying to convince their partner to participate. Your role is to help them explore options and stay safe as a couple.

Give them permission to explore this aspect of their sexuality. That's why they called you!

Teach "safety first." Help them develop safety guidelines, including knowing their partners, avoiding legal risks (for you too—don't join in), and using safer sex practices (condoms at a minimum).

Sanction exhibitionism/voyeurism. It's okay to watch without participating at a swinging party—or to perform without actually experiencing intercourse.

Encourage them to use personal referrals. Trusted sources are more reliable than anonymous online or printed personals. Help them minimize their risk of entrapment or involvment in dangerous situations.

Give them permission to fantasize rather than act. Sometimes fantasy is better than the reality. Many couples savor the sheer idea of swinging with a third person or another couple, or even attending a swingers' party, without ever having to face any negative repercussions or risks.

Have them assess their motives. Sometimes clients interested in swinging really want a bisexual or homosexual relationship. Other times they are looking for a form of outside stimulation to enhance their own erotic thoughts or behaviors. You will also meet couples for whom swinging is an authentic way to express love to a partner outside of their primary relationship. Help your couple clients develop a set of critical questions about jealousy, loyalty, trust, and disease, to evaluate in advance the impact expanding their sexual experience will have on the relationship. Swinging can really change a relationship. As a sex coach, you must strike a balance between encouraging new exploratory behaviors and preserving the integrity of the couple's intimate relationship or lifestyle requirements.

INSIDE STORY: THE BAILEYS AND THE LAP DANCER

The Baileys sought coaching for enriching their sex life. "We have good sex," Mrs. Bailey said. Mr. Bailey agreed. "But we would like more sexual variety."

Following one of our sessions, the Baileys went to an erotic dance club, where Mrs. Bailey was attracted to a female lap dancer who reciprocated the feeling. Hot and heavy kissing between the two women left Mrs. Bailey wanting more. He was thrilled. She was scared.

When they asked me if they should invite this woman into their home, I advised against it. I coached them to carefully answer a long set of questions, including: Was this a possible sex-for-sale setup that could be a problem financially? Could they be accused of pandering? Would she really enjoy acting on her fantasy? Would he mind if she had sex with a woman in front of him? Would he ask to participate in the sex? If so, how would she feel watching him be sexual with another woman? Was this new woman a trustworthy partner? Shouldn't they investigate her health status and sexual past? How could this decision harm their emotional bond?

Once they examined the possible ramifications, the couple decided not to issue that invitation. Instead, they enjoyed getting aroused at the dance club and going home to have intense sex. They used the dance club as erotic fuel for their personal fire.

"Thank you for saving us from serious grief and maybe jail time!" Mr. Bailey said. "Your sex coaching has given us the encouragement to go out into the world as sexual explorers and the skills to come back home as world-class lovers."

Erotic Indulgences

Any erotic indulgence taken to the extreme can and probably will be defined by someone as *sex addiction* or *compulsive sexual behavior*, with the terms often used interchangeably. Men and women who devote significant time and energy—to the detriment of relationships, work, and other life goals—to Internet porn, X-rated videos, or multiple sexual partners are often labeled as sex addicts, porn addicts, or, the newest, Internet addicts. I don't believe that compulsive sexual behavior is the same thing as addiction. You might lose your job over Internet porn, but that doesn't make you an addict. The following inside story illustrates how pervasive and damaging the porn addiction theory is.

INSIDE STORY: CHARLIE THE PORN ADDICT

I was a panelist on a national television show. The controversial topic of the day was porn as adult entertainment. Some of the other guests and audience members were antiporn zealots. One professor with a PhD opposed all adult entertainment, claiming that all of it exploited women, a common misperception about porn.

Insisting that using triple-X material can enrich a couple's sex life, I stood for adult rights and free expression in sexual materials. I believe adults—individuals and couples—should be able to indulge in adult entertainment for solitary pleasure or sexual enhancement. But I was a small voice in a chorus of bitter moral judgment that day.

I rode home with some other guests, mostly adult performers. Two expressed their outrage at being victims of a witch hunt and I tried to assuage their hurt feelings. But I, too, felt like I'd been set up for an ambush on camera. I watched the show air 2 weeks later and was appalled all over again at the ignorance some of those people displayed about explicit sexual entertainment. What a waste of my professionalism!

No more than 5 minutes after the show ended, my phone rang. The caller, Charlie, asked in a hushed and tender voice if this was the real Dr. Patti he'd seen on the show. When I said I was, he begged me to hear his story.

Ashamed and mortified by his enjoyment of X-rated videos and online adult sites, Charlie had feared he was addicted to porn when he turned on that program. He said, "You are the first professional who made me feel clean. I thought I was a scumbag, a pervert. I no longer feel that way. You helped me in ways you'll never know. I hope that I can meet you and work with you."

Charlie showed up a week later. We worked together for a year on his issues surrounding porn—and much more. I will always be grateful for that horrible television show for allowing healing about porn to take place, at least for one man. I'm sure he wasn't the only one!

A FEW QUESTIONS ABOUT PORNOGRAPHY

Probably one of the least understood and most maligned aspects of sexuality is pornography. Call it what you wish—erotica, porn, trash, or treasure—people choose to enjoy this form of erotic entertainment to the tune of billions of dollars each year.

Is it porn, or is it erotica? We could devote another book to defining the differences between porn, erotica, and sexually explicit materials. Pornography is often an umbrella term all three categories. I define the terms as follows: Porn and erotica are meant to arouse. I usually refer to *erotica* as porn's soft side, whereas *porn* is hard-core. *Sexually explicit materials* are not meant to arouse but rather to educate and explain (like sex education videos, books, and articles) or to stimulate the intellect, like erotic art. However you define it, the term *porn* shouldn't bear negative connotations.

Your clients' attitudes toward porn will probably be split down gender lines, with men being porn-friendly (or porn-dependent) and many women being antiporn. Bringing couples into alignment on this charged topic isn't easy. One of your tasks as a sex coach will be to prescribe some kind of mutually acceptable pornography to educate and arouse.

Does pornography help or harm? No, porn did not *make him do it.*
Don't let clients blame sexual misconduct on porn. Porn helps not
harms an individual's or couple's sexual development and expression. Numerous studies have shown that there is no causal link
between viewing pornography and committing acts of sexual violence, including rape. Porn is designed to create sexual arousal in the
viewer, and that's what it does. If images could change people's
behaviors that easily, the safer sex seminars of the late 1980s would
have stopped the spread of HIV.

I often prescribe porn for individuals and couples, especially those
suffering from low or no desire, boredom, lack of technical skills, and
arousal concerns. Yes, it's radical for a woman to say porn is *not* dirty
and shameful. But I have seen many people improve their sex lives
through using porn.

But doesn't porn present a distorted view of sex? Porn does leave
steady viewers, particularly young men, with distorted images of sexual reality. Not all real women are endowed with huge breasts and
insatiable erotic appetites. Most men don't have enormous penises or
ejaculate copiously on command, nor do they maintain rock-hard
erections for hours. Help your client become desensitized to these
images and, particularly in the case of single men, quell expectations
of busty women eager for them to ejaculate on their faces. Many
porn-dependent men also need to be educated about average penis
size and performance so they will feel better about themselves.

*But can our clients become addicted to porn or to other sexual behav-
iors, especially cybersex?* Opinions differ on what constitutes "too
much" and whether or not that "too much" is a true addiction. For
example, some experts say that watching porn on the Internet for
8.5 hours per week is an addiction. Although I respect my colleagues
in other fields who define certain behaviors as mental health concerns,
I do not agree with their conclusions. I label that behavior as *porn dependency.* The real issue is not the porn—it is the compulsion. Many
men who use the computer for sex—whether they are in relationships or not—handle stress by transferring that tension to a sexual
release without a partner. They masturbate—with or without the
Internet. Why? They are exhausted, overworked, anxious—and may
be having relationship problems. A no-demand sexual outlet seems

perfect for that man. However, when he takes energy away from his work, family, and primary relationship and puts it into compulsive sexual behavior, he has a problem. As a sex coach, you must work with him to reduce the compulsive behavior and return more of his energy to his relationship. In some cases, you may need to refer out for therapy or medications.

Sex addiction: fact or myth? *Sex addiction* is one of the most controversial topics in sexology today. I never use the term, preferring instead, as other sexual researchers and therapists do, the term *compulsive sexual behaviors.* The sex addiction model developed by Patrick Carnes has spawned 12-step programs including SAA (Sex Addicts Anonymous), SLAA (Sex and Love Addicts Anonymous), and others.

I do not refer clients to those programs, which attempt to stop sexual thoughts and behaviors. In fact, I often see men and sometimes women who have *failed or been failed* by such programs. Instead, I help clients discover and understand the cause of their urges, detect their patterns, and break those negative patterns—without making sex "bad" or "evil." The compulsive behavior (which many overlap into alcohol, drug, and food dependency) becomes the focus of the work.

Sexual compulsives can be delicate and difficult clients. They may need more help than you can or want to provide, including daily check-ins by phone or email, aversive conditioning assignments, and positive support networks of friends, partners, relatives, and even groups who encourage them to manage their compulsive tendencies.

If you can help these clients manage their compulsivity without denying themselves sexual pleasure, you have dramatically changed their life.

OPTIONS FOR RESOLUTION

To resolve concerns related to pornography and compulsive sexual behaviors, you must be very tolerant and comfortable with eroticism.

Use porn/erotica in sex education for clients. Many individuals and couples get new ideas for sexual positions and techniques from watching porn. The actors and actresses are their role models for initiating sexual acts. Couples can jumpstart sagging libidos by watching videos together.

Don't be afraid to use these materials in treating clients with all sexual concerns. Recommend some of the videos by women producers like Candida Royalle (Femme Productions) and Veronica Hart. Sometimes individuals or couples who simply enjoy porn will express fear that they are addicts—reassure them that they are not.

Encourage couples to compromise in resolving conflicts about porn. You will often see couples with a conflict about the type of porn or erotica used, the time devoted to porn by one partner (usually the man), or about using porn at all. I coach couples to accept that porn can add something to their relationship, not detract from it. Steer them to better porn, the kinds of materials they can share to become aroused together. Porn, or erotica, is often the missing ingredient in a couple's busy sexless life.

Help clients identify the reasons behind their compulsive behavior. What makes a man devote hours a week to Internet porn while his wife complains about their sexless marriage? Compulsivity is driven by fantasy, including the fantasy of living in a world where sex comes with no expectations, no demands, and no time constraints. The Internet porn lover is avoiding responsibilities or problems in his relationship. Help these clients decide whether cybersex is real or perceived intimacy—and whether it is cheating.

Don't leap to cyber-conclusions. You will probably have to address questions about online sexuality with clients. Know your limitations. The almost limitless realm of online sexuality is another world with its own rules; understanding its nuances requires considerable research. Help your clients talk honestly about whether cybersex is really sex. Focus on the real issues: How much time and energy does this activity take away from the relationship?

Be on the lookout. Watch for signs of a porn recluse. Some men use porn to safely hide from real relationships. I've met women who spend all their free time devouring romance novels as their fantasy lifestyle of choice. Help your clients avoid isolation and prevent themselves from using erotic—or romantic—entertainment as their escape from intimacy or physical pleasure.

Code It! Code It!, my behavioral program for clients who watch too much porn, has a slightly ironic twist. Unlike the abstinence-only approach to sexual compulsivity, I have my porn-or Internet-dependent clients use a special coding sheet while watching their arousal materials. On the sheet they must note the number of sexual acts, the running time in minutes per sex act, and who did what where and when. The sheer amount of mental work involved in this exercise deeroticizes the activity of watching adult entertainment.

INSIDE STORY: TEDDY AND THE JOGGERS IN THE PARK

Referred as a "hopeless case" by a renowned psychologist specializing in obsessive compulsive disorders, Teddy was indeed a complex client, but I was able to help him. A shy, withdrawn man, he put his trust in me completely, enabling me to help him grow beyond both our expectations. Trust is the key to any healing relationship.

"I have problems with compulsivity," he said in a whisper, twisting his hands nervously. "I have an awful thing I do, and my doctor says I've got to stop it."

I smiled at him warmly and said, "Anything you say here is okay, Teddy. I'm hoping I can help you! Are you willing to tell me more?"

And so began Teddy's story. He had a dangerous habit of lying on the grassy knolls in the local park, watching women in sports bras and leggings jog past. He achieved orgasm and ejaculation by rubbing his belly on the hard ground and rolling side to side. Teddy was already aware that this behavior could get him arrested. But discovering through sex coaching that it also created a masturbatory pattern that made it difficult for him to be sexual with a woman quickly caught his attention!

I coached Teddy to take the thrill out of his habit through using an immersion technique. In his home assignments he watched hours of television (his other favorite pastime), looking for images similar to the jogging women and engaging in his solo sexual practice whenever he did. He recorded each show by title, how many minutes the key segment lasted, and what he did as he masturbated. He loved doing the assignments. The more he masturbated to television, the less time he spent in the park.

His way out of compulsivity was intensively focusing on, not away from, his behavior. By depathologizing his masturbation—not making it shameful or dirty—sex coaching helped him to change. Eventually he simply lost interest in masturbating to jogging women. And, finally, he changed his masturbation pattern away from that secret boylike pattern of rubbing his tummy on the sheets so that Mommy wouldn't see or hear him. He began to lie on his back and learned a new way to use his own hands for self-pleasuring. At last he was ready for sexual intercourse in a way that wouldn't scare off the average woman. By never pathologizing his behavior, I got him to trust the sex coaching journey and himself.

As I do with all my clients, I said to Teddy when he left: "The phone line is always open. I'll always be here for you." Every now and then I get a note from him letting me know he is doing well.

I hope that by now you feel empowered to do the work of a sex coach. We need you! If you don't feel prepared, you may need to seek further experience, along with professional training and a SAR, to get ready to tackle the fascinating panoply of human sexual concerns.

Get It!

1. Describe a hypothetical BDSM client, what they might ask of your services, and how you would respond.
2. What is a fetish client and how would you handle this?
3. What feelings does this chapter evoke from that are different from those the other chapters evoked? Why is that? What can you do right now to better align yourself with this client population?

Epilogue

SEX COACHING IS truly a thrilling profession, one that demands regular maintenance (including networking with peers), access to new ideas, and ongoing skill development. I know that you, if you're anything like me, wouldn't be able to do this work if it didn't evoke your passion. Passion is the element that lights the fire of desire for more knowledge and for expanded opportunities to apply our craft. Passion is what gives us that feeling that even if we didn't get paid for doing this work, it still would be worth it.

Before you launch your new sex coaching practice, I'd like to share a few final thoughts—some helpful reminders of things to remember as you sex coach your clients.

Think big! Don't set restrictive limits as you envision your sex coaching practice. And don't underestimate the positive influence you can have on the world through your work.

Be gentle with yourself as you grow your practice. Establishing a successful practice takes time. Don't beat yourself up if things happen slowly.

Enjoy the process. As you will tell you clients, sex coaching is a process, not an event. Record your daily coaching accomplishments in a journal. Savor every victory, no matter how small.

MORE ABOUT THAT

I spoke with a young man Tom, a few weeks ago and coached him on becoming a sex coach. I just did what I always do . . . give freely and orient a newcomer into this field as best as I can. Here is what he sent to me, after our call—lettered in ink on a beautifully handwritten note tucked inside a handmade greeting card. When I read it, I cried I was so touched.

"Dr. Patti,

I can finally say that my path is illuminated. No longer must I walk in relative darkness, bumping into most everything, unsure of where the next door in my journey leads. While you might not recognize just how powerful our conversation was, in a way, you guided me to the light switch. While nerves and uncertainties still remain, I can now, at least, see the doors in the distance.

My oldest sister tells me all the time that in order to get the answers you need, you've got to find the "oracle". She reminds me that it is often a journey within itself to find them, but once you do, you'll know. I've been searching for months now, calling, emailing, speaking to people at least three times removed from someone who actually knew what they were talking about. But, by some stroke of uncanny luck, you came into the picture. Your charisma, knowledge and experience are so refreshing after dealing with so many completely inane individuals that I really can't thank you enough. You, Dr. Patti, are my oracle.

I find it no small coincidence that you have chosen coaching a profession. A coach is one that guides, suggests, counsels, mentors, educates and enlightens. And, if our half-hour conversation is any indication, you were meant to do this.

With deepest respect and appreciation, Tom"

Keep growing yourself. Learn more each day. Expand your boundaries whenever you can. Challenge yourself to grow beyond your own *comfort zone.*

Invite others to help you. Establish an active network. Keep it alive by contacting your peers and seeking others to join with you.

Dare to do it your way. Take the risk to be unique and different in your approach as a sex coach. Creativity is a must in this field!

Be joyful for the misses as well as the hits. Your misses are your greatest teachers. Your hits are your anchors and your friends.

Keep the boundaries clean and your vision clear. Move toward your own vision for whom you can be and what you can do for others. Don't compromise the professional boundaries that you set.

Be all that you can be. Treat yourself like your own coaching client. Hold the bar high for yourself!

Celebrate your sexual self! Don't forget that you, too, need to enjoy pleasure. Celebrate everything that your delicious sexuality brings to your own life. I give you permission!

Above all else, remember this: The art of anything requires attention, both to your own brush strokes and to the bigger picture painted by everyone around you. Find all the fabulous colors you can, and paint up a sex coaching storm!

Appendices

Guided Imagery
The Pond on the Hill

THIS TECHNIQUE sends clients on an inner journey. For clients you identify as requiring a means for uncovering as-yet-to-be-revealed emotions or memories relevant to your sex coaching work (especially the ST client), this can be particularly useful. It is also an effective tool for promoting relaxation and enhanced self-awareness, or as a peaceful meditation the client can use on his or her own. You can record it in your own voice on a tape that you give to clients, or you can give clients a printed version and allow them to record it in their voice for use as a home assignment. Allow plenty of unrushed time to complete the exercise—at least 10 to 15 minutes.

Say in a soft voice:

Close your eyes. Now, take a deep breath. Breathe with me. Slowly now. Use your breath to go up the back of your body, then down the front, slowly and gently. Breathe, in . . . now out . . . now in . . . now out. That's it. Now, let yourself relax. Relax into the flow of your breath going in and out, slowly and gently. Drifting now, move into the sound of your own breathing. . . . Now let yourself imagine going to a green meadow and seeing a glistening pond on the hill. Walk along the path you find, letting yourself notice things along the path that may give you insight into how you feel inside. Pick up any objects that you see along the path—flowers, sacred objects, pine cones, or even litter. Anything you find is a part of your journey. Along the path you find a little brook. Listen to its babbling sound. Feel the warmth of the sun on your skin, taking deep breaths along the way. Walk with each step, one at a time, feeling the earth under your feet as you move one, two, three, four steps forward to the pond on the right. As you approach the pond, you lie down on the ground beside it and look into the pond at your own reflection. What do you see? How do you feel? What thoughts come up for you? Make a mental note of how this makes you feel. Breathing naturally now, you take your hand, dip into the bottom of this pool and take out something that tells you about your inner self. Ask yourself: Why am I here? What message is here for me? Keep asking yourself these questions as you feel the glow of sunlight on your face and smell the freshness of the pond and grassy knoll. Listen to the sounds of nature—the birds, the insects, the breeze. Imagine now that you have rolled onto your back and are drinking in the warmth of the sun, the sights, smells, sounds, and feel of this beautiful place. Let yourself lie there in peacefulness. When you are ready, start with me counting backwards from 5-4-3-2-1. At 1 slowly open your eyes and let's talk about your journey.

APPENDIX B

Guidelines for Clients

CLIENTS OFTEN SEEK sex coaching without really understanding what the work involves. I give a printout of the following guidelines to all my new clients.

Welcome to Dr. Patti's Sex Coaching. I am so happy you have taken the time and allocated resources to let me be your guide and sex coach.

WHAT IS SEX COACHING?

Sex coaching is a mix of these elements:
• Personalized sexuality information and education
• Redirective cognitive processes and mental reframing
• Emotional balancing
• Intuitive guidance
• Behavioral training
• Resources and referrals

Sex coaching involves all of these parts of you:

Mind. Information. Your "self-talk," thinking about sexual performance, capacity for fantasy, and troubling thought patterns, such as compulsivity.

Emotions. Feelings. Feelings that you carry from the past, about your body and body image, what you suppress and express, how you express your emotions, and your capacity for intimacy.

Body and body image issues. Your physical self. Knowing how your own sexual pattern works, understanding your own body's sexual architecture and function, acknowledging your own sexual functions and dysfunctions, and learning skills for how to be a successful lover alone or with a partner.

Energy. Sex is all about energy! The buildup, the containment, and the expression of energy. In my one-on-one work I observe energy patterns with the individual and with a partner, and I give coaching feedback for handling this often overlooked part of sexuality.

Spirit. The essence of self. Esoteric moments or practices that transcend the moment, such as peak orgasms; sacred sexuality; the more subtle and delicate manner in which people deny or reflect their inner self through sexuality; and the path of sex to experience the divine or God.

WHAT ARE MY RESPONSIBILITIES?

• To guide, direct, and protect you from harm
• To empower you to attain the dreams you desire
• To empower you to overcome any sexual difficulties you may have or fear you have
• To help you reach your sexual/relationship goals and together find results that satisfy you

WHAT ARE YOUR RESPONSIBILITIES?

• To be on time for your scheduled appointments
• To pay on time
• To provide a comprehensive history on sexual relationships
• To be authentic and share your truth with me

WHAT ARE THE FEES?

Fees are set at $120/50-minute talk-only session and pro-rated for longer or shorter sessions. Bodywork fees are set at $125/50-minute session and pro-rated for longer or shorter sessions. Payment is expected at the conclusion of each session by check, cash or credit card. If finances are a problem for you, a sliding fee scale and payment programs are always available. For telephone sessions, payment is required via credit card at my website or by check in advance.

HOW DO SESSIONS WORK?

Most sessions are conducted in person. Some are conducted by telephone, which can be highly effective. Most sessions are about an hour in length. Sessions may be scheduled for once a week, or less or more frequently depending on your schedule, my availability, and your needs for sex coaching.

WHAT ABOUT MISSING OR CHANGING APPOINTMENTS?

There is a 24-hour-advance cancellation policy. If you fail to cancel or reschedule within that time frame, a 50% charge will be asked of you for the missed appointment. Of course, in the case of extraordinary circumstances, there is no charge for the missed appointment. Due to my participation in live media (radio, television, etc.), I may have to move appointments. In those situations, I will do my best to give a 24-hours notice as well.

WHAT CAN YOU EXPECT?

This type of work can be transformational for your whole life, not just your sexuality. By trusting the process and allowing me to be your guide, you will grow, learn, and become a more empowered person, I assure you. Thank you so much for choosing me as your sex coach. It is always my honor and privilege to do this work. I am thrilled that we are going down this path together.

Intake and Assessment Forms

BRIEF SEXUAL HISTORY-MALE

Personal Data

Name:

Telephone Home or Work: Cell:

Address:

Okay to call? Yes/No

Email: Okay to send mail? Yes/No

Date of birth:

Relationship status: single/dating/married/separated

Present sexual identity: heterosexual/homosexual/bisexual/
    crossdresser/transsexual/other: _____

Present living situation: alone/with my spouse/with a lover/with
    friends/with a roommate/with my parents/other: _____

Sexual History

Age of first sexual feeling: Age of first wet dream:

Age of first masturbation: Age of first sexual attraction:

Age of first date: Age of first sexual intercourse:

Age of first orgasm: Date of last orgasm:

Write brief answers:

1. What childhood messages about sex/sexuality did you receive? How might they affect your sexuality today?

2. What are any concerns you may have about your sexuality right now? Why are you here (for example, feelings about your sexual performance, feelings about your relationship, your body, or about masturbation)?

3. What are any concerns you may have about being male?

4. What have been your experiences with orgasm? Alone? With a partner?

5. What have been your experiences with self-pleasuring or masturbating?

6. What is your present pattern for and frequency of self-pleasuring/masturbation?

7. How did and how do you feel about your body (as a child, growing up, as a young adult, and now)?

8. Describe the history of your sexual relationships. (Take extra paper or use the other side if you need to.) Talk about the number of partners, what sexual activities you have experienced, and the issues and conflicts that have emerged for you in intimate relationships.

9. Describe any feelings you may have about having sexual contact with your present or possible sexual partner(s).

10. Describe your present sexual interactions, such as intercourse or masturbation, turn-ons, your present pattern for sexual pleasure, frequency of sexual interactions, your current number of partners, and so on.

11. How often do you think about or desire to have sex?
    ____ once a day   ____ 2-3 times a day
    ____ more than four times a day
    ____ once a week   ____ 2-3 times a week
    ____ more than four times a week
    ____ less than four times a month

12. Check off which of the following are sexual turn-ons for you:
    ____ erotic/porno magazines
    ____ erotic/porno videos
    ____ fantasy during masturbation
    ____ phone sex lines (1-900 numbers)

___ message parlors
___ online sex chats
___ Internet sex (live)
___ other online sex with others
___ prostitutes
___ S&M play
___ cross-dressing
___ swinging
___ exotic dance clubs
___ voyeurism
___ erotic books
___ romance novels
___ dirty talk
___ other

13. Are you interested in being trained in bodywork, such as masturbation or other sexual enhancement techniques? Yes/No

14. Do you want to work with a sexual surrogate? Yes/No

15. Are you currently seeing a psychotherapist or body worker? Yes/No

16. Do you want a referral to a psychotherapist or body worker? Yes/No

17. Do you have any preexisting medical conditions that may affect your sexuality (for example, diabetes, hypertension, heart disease, etc.)? Yes/No

18. Are you currently taking any prescribed medications (such as for hypertension, diabetes, depression, anxiety, or cardiovascular disease)? Yes/No. If yes, list: ___

19. What are your long-term sexual goals?

20. What is your primary goal for our work together?

21. Are you willing to commit to your sexual success? Do you agree to do the assignments and allow yourself to your sexual pleasure? Yes/No/Not sure

22. I hereby release Dr. Britton and/or her associates for any damages that may result from sexual coaching: Yes/No/Not sure

23. Describe anything else related to your past or present experiences. Include anything that may be important for me to know, so that I may assist you in reaching your sexual goals.

BRIEF SEXUAL HISTORY (FEMALE)

Personal Data

Name:

Telephone Home or Work: Cell:

Address:

Okay to call? Yes/No

Email: Okay to send mail? Yes/No

Date of birth:

Relationship status: single/dating/married/separated

Present sexual identity: heterosexual/homosexual/bisexual/
crossdresser/transsexual/other: _____

Present living situation: alone/with my spouse/with a lover/with
friends/with a roommate/with my parents/other: _____

Sexual History

Age of first sexual feeling: Age of first erotic dream:

Age of first masturbation: Age of first sexual attraction:

Age of first date: Age of first sexual intercourse:

Age of first orgasm: Age of first period:

Date of last orgasm: _____

Age of menopause: _____   Type of hormone supplement used:
                                for how long? _____
                                (RX or natural/OTC)_____

Write brief answers:

1. What childhood messages about sex/sexuality did you receive?
   How might they affect your sexuality today?

2. What are any concerns you may have about your periods or
   pregnancy?

3. What are any concerns you may have about being pre-/peri-/post-
   menopausal?

4. What have been your experiences with orgasm? Alone? With a
   partner?

5. What have been your experiences with self-pleasuring or
   masturbating?

6. What is your present pattern for and frequency of self-pleasuring/masturbation?

7. How did and how do you feel about your body (as a child, growing up, as a young adult, and now)?

8. Describe the history of your sexual relationships. (Take extra paper or use the other side if you need to.) Talk about the number of partners, what sexual activities you have experienced, and the issues and conflicts that have emerged for you in intimate relationships.

9. Describe any feelings you may have about having sexual contact with your present or possible sexual partner(s).

10. Describe your present sexual interactions, such as intercourse or masturbation, turn-ons, your present pattern for sexual pleasure, frequency of sexual interactions, your current number of partners, and so on.

11. How often do you think about or desire to have sex?
    ___ once a day   ___ 2-3 times a day
    ___ more than 4 times a day
    ___ once a week   ___ 2-3 times a week
    ___ more than 4 times a week
    ___ less than four times a month

12. Check off which of the following are sexual turn-ons for you:
    ___ erotic/porno magazines
    ___ erotic/porno videos
    ___ fantasy during masturbation
    ___ phone sex lines (1-900 numbers)
    ___ message parlors
    ___ online sex chats
    ___ Internet sex (live)
    ___ other online sex with others
    ___ prostitutes
    ___ S&M play
    ___ cross-dressing
    ___ swinging
    ___ exotic dance clubs
    ___ voyeurism
    ___ erotic books
    ___ romance novels

___ dirty talk

___ other

13. Are you interested in being trained in bodywork, such as masturbation or other sexual enhancement techniques? Yes/No

14. Do you want to work with a sexual surrogate? Yes/No

15. Are you currently seeing a psychotherapist or body worker? Yes/No

16. Do you want a referral to a psychotherapist or body worker? Yes/No

17. Do you have any preexisting medical conditions that may affect your sexuality (for example, diabetes, hypertension, heart disease, etc.)? Yes/No

18. Are you currently taking any prescribed medications (such as for hypertension, diabetes, depression, anxiety or cardiovascular disease)? Yes/No. If yes, list: ___

19. What are your long-term sexual goals?

20. What is your primary goal for our work together?

21. Are you willing to commit to your sexual success, Do you agree to do the assignments and allow yourself to your sexual pleasure? Yes/No/Not sure

22. I hereby release Dr. Britton and/or her associates for any damages that may result from sexual coaching: Yes/No/Not sure

23. Describe anything else related to your past or present experiences. Include anything that may be important for me to know, so that I may assist you in reaching your sexual goals.

INTAKE AND ASSESSMENT FORM-TRANSGENDERED PERSONS

(Note: This is a necessary and confidential part of our work together. Please answer it as completely as you can. We will have a chance to discuss it in detail during our first session.)

Personal Data

Date: Referred by:

Birth Name: Transgendered name
                                         (if different):

Address

Telephone (w)   (h)   (cellular)

Okay to call? Yes/No

Email: Okay to send email? Yes/No

Occupation: Present employer:

Date of birth: Age:

Yearly income (estimated): $ Insurance status:

Relationship status: single/dating/married/separated/other:

Presenting gender at first visit: male/female/other:

Sexual orientation/preference/identify: (circle any that apply)
    heterosexual/homosexual/bisexual/crossdresser/transsexual/other:

Present living situation: alone/with my spouse/with a lover/with
    friends/with a roommate/with my parents/other:

Current medical treatment (MD/clinics/RX by type and location):

Emergency contact (name):   Telephone:

Assessment of Concern(s)

Treatment/therapy history:

History of suicidal ideation or behaviors:

Nature of social support system:

Hormonal use history:

Alcohol/drug usage history:

Involvement in social, recovery/12-step programs:

Gender identity conflict/sexual orientation history:

Age of first awareness of TG (circle one):

before 5   5–11   12–18   18–25   over 25 years

Medical/vocational/legal issues:

Family history (psych/drug/alcohol/sexual abuse history):

Recent losses and crises in past year:

Your Goals

In your own words, please state why you are here today:

What are your goals for our work together?

Stop here.

Referrals Made at Intake (for Dr. Patti to fill in)

APPENDIX D

The PC Exercise Model

THIS IS A BASIC sexual skill that you can teach almost every client, male or female. Exercising the pubococcygeal muscles, or the love muscles, (I don't like to call them by their proper name, the Kegels, because it sounds too clinical) benefits women who are not orgasmic and men who have difficulty sustaining erections. Men can use it for enhanced firmness in their erections, especially when erections wane. Women who regularly practice their "PC's" are more likely to reach orgasm, with tighter vaginal walls. Often they can flex the PC muscles during sex, too, to heighten their own and their male lover's sensations. Both men and women can learn to use their strengthened PC muscles as *power pumping* in sex play. In one ancient sexual secret technique, aptly named *pompoir power*, the woman flexes her muscles around the penis (or "pumps" it) making the man feel like she's milking his ejaculate.

Strong PC muscles mean better sex—improved erectile functioning, quicker orgasmic response, and intensified pleasure. By integrating regular exercise of the PC's into daily life, after three weeks both men and women astoundingly report that they feel an elevated sense of self, increased sexual desire, and greater sexual confidence—not to mention longer-lasting acts of sexual pleasure and greater sexual satisfaction overall.

My PC exercise coaching method:

Locate the PC muscles of the pelvic floor by stopping and start-ing the flow of urine. But never use that technique again! Use the following pattern for daily practice:

1. Locate those muscles and squeeze them tightly on a two-count. Say one potato, two potato for the count.
2. Release them for a one-count (one potato).
3. Repeat this 20 times.
4. Take a short rest—20 seconds.
5. Do the whole thing two more times for a total of 60 repetitions.
6. Do the *every* day of 3 weeks without fail and you will find a marked positive change with sex.

Resources

ORGANIZATIONS AND ASSOCIATIONS

Adult Children of Alcoholics
  (ACA)
www.adultchildren.org

Advocacy for First Amendment
  Free Speech: Feminists for Free
  Expressions (FFE)
www.ffeusa.org

American Association of Sex
  Educators, Counselors and
  Therapists (AASECT)
www.aasect.org

American Board of Sexology and
  American Association of Clinical
  Sexologists
www.sexologist.org

Centers for Disease Control &
  Prevention
www.cdc.gov

Coach University
www.coachu.com

CoachVille
www.coachville.com
  or www.cvcommunity.com

Codependents Anonymous
  (CODA)
(check local listings)
www.codependents.org

ETR Associates
www.etr.org

Gloria Brame on S&M/Different
  Loving
www.gloria-brame.com

Go Ask Alice: Columbia
  University's Health Education
  Program
www.goaskalice.columbia.edu

Harry Benjamin International
  Gender Dysphoria Association
www.hbigda.org
email: HBIGDA@famprac.umn.edu

Humboldt-Universitat zu Berlin
Magnus Hirschfeld Archive for
  Sexology
www.sexology.cjb.net

Institute for the Advanced Study of
  Human Sexuality (IASHS)
  (graduate programs in sexology)
www.iashs.edu

Institute for Life Coach Training
  (Pat Williams)
www.lifecoachtraining.com

International Academy of Sex
  Research
www.iasr.org

International Association of
  Coaches
www.certifiedcoach.org

International Coaching
  Federation
www.coachfederation.org

International Foundation for
  Gender Education (IFGE)
www.ifge.org

International Professional
  Surrogates Association
www.surrogatepartners.org

Lifestyles Organization
www.lifestyles.org

Miss Vera's Cross-Dressing
  Academy
www.missvera.com

Gyn Help: Vulvar Pain
www.ourgyn.com

Planned Parenthood Federation
  of America
www.ppfa.org

Sex Coach University
www.sexcoachu.com

Sexual Health.com (includes
  information on disability)
www.sexualhealth.com

Sexuality Information and
  Education Council of the U.S.
www.siecus.org

Society for Human Sexuality
www.sexuality.org

Society for the Scientific Study of
  Sexuality
www.sexscience.org

T. Harv Eker
www.peakpotentials.com

The Kama Sutra Temple (tantra)
www.tantra.org

The Kinsey Institute
www.kinseyinstitute.org

University of Minnesota's
  Program in Human
  Sexuality
www.med.umn.edu/fp/phs.
  phsindex.htm

Widener University (graduate
  school in sexology)
www.widener.edu

World Association for Sexology
www.worldsexology.org

SPECIAL REPORTS

Special Issue on Sexual Health in
Minnesota Medicine
www.mmaonline.net/publications/
MNMed2003/July/0307.htm

The U.S. Surgeon General's Call to
Action to Promote Sexual Health
and Responsible Sexual Behavior
www.surgeongeneral.gov/library/
sexualhealth/

WHO Working Definitions of
Sexual Health
www.who.int/reproductive-
health/gender/sexual_health.
html

RESOURCES FOR CLIENTS

Instructional Sex Teaching Videos/DVDs

Alexander Institute
www.lovingsex.com

Dr. Patti's Website
www.yoursexcoach.com

Pacific Media Entertainment
www.loveandintimacy.com

Sinclair Institute
www.bettersex.com

Eve's Garden
www.evesgarden.com

Erotic and Porn Videos/DVDs

Candida Royalle: Femme Collection
www.royalle.com

Veronica Hart: Triple-X
videos/DVDs
VCA Pictures
www.vcapix.com

ONLINE STORES

Good Vibrations
www.goodvibes.com

Grand Opening
www.grandopening.com

My Pleasure
www.mypleasure.com

Xandria Collection
www.xandria.com

References

CITED SOURCES

Bandler, R. & Grinder, J. (1979). *Frogs into princes: Neurolinguistic programming*. Meab, UT: Real People Press.

Barbach, L. (2000). *For yourself: The fulfillment of female sexuality* (Rev. ed.). New York: Signet.

Berne, E. (1996). *Games people play: The psychology of human relationships*. New York: Random House.

Blank, J. (1993). *Femalia*. San Francisco: Down There Press.

Britton, P. (2001). *The adventures of her in France*. Beverly Hills, CA: Leopard Rising.

Britton, P. & Hodgson, H. (2003). *The complete idiot's guide to sensual massage*. Indianapolis, IN: Alpha.

Chia, M. (1996). *The multi-orgasmic man: Sexual secrets every man should know*. New York: HarperCollins.

Dodson, B. (1996). *Sex for one: The joy of selfloving*. New York: Crown.

Dodson, B. (2002). *Orgasms for two: The joy of partnersex*. New York: Harmony.

Edwards, B. (1999). *The new drawing on the right side of the brain*. New York: J.P. Tarcher.

Gray, J. (1992). *Men are from mars, women are from venus*. New York: HarperCollins.

——— (1984). *What you feel you can heal: A guide to enriching relationships*. Mill Valley, CA: Heart Publishing.

Harris, T. A. (2004). *I'm ok, you're ok: The transactional analysis: breakthrough that's changing the consciousness and behavior of people who never before felt ok about themselves.* NY: HarperCollins.

Hartman, W. E. & Fithian, M. A. (1972). *Treatment of sexual dysfunction: A - bio-social approach.* Long Beach, CA: Center for Marital & Sexual Studies.

Keesling, B. (1995). *How to make love (and drive your women wild).* New York: HarperCollins.

Kinsey, A. et al. (1998). *Sexual behavior in the human male.* Bloomington: Indiana University Press. (Originally published 1948).

Klein, F., Sepckoff, B., & Watt, T. J. (1985). Sexual Orientation: A multivariable dynamic process. *Journal of Homosexuality, 11* (1–2), 35–49.

Lauman, E., Gagon, J. H., Michael, R. T., & Michael, S. (1994). *The social organization of sexuality: Sexual practices in the United States.* Chicago: University of Chicago Press.

Leonard, T. J. (1998). *The portable coach: 28 surefire strategies for business and personal success.* New York: Scribner.

Morin, J. (1995). *The erotic mind: Unlocking the inner sources of sexual passion and fulfillment.* New York: HarperCollins.

Myss, C. (2001). *Sacred contracts: Awakening your divine potential.* New York: Harmony.

Pasahow, C. (2003). *Sexy encounters: 21 days of provocative passion fixes.* Holbrook, MA: Adams Media Corporation.

Queen, C. (2002). *Exhibitionism for the shy: Show off, dress up and talk hot.* San Francisco: Down There Press.

Savage, L. (1991). *Reclaiming goddess sexuality: The power of the feminine way.* Carlsbad, CA: Hay House.

Schnarch, D. (1998). *Passionate marriage: Keeping love and intimacy alive in committed relationships.* New York: Henry Holt.

Stubbs, K. R. (1994). *Women of the light: The new sacred prostitute.* Larkspur, CA: Secret Garden.

Tolle, E. (1999). *The power of now: A guide to spiritual enlightenment.* Novato, CA: New World Library.

Williams, P. & Davis, D. C. (2002). *Therapist as life coach: Transforming your practice.* New York: Norton.

ADDITIONAL READING

Anand, M. (1989). *The art of sexual ecstasy: The path of sacred sexuality for western lovers.* New York: Putnam.

Barbach, L. (1984). *Pleasures: Women write erotica.* New York: Harper-Perrenial.

Berman, J. & Berman, L. (2001). *For women only: A revolutionary guide to overcoming sexual dysfunction and reclaiming your sex life.* New York: Henry Holt.

Boston Women's Health Book Collective. (1992). *The new our bodies, ourselves: A book by and for women.* New York: Simon & Schuster.

Brockway, L. S. (2003). *A goddess is a girl's best friend: A divine guide to finding love, success, and happiness.* New York: Perigee.

Castleman, M. (2004). *Great sex: A man's guide to the secret principles of total-body sex.* Emmaus, PA: Rodale Press.

Crenshaw, T. L. (1996). *The alchemy of love and lust: How our sex hormones influence our relationships.* New York: Pocket Books/Simon & Schuster.

Davidson, J. (2004). *Fearless sex: A babe's guide to overcoming your romantic obsessions and getting the sex life you deserve.* Gloucester, MA: Fair Winds Press.

Dyer, W. (2003). *There's a spiritual solution to every problem.* Carlsbad, CA: Hay House.

Ellis, A. (1998). *A guide to rational living.* North Hollywood, CA: Wilshire Book Co.

———— (1988). *How to stubbornly refuse to make yourself miserable about anything—yes, anything.* NY: Kensington Publishing group.

Ellison, C. R. (2000). *Women's sexualities: Generations of women share intimate secrets of sexual self-acceptance.* Oakland, CA: New Harbinger.

Foley, S., Kope, A. A., & Sugrue, D. P. (2002). *Sex matters for women: A complete guide to taking care of your sexual self.* New York: Guilford.

Hollander, X. (2002). *The happy hooker, 30th anniversary edition.* New York: Regan Books/HarperCollins.

Joannides, P. (2004). *Guide to getting it on* (2nd revised edition). Waldport, OR: Goofyfoot Press.

Kapit, W. M. & Elson, L. M. (1993). *The anatomy coloring book* (2nd ed.). New York: HarperCollins.

Kuriansky, J. (2001). *The complete idiot's guide to tantric sex.* Indianapolis, IN: Alpha.

LaCroix, N. (2001). *Tantric sex: The tantric art of sensual loving.* New York: Southwater/Anness Publishing.

Leiblum, S. R. & Rosen, R. C. (2000). *Principles and practice of sex therapy* (3rd ed.). New York: Guilford.

Milsten, R. & Slowinski, J. (1999). *The sexual male: Problems and solutions.* New York: Norton.

Northrup, C. (2001). *The wisdom of menopause: Creating physical and emotional health and healing during the change.* New York: Bantam.

Ogden, G. (1999). *Women who love sex: An inquiry into the expanding spirit of women's erotic experience.* Cambridge, MA: Womanspirit Press.

Paget, L. (2000). *How to give her absolute pleasure: Totally explicit techniques every woman wants her man to know.* New York: Broadway.

——— (2001). *The big O: Orgasms, how to have them, give them and keep them coming.* New York: Broadway.

Robbins, A. (1986). *Unlimited power.* New York: Fawcett Columbine. Available only on audio.

Sheiner, M. (Ed.). (1999). *Herotica 6.* San Francisco: Down There Press.

Tannen, D. (1990). *You just don't understand: Women and men in conversation.* New York: Ballantine.

Westheimer, R. K. (2000). *Encyclopedia of sex.* New York: Continuum.

Winks, C., & Semans, A. (2002). *The good vibrations guide to sex: The most complete sex manual ever written* (3rd edition). San Francisco: Cleis Press.

Zilbergeld, B. (1999). *The new male sexuality* (Rev. ed.). New York: Bantam.

Index